# JAZZ MAN

John Fordham is a jazz critic, writer and broadcaster, who has been writing about jazz for twenty years, initially for the London listings magazine, *Time Out*, and then for a variety of music papers including *Melody Maker, Sounds, Zig-Zag, Wire* and *Q*. Since 1978 he has been a regular jazz correspondent for *The Guardian*. He has acted as jazz adviser for the Arts Council of Great Britain, and the former Greater London Arts Association, and was also editor of *Time Out* from 1978 to 1981, and co-editor of *City Limits* until 1987. He is the author of an illustrated jazz history, *The Sound of Jazz* (1989), *Jazz* (Dorling Kindersley, 1994) and *Jazz on CD* (Kyle Cathie, 1992).

# JAZZ MAN

## The Amazing Story of Ronnie Scott and his Club

JOHN FORDHAM

KYLE CATHIE LIMITED

First published 1986 by
Elm Tree Books/Hamish Hamilton Ltd
under the title *Let's Join Hands and Contact the Living*

This revised and updated edition published 1995 by
KYLE CATHIE LIMITED
7/8 Hatherley Street, London SW1P 2QT


ISBN 1 85626 171 9

A Cataloguing in Publication record for this title is
available from the British Library.

Typeset by Heronwood Press
Printed by Biddles Ltd, Guildford, Surrey

*For My Mother*

# Contents

# Foreword

WHEN I WROTE the foreword to the first edition of this book in 1986, I declared three personal enthusiasms that drew me to write it. Firstly for jazz, which has given me more pleasure than any other art, as well as providing what has seemed to be a remarkably fitting musical score for urban living in the twentieth century. Secondly for London, and the transformations in it since the years of the Second World War. Thirdly for Ronnie Scott, a man who not only remains one of this country's finest jazz musicians but whose proprietorship of one of the world's most celebrated jazz clubs helped me to witness many of the legendary originals of the genre making music in an environment in which they could mostly feel relaxed, respected, often loved.

When Ronnie Scott began his career, serious jazz playing was in its infancy in this country, and for many years its British practitioners stood blushingly in the shadows of the mainly black American pioneers. As Scott approaches his seventies, much has changed. Gifted players like him, with a deep respect for the music and its origins, have helped in every part of the globe to spread the word.

Though the relatively buoyant condition of jazz in this country today is a tribute to the work of all its performers and adherents, it's hard to imagine that either the profile it has in 1994 – still marginalised, but a long way further forward than a quarter of a century ago – or the raised ambitions and hopes of its up-and-coming players could have been the same without Ronnie Scott and his partner Pete King. I hope this book goes some way toward expressing my gratitude for that.

Thanks are due, above all, to Ronnie Scott and Pete King for their help, hospitality and cooperation. Also to all the people who helped me to tell this story, and especially to the following: Ron Atkins, Derek Bailey, Alfie Benge, Rachel 'Ray' Berger, Brian Case, Harry Conn, Joan Crewe, Tony

Crombie, Jeff Ellison, Bernie Fenton, Nigel Fountain, Charles Fox, Ilsa and Nicholas, Benny Green, Coleridge Goode, Kitty Grime, Roxy Hoffman, Ted Hughes, Barbara Jay, John Jack, Bernard Kops, Nissel Lakin, Issac 'Mitch' Mitchell, Laurie Morgan, Julia Pascal, Mary Scott, Vic Schonfield, Stan and Jackie Tracey, Françoise Venet, Val Wilmer, Richard Williams, Cecil 'Flash' Winston and Robert Wyatt.

Thanks also to Theresa Allan, who helped with the research on the first edition, to *The Guardian* for the space it gives to jazz, and to Kyle and Beverley at KC for their forbearance. Love and thanks to Ros, to Vivien and to Fred and Leo.

*Name of the Rose* author Umberto Eco wasn't writing about jazz in his book *The Open Work* when he described 'a different status for the artistic product in contemporary society. . .far from being fully accounted for and catalogued, it deploys and poses problems in several dimensions. In short it is an "open" situation, in movement.' Eco was talking about the contemporary music of Stockhausen and Berio, in which improvisation and chance play a part, and also about modern writers like Mallarme and Joyce. But he could just as easily have been talking about jazz. Respected for this unique identity at last, jazz is becoming recognised as one of the most significant musical developments of the twentieth century as the millenial year approaches, and in their own ways Ronnie Scott and Pete King have inestimably helped to secure that belated recognition.

Groucho Marx said to Greta Garbo when she rounded indignantly on him from under her hat, 'I'm sorry, I thought you were a fella I once knew in Philadelphia.' Mistakes happen, but I sincerely hope that Ronnie Scott's friends and associates will recognise the man who travels the following pages. But such short-comings as this book reveals are nobody's fault but my own.

*John Fordham*
London, November 1994

# 1

# Exiles

'I could see that Jewish people couldn't afford the luxury of being merely mediocre. They were like other people only more so. They were either angels or bastards and sometimes angelic bastards.'
(Bernard Kops, *The World is a Wedding*, 1963)

*Friday, 28 January 1927. Aldgate, London*

IN THE RIPTIDE of migrating humanity flooding through London's docklands in the early years of this century, an uprooted traveller needed love or money for a lifeline, preferably both. It had to be the kind of fierce love that embraced a bigger family than could be squeezed between four walls, a survivor's love that could hearten the whole fleeing family of Jewish migrants leaving the increasingly inhospitable lands of Eastern Europe.

For three decades, the east End had seen them come. Exhausted, frightened, uncomprehending, as rich or poor as whatever they could carry, the lucky ones were swept off the ships into the embraces of relatives, bustled chattering down grey alleys, through busy market places hissing with the sound of the naptha lamps, past sweatshops, past the modest premises of hopeful jewellers, tailors, restaurateurs, even brothels run by Jewish mamas and daughters.

Trams clanged, ships hooted on the river, freight trains clattered in the docks, out-of-work tailors argued furiously on street corners while they waited for news of sweatshop jobs. The Prince of Wales had visited the district that week, an event which had intensified the streetlife philosophising – particularly amongst the knots of Russian exiles in the doorways and the little restaurants still claiming personal acquaintance with Trotsky.

Another uprooted traveller arrived that day. Ronald Schatt came into the world of Joseph Schatt, musician, and Sylvia 'Cissie' Schatt, saleswoman, of number 33 South Tenter Street, a tiny terraced house at the southern edge of a labyrinth behind Aldgate station, not more than a quarter-mile from Tower Bridge and London's Western Dock, in the heart of one of the biggest Jewish communities in Europe. The boy was the couple's first and only child. They had married at the end of August 1926, when Jock was twenty-three and Cissie twenty-five, and four months' pregnant.

Amid the small ads for dancing teachers offering proficiency in the Charleston and the Black Bottom, and scullery maids pursuing the £30 or so per annum that was the going rate, Prime Minister Baldwin declared that he was the 'loneliest man in the country'. These weren't familiar emotions to Joseph Schatt, who didn't let himself get lonely that often. A handsome, elegant man with humorous eyes, in whom enthusiasm for music, gambling and women competed on more or less equal terms, Schatt was a dance band saxophonist, and a good one. He played the alto, with the sweet, pure tone that was fashionable for the day, and had served an apprenticeship in the music of the Jazz Age that could handle the most obscure requests without a blink.

Joseph Schatt's profession was a glamorous one. A worldwide explosion of interest in a vivid new music from America paralleled huge changes in society – the coming of the movies, the phonograph record, network radio and the automobile were transforming notions of time and place, reality and dreams, whether truth could be found in a book, or in a church or a synagogue, or in the word of elders, or in a talking box in the corner. Jazz reflected the speed and hungry disruptiveness of these changes, as well as the desire to cauterise the wounds of the Great War.

Everybody danced. Bandleaders with slicked-down hair, tail-coats and professional simpers led platoons of section players through the hits. Dance band players were pop idols.

For Joseph and Cissie Schatt's relationship, this wasn't an unmixed blessing. Joseph was a man people remembered. He was sharp, a fancy dresser, a practical joker, a gambler, a shrewd immigrant in an unwelcoming world, and he knew the score. He was one of countless gifted Jews for whom the careers of overnight fame – notably, as far as the East End was concerned, boxing and music – were the route to a decent life, most of the more respectable professions being virtually inaccessible to non-Gentiles at the time. He travelled widely to play, and around the time of Ronald's birth was leading a palais band in Scotland, the Glasgow Plaza Band. Like many of his generation – and the one that followed – Joseph Schatt thought it prudent not to work under a Jewish name. He was always known professionally as 'Jock Scott'.

For Cissie, Jock's style and the demands of his working life were both fascinating and unsettling. The house at South Tenter Street had to become a traditional Jewish home with the birth of the baby. Cissie was always close to her mother and stepfather and to her brother Mark, even if he was a compulsive gambler forever convinced he was on the verge of the Big Deal. Jock Scott loved the races too, and spent a fortune on them over the years.

Jock was descended from a Russian Jewish family, a community turned into refugees in the 1880s when anti-Jewish riots in southern Russia and Poland – followed by laws that crippled Jewish businesses – drove them across Europe to seek safety and a new start in the West. Some were joining relatives already living in the Jewish ghetto of the docklands of London's East End. Most were heading for America. Some stepped off the boats in London *en route* to the States and never left. Some actually thought they *were* in America. The area was populated with exiles exchanging imprecations and anecdotes in the cosmopolitan shorthand of Yiddish, or a mixture of Yiddish and Cockney. The language itself was an inspiration to music – so many of its meanings emerged from intonation as significantly as from vocabulary. The East End became a second home. The locals even ironically dubbed one thoroughfare 'Christian Street' because there wasn't a single Gentile living in it.

For a Jew, it was a good time and a bad time to be born. While Cissie was waiting through the last days of her confinement, the *Daily Express* was asking 'How Long Can Fascism Last?'. But though unemployment in Britain touched a million and a half, London was doing well at the end of the 1920s and many of its Jewish community could feel it. The entrepreneurs of the ghetto were geniuses of popular taste because they were starting from the people they knew, understanding a market place the dynamics of which could be measured simply by consulting the needs of mothers, fathers, brothers, sisters. The Joseph Lyons organisation became the virtuoso of street corner catering, Marks and Spencer's of affordable quality clothing. The Grade brothers, music-hall tap dancers both, ended up running television stations.

Survival demanded a delicate mix of risk and family stability. For Jock Scott, it was important to believe that life would – given a few lucky breaks – pan out fine. Though he wore evening dress and moved in the respectable circles of dance hall and hotel entertainment, his work and life belonged to the tradition of the Jewish *kletzmorim* of centuries past, the travelling players. Thousands of them came during the migrations. They were descendants of a rich seam of itinerant Jewish musicianship, a culture that had developed

out of the obligation to assimilate non-Jewish life in order to survive; clar-
inettists, fiddlers, mandolin and dulcimer players who could play polkas
for the locals or waltzes for the aristocracy, and still reel through the traditional repertoire for bar mitzvahs and weddings. In its demand for flexibility and quick reflexes, its bridging of the worlds of popular entertainment
and idiosyncratic creativity, and its dependence on a massive and constantly changing stock of memorised materials, it had a lot in common with
jazz. Jock's brother Dave was a violinist too, and played successfully in the
dance bands.

Both sides of Ronald Schatt's family were bursting with opportunists,
resourceful people riding with the waves of a strange new sea, and navi-
gating it with mixed results. There were Aunt Julie and Uncle Muchie – an
olive-skinned, dark-eyed, gypsy-looking couple who bore unmistakable
signs of Cissie's Portuguese ancestry – who ran a hotel in Brighton. There
was Uncle Harry, who made what living he could at the Brighton race-
tracks, and who was eventually to serve prison terms for fraud and con-
artistry. Uncle Markie, who never had a job, lived when he felt like it in the
South Tenter Street house, forever borrowing money from Cissie to back
another dream. Uncle 'Gypsy' Rafie wore a bandana and a gold earring
though nobody could trace much Romany ancestry in him; he sold racing
tips for sixpence a shot down Petticoat Lane.

But the hazard in the path of Cissie's journey with Jock loomed only too
soon. One day in 1930 or 1931, Cissie travelled to Glasgow where Jock was
at work, and found him with another woman. All the blandishments and
charm that her husband could unwrap – just the kind that had sparked a
love for him that would never really die – were not enough to persuade her
to find a way around what seemed to her a most irrefutable betrayal. She
deliberated, then asked him not to return to the family house, and began
divorce proceedings.

For the young Ronald, Jock was an exotic but elusive figure. The dominant people in his life were his mother and his grandmother, and from
either of them he could get whatever he asked for, if it was available and
affordable. One night Cissie did take the child to see Jock play with a band
that he was running in the East End, sat Ronnie at a restaurant table, heard
the indefatigable charmer sound as convinced as ever that everything
would be all right, that it would be worth another try, heard herself insist
that it was all too late. But one memory of Jock that lingered after he had left
was the glamorous aura of the saxophone.

By 1931 Jock had gone for good, swept off into the tempestuous dance
band scene, into the famous Jack Hylton band and then into the outfit led

by Hylton's wife Ennis (her signature tune was 'This Is The Missus, Just Look Her Over') with whom Jock eventually lived until her death in the early 1950s. He was not to reappear in his son's life until the boy's teens – when Ronnie Scott was on the verge of following in his footsteps.

The East End years were a happy childhood. Young Ronald was enrolled at the Buckle Street Jews Infant School in Aldgate aged three, in a class built to the needs of busy parents, operating as a playgroup in the morning and a nursery after lunch, the children all put down in cots to sleep for the afternoon until they could be collected. Cissie, the breadwinner, was at work behind a shop-counter all day, and Ronald's grandmother Becky did the collecting. The staff were warm, and tolerant and Ronald sometimes could raise a laugh from them, like the day he turned up late with the excuse: 'I'm sorry, I had a long wash.' They laughed too when during a school trip to Devon his curiosity was gripped for the first time by something distinctly different about the little girls on the beach.

There was a stables in Cable Street, and a dairy where the boy and grandmother would take a jug to collect fresh milk from the cows. A horse-drawn roundabout would pass down the street, rides for 'a halfpenny or a jamjar' (the owners could get money back on the jars); Indians sold a candyfloss-like toffee off trays, wrapped in cones of newspaper; fresh ice-cream was sold off a barrow. When he was seven, Ronnie and the local children would go swimming underneath Tower Bridge. At Christmas, the landlord of the house would visit, like a Jewish Santa Claus, with presents for all the children in his properties. One year Ronald had the choice of a clockwork truck or lead soldiers, chose the soldiers and then regretted it as soon as his benefactor had left the house.

Tradition and spectacle were part of life. Grandpa Samuel took the young Ronald to the Portuguese synagogue in Great Alie Street when he was five, and it left indelible memories – music, song, the passionate chanting of the cantor, bearded old men in black, musty clothes, dust, history. Ronnie liked Samuel, and it was mutual. The old man's reputation with other members of the family was more variable, as were his aspirations to respectable citizenry, but he was a glamorous figure to a child. When the policeman came to the door one December night in 1935 to tell the family Samuel was dead, it distressed the boy greatly as a first intimation of mortality and loss.

There was Great Aunt Leah in a tenement nearby, who had a withered hand and who saw her sailor son repeatedly at the foot of the bed, the one who had been blown to pieces in the Great War. There was Ronnie's great-grandfather, secretary of the local British Legion branch, a man whose exquisite copperplate handwriting survived into great old age. The household in South Tenter Street was hardly orthodox but Nana Becky guarded as much of the tradition as could decently be observed – candles were lit on Friday nights, the fast of the Passover steadfastly observed.

Petticoat Lane was a magical place, particularly at night when the lamps whispered and threw thrilling shadows. Ronnie's grandmother was a streetwise Eastender to the tips of her toes and never let a purchase go by without a haggle over the price. There was Bennett's the salt-beef emporium, which sold only salt-beef sandwiches and soup. There was the beigel lady who sold her wares out of a canvas sack from a chair in a sidestreet.

It was a familiar stamping ground too, for Uncle 'Gypsy' Rafie, the tipster. He sometimes drew his young nephew into the act, pretending not to recognise Ronnie, saying: 'Hello, little boy, go and get that gentleman's money and take him this for me,' little Ronnie scuttling to and fro in the crowd of men, and wondering not so very much later why his Uncle Rafie wasn't as rich as Croesus if he knew so much about the horses.

Very little disturbed the calm of these early years in a warm and embracing community, among women who doted on him. Nobody was rich, but nobody went short. After Jock's departure, Cissie's job as a saleswoman at the Jewish-owned Aldgate department store Burstein's (it later became the Houndsditch Warehouse Company) was the only support for the household, but it was enough.

Cissie met her second husband whilst working there, a slight, bespectacled tailor called Solomon Berger. Sol was the diametric opposite of Jock Scott in every conceivable way. Hardworking, straightforward, affectionate and businesslike, he was as reliable as Jock had been mercurial, and he took to Ronnie instantly. Sol and Cissie were married in 1935, when Ronnie was eight. He wasn't taken to the ceremony, and indignantly protested: 'I bet all the other kids went to their parents's weddings.' Not long after, Ronnie's stepsister Marlene was born. The boy was fascinated by the new arrival, watched Cissie play with her for hours.

The family left South Tenter Street. It was already a well-worn path out of the ghetto of the docks for Jewish families – and the move came just in time, with the Mosleyite race riots and growing anti-Semitic violence not far behind. Stoke Newington and Stamford Hill were more spacious, more green and more forgiving parts of town for those who could afford the trip.

But though music was still not a part of the young Ronnie's world he did discover it in the family's flat at Benthal Road, Stoke Newington. Two brothers – about Ronnie's age – lived upstairs. One played the guitar, the other the alto saxophone. The altoist's influence, which permeated the building (the saxophonist was Paul Bennett, later to become a professional), may have awakened dormant memories of the glamour of a musical life in a child otherwise preoccupied with aeroplanes and racing cars.

Ronnie Scott went to the elementary school in his street for two years, then passed the Junior County Scholarship to Central Foundation School in the City. A devoted reader of boys' comics like *Hotspur* and *Wizard*, Ronnie was gratified to find that at last the teachers looked like the teachers in the fictitious Red Circle School in his magazines, grave-looking men in black gowns. There was even *Boys' Own* heroism. In one school boxing tournament, a slight Jewish boy drew the local anti-Semitic bully as his opponent, and wiped the floor with him. Ronnie and friends celebrated a triumph.


September 1939 saw the family in Bognor on holiday when war was declared. Sol and Cissie feared returning to the family house at first. Aunt Annie and Uncle Muchie's hotel in Brighton seemed a safer bet. For a twelve-year-old, Brighton was a pleasant enough place to be, and young Ronnie took to rugby, captaining the school second team, telling himself they needed one good player in it. The war seemed to him not the threat of loss and trauma that it was for his parents. Ronnie wanted to be the rear gunner in a bomber, and was fascinated by aviation and aeronautics.

When the family moved back to London in 1940 (this time to Edgware – and the Blitz began on the very same day, an event that they steadfastly maintained couldn't be a coincidence) the young Ronnie Scott went to a local elementary school and did well there. A report told Sol and Cissie he was likely to be the next head boy, he was allowed to take care of younger classes when teachers were absent (entertaining them with Richmal Crompton's *Just William* stories), and he won a prized Conway Stewart fountain pen in a national essay competition. A master said to him: 'You write very well, why don't you make it a career?' It sounded like a suggestion that involved hard work and study, and the young Ronnie's temperament didn't embrace that. He began a course in aeronautics at Hendon Technical College instead, and also joined the local Air Training Corps, spurred on by a regular march to Hendon aerodrome with the irresistible promise 'You're going to fly this week' – one that never materialised. This and architecture – a subject he had adopted to the extent of reading widely about it – were Ronnie Scott's main speculations about his future. He also used to visit Elstree Film Studios with a friend, asking the staff if there were odd jobs they could do. But something altogether more seductive was soon to replace these ever-evaporating promises.

On the way to school one morning, Ronnie Scott bought his first musi- cal instrument. In the window of a junk shop was an ancient cornet held together with black tape. Though the cornet didn't work, the boy was proud to take it on for five shillings. A little later he came by a soprano sax- ophone the same way. Like the cornet, it was barely good enough to extract a sound from, but it worked well enough to produce a handful of phrases that were recognisable as a tune. Sol and Cissie were delighted, and they could see how keen Ronnie already was. If this was what their boy wanted to do, he couldn't make it with second-rate equipment. And if Cissie was troubled by the possibility that young Ronnie might turn into a man in the image of the father he hardly knew, she wasn't showing it.

She went to Archer Street, the West End open-air job centre where the commercial musicians plied their trade, compared notes, gossiped. She took some advice from old friends of Jock, men she had known from the dance bands. After some thought, she and Sol then bought Ronnie a silver-plated Pennsylvania tenor saxophone with a gold-plated bell. Sleek and smooth and gleaming as Jock's had been in the dockland house so long ago, soft yielding pads under pearl inlays, as sensuous as a human form and yet as thrilling in its mechanics as an aeroplane, a miraculous conjunction of wires and levers and flaps capable of producing a sound – somewhere between that of the brass instruments and reeds – which came close to defining the character of the dance band era.

It was also the instrument of Jewish social life, played by balding moustachioed men with twinkling eyes, pragmatically mixing the pop tunes of the day with the music of the Jewish dances. It was the instrument that had gleamed behind the lace curtains in the moody lighting at the Phoenix Theatre in Charing Cross Road when Cissie had taken Ronnie there because the Jan Ralfini orchestra was playing – and because Jock was somewhere in the saxophone section. But though Cissie was still in love, she never went backstage or sought him out.

There was also the world of the saxophone that Ronnie Scott did not yet know, but when he discovered it would devour it so voraciously that his companions would be astonished by how fast he absorbed the music of the best players of the day. Sidney Bechet, the great Creole musician, had transferred from the clarinet to the soprano saxophone, playing a music of sweeping passion that could make you shiver. But it was Coleman

Hawkins, the saxophonist who had come up with the bands of Louis Armstrong and orchestra leader Fletcher Henderson, who had virtually single-handed created the tenor. He had rescued the larger horn from the wilderness of sensationalism and special effects it had been relegated to, and turned it into a vehicle for warmth, sardonic humour and a kind of brusque tenderness.

Ronnie Scott thus found himself catapulted into a musical age in which the cooings and flouncings of the dance orchestras were increasingly being charged with a new and irresistably exciting ingredient. 'Hot' music. Jazz. The first recordings of a young trumpet genius from New Orleans, Louis Armstrong, had trickled into Britain in the mid-1920s, and a newspaper, *Melody Maker*, had come into being the year before Ronnie's birth, to cater for both the regular music business and a buff's readership of 'hot jazz' lovers, the devotees of the genuine article.

And in the year he was born, and not a five-minute walk from the South Tenter Street house, Britain's first specialist jazz record shop – Levy's in Whitechapel Road, an establishment founded by a dealer who had been selling records in the local street markets for years – opened in response to the growing popularity of a music that had been forged by another ghetto community thousands of miles away.

What British fans experienced as the 'hot' quality of jazz was unmistakable, if imperfectly understood. It was the fierce glow of a music thrown up by the experience of recently emancipated slaves migrating from the southlands to the northern cities. In the process they accelerated the rambling, conversational tempo of back-porch folk-blues into a taut and clamorous urbanised band music that sounded like the clatter of mechanised transport, the hum of street markets, the cadences of street corner badinage, the stridency of marching bands, the pragmatism and casual tragedies of the blues.

But to most Western whites, jazz was not much more than an interesting musical accident valuable mainly for those bits of its rhythmic originality that could be refined by the upmarket orchestras. It was thought to need 'improving', it was a phenomenon altogether too crude and feverish for those of more tender sensibilities. Its creators might be described as 'niggers' or 'coons' by anyone from band leaders to critics to politicians. When Ronnie Scott was six months old, the dance band leader Bert Ambrose was performing a work at the London Palladium called 'Heart of a Nigger'. An outcry about its derogatory overtones had it altered. They changed the title to 'Heart of a Coon'.

But in Ronnie's early childhood, jazz began to get a real foothold in

Britain. The white Original Dixieland Jazz Band had toured the country successfully years before, and many performers of his father's generation had heard the band on its long residency at the Hammersmith Palais and decided on a musical career there and then. The great Sidney Bechet had appeared during the 1920s. But the visits of Louis Armstrong and Duke Ellington to London in 1932 and 1933 were unquestionably a turning point. Armstrong had triggered a mixture of responses, from *Melody Maker's* 'tremendous force in modern dance music' to the *Daily Herald's* account of an 'untrained gorilla . . .' who 'might have come straight from some African jungle'. The *Herald's* correspondent observed 'the young Jewish element at the back were enthusiastic' as if this was explanation enough.

The pressure to campaign for the authentic originators of the music was coming from the dance bands themselves. Bandleader Jack Hylton had brought Ellington over. Though the dance band artists were a mixed bunch – immigrants, survivors of purges, inheritors of the music hall traditions, artisans of the business who knew their way through the tunes and the keys the way a cab driver knew the back doubles – they knew a good thing when they heard it. That world – where 'entertainment' was being laced by a twentieth century musical revolution from a source considered incapable of serious art – was where Ronnie Scott was headed.

The East End youth clubs were the place to start. The notion of a 'teenager' wasn't invented, so you were either at school, or you were at work, or looking for work, and in the clubs there was the chance to talk to somebody older about what it might be like, try to wring out a feasible future from the fantasies of the *Wizard* and *Hotspur*, find out what adulthood meant from somebody maybe six months older over a game of billiards. Clubs like the Stepney and the Oxford and St George's had games rooms with billiard tables, gramophones and records, as well as a dance hall. Kids who could sing stood the best chance of getting a break and a chance to entertain their friends – and maybe even take a step on the first rung to the big time. The Oxford and St George's, Ronnie's regular, was the brainchild of Jewish philanthropist Basil Henriques and his wife, key figures in the development of London's Jewish community.

Ronnie encountered plenty of urgent achievers on the way up, though not always to where they expected. Sonny Herman, a youth club trombonist, became a rabbi in Amsterdam. Mike and Bernie Winters, youth club regulars, came up through the music halls and variety shows. Vidal Sassoon went to the Oxford and St George's, where Ronnie Scott spent much of his teens. For Ronnie's father to have been a professional saxophonist was glamorous, but not exceptional. Tony Crombie, the young

10

furrier's apprentice who wanted to be a pro drummer and who formed a lifelong friendship with Ronnie from those days, had a cinema organist for a mother, a drummer for an uncle and a father who was an instinctive, if rudimentary, piano player.

To learn to play like a dance band musician was tough, but there was always someone on hand with advice. Stock arrangements could be bought from the sheet music shops for a shilling apiece and there was no shortage of older kids who knew just that little bit more. Sol and Cissie could see that Ronnie was determined to take his new hobby seriously. Ronnie Scott had lessons with Jack Lewis, a recommendation Jock had made to Cissie, and who taught saxophone from the front room of a house in Stamford Hill. Lewis was a genial old man, happy to help a youngster as obviously keen as his new pupil. Lewis's own son was a musician, and a successful one – he was also to marry one of the biggest names in Tin Pan Alley, Vera Lynn.

Jack was a realist. Knowing what your instrument could do and what it couldn't do, not getting fancy ideas, drawing out the best of that lush, romantic sound that the tenor seemed to be made for, that was the secret. Ronnie made the awkward journey from Edgware to Stamford Hill once a week for six months, and soon felt he was beginning to understand the subtle potential of the instrument. He was a quick learner, and a good mimic, if an indifferent theorist. He had also learned to play 'Honeysuckle Rose', which could get you a long way.

The circuit of Ronnie's existence from school to Jack Lewis's house and back to the East End on Saturdays to the clubs, now embraced a London increasingly ripped apart by the war – but still gloriously unthreatening to a boy confident of immortality. In the summer of 1941, unsure of his future but by now in love with the silver and gold Pennsylvania tenor, Ronnie left school and got a job in an establishment that seemed to promise a more useful education as his interest in music grew. He went to the Keith Prowse Organisation, the biggest company in London dealing in records, instruments and sheet music.

Ronnie Scott started his working life as a packer in the basement of the Prowse Coventry Street store but hated it. The staff took pity on him and he was sent to the Kensington High Street branch, where he was put on the record sales desk. He sold a lot of records there, listened a great deal and helped himself to some that ended up on the gramophone at home – Tommy Dorsey swing discs, the swagger and bravura of Benny Goodman's account of 'Sing Sing Sing'. Ronnie moved from Keith Prowse to Lou Chester – Dance band Instrument Suppliers in Soho's Rupert Street, a shop run by an ex-dance band trombonist. It was a storeroom job again, but by

' this time Ronnie's rudimentary expertise on the saxophone was beginning to win him occasional gigs on the East End youth club circuit, beginning with an opportunity arranged by Jock's violinist brother Dave. It was an insight into music business ways. Making up the numbers in Felix Mendelssohn's Hawaian Serenaders, Ronnie found the fiddle players could retune to a piano a semitone out, but he couldn't. But dances, weddings and barmitzvahs ensured that a sax-playing Yiddisher boy needn't feel neglected. And there were soon enough of them to ensure that store-clerking for Lou Chester would be the last day-job that Ronnie Scott would ever need to have.

London was a town bursting with the desire to survive. Entertainment was like a form of war-work, helping to make every laugh, every moment of euphoria a bigger and better one because it might just be the last. Bandleaders told stories of revellers dug out of wrecked houses making it to the clubs and dance halls with the dust still in their hair, patched up, determined to forget. It was risky for everyone, but if you were a Londoner, you might as well be in a club as anywhere else, if you could afford it. Many couldn't, and discontent was rife between poor Eastenders, badly hit by the bombing, and the more fortunate West End.

In the East End, Ronnie was beginning to hang out with kids who were already on the brink of showbusiness, and some of them were even habitués of that glamorous underworld of the Soho dives. Flash Winston, a diminutive, fast-talking young drummer, was one such, already working the West End. Tony Crombie, the reluctant furrier, would get a taste of the action by carrying Flash's drums to gigs. Crombie himself, a little older than Ronnie, soon began to work, notably in the Bouillabaisse, a black club that presented a mixture of swing-based jazz and calypso music.

The West End was the magnet. All the semi-pro, thirty-bob-a-throw gigs on the wedding-and-barmitzvah round would be just treading water compared to the irresistible life of the professional. If they got close enough, perhaps some of the mystique would rub off.

The boys more or less camped out on the club scene. Hanging around those seductive doorways at night, peering down rickety stairways into blaring, deliciously dangerous basements, lurking around back entrances. Catching the last tube home, or missing it and spending the rest of the night in the Lyons Corner House, drinking tea, hearing tales of the night's work from one of their number lucky enough to be playing, catching the first

12

train of the morning home. Cissie didn't like it. But she didn't like the thought of holding her son back either.

That square mile was run on hedonism and fast turnover. Soho then was the nearest London could get to the twilight world of fringe life in Chicago and New York. The licensing laws in these one-room drinking clubs (home for what were usually described as 'bottle parties') were that the clients were supposed to have bought or ordered their drinks twenty-four hours before their visit to the premises. This didn't often happen, but as fast as the police would close one establishment down its organisers would reappear somewhere else.

Stark, dirty and run-down in the daytime, these dim and smoky rooms were at night a focus for every kind of drifter and square peg who didn't, or couldn't, relax in polite society. London's small West Indian community and the passing black seamen from the docks came in. So too did service-men on leave with no homes to go to, GIs, crooks doing deals, black mar-keteers, billiard players, aristos slumming it.

And because it was a scene in which so many wired and nervy people, speeding on the ever-present proximity to death, were fixing and manipu-lating and patching up their roller-coaster lives, it was also a scene in which the young musicians, ignored by all but the true fans, who perched them-selves attentively at the edge of the bandstand, had an immense amount of freedom. The tradition was that when you heard the whistle of the bombs the band kept playing, unless it was *very* close.

With the anxiety and exhilaration, and the long hours, came drugs. The clubs were like sweet shops; variations of speed and heart stimulants intended for war-zones, benzedrine inhalers dismembered and dropped into teacups, marijuana. Availability and adventurousness were leading the new generation to experiment with drugs seriously for the first time in Britain.

London was being forced to change in many other ways. Though the inescapable truth that bombs were no respecter of social class had helped to melt (at least temporarily) the worst of the country's social taboos, others were growing. By the late summer of 1942 the war had brought 10,000 black American servicemen to the country. They had received a mixed reception. MP Tom Driberg had asked Winston Churchill in the Commons in September of that year 'whether he is aware that an unfortunate result of the presence here of American forces has been the introduction in some parts of Britain of discrimination against negro troops'.

Churchill seemed hardly impressed. The argument went to a Cabinet-level discussion in which the Colonial Secretary cited the case of a black official on his own staff now barred from his regular restaurant at the insistence of white American officers patronising it. Churchill responded: 'That's all right. If he takes his banjo with him, they'll think he's one of the band.'

The Cabinet eventually endorsed a document that ostensibly deplored discrimination but none the less discouraged 'close contact with English home life or English women'. Some American soldiers were even reported to be aggressively confronting West Indian troops with white wives as they walked along the streets. Black soldiers – from the States and from the colonies – found themselves in many cases fighting for a strange kind of freedom.

The clubs were a haven for both the Archer Street professionals and the eager congregation of teenage hopefuls following them around. Where the early evening would pass to the clink of decanters in the plush restaurants and the steady swell of small talk, the after-hours low-life atmosphere would be a tumult of noise, blandishments, importunings, marijuana, indulgence, survival, villainy. The club owners welcomed the informality of the musicians' way of working, bustling around Soho all night with their instrument cases, dropping in and out of clubs, playing a few tunes, moving on. After all, if somebody wanted to turn up and play for the hell of it, they needn't expect to be *paid* as well.

Ronnie Scott, fifteen years old, began to be one of them. He knew his grip on the music was tenuous and that playing the tunes was more complicated than it sounded, but it was a start. And as he began to come to the West End regularly, he looked out for Jock, wondering what his father would be like, watching the pavements from the top decks of buses, knowing that this was Jock's patch, glimpsing this or that elegant, grey-haired figure, a man with an instrument case, wondering how he would start a conversation if he found him.

One night towards the end of 1942, in a sudden rush of revitalised confidence, Ronnie Scott came 'up West' and asked for a blow with a band run by drummer Carlo Krahmer. In a musical world where most of the practitioners were hard-bitten professionals with no time to lose and little appetite for fancy ideas that wouldn't pay the rent, Krahmer was both a pro and an enthusiast. In almost every respect he was a rare bird in an environment already teeming with eccentricity.

Krahmer was approaching thirty at the time, a prolifically busy performer and bandleader running groups at many of the London dives and legendary for operating several gigs in the course of the same night. What made Krahmer's negotiation of this obstacle course more remarkable was that he was almost totally blind, unable to drive, and obliged to hump his kit around the city on the buses and the underground, though he partly solved the problem by leaving bits of innumerable kits all over town.

He was a also one-man recycling agency for every kind of commodity that London's itinerant population was anxious to convert into cash – ties from America, records, musical instruments. He was rumoured to be the first exponent of the art of hi-hat playing amongst the city's drummers, a 'cymbal man' in a forest of snare-drum rollers, rimshot artists and boom-boom bass drummers reared on the swing players. And he had courage. In an altercation one night with the owner of the Gremlin Club, Krahmer was felled by his employer despite warnings from the proprietor's minders that his opponent couldn't see. Krahmer was spirited, energetic, and loved music – and he was a jazz enthusiast. He had a collection of thousands of records, he kept pace with what was happening in America, and he had an ear for musicians who grasped the spontaneous and invigorating spirit of jazz. Krahmer later recalled that first encounter with the East End boy with the tenor, remembering he'd said, 'He's got a good sound, this lad; sounds promising, make a note.'

Ronnie Scott began knocking on the door of the music profession at a time when its composition was changing. The great age of the big bands was passing, partly as conscription and the dwindling male population was knocking serious holes in the line-ups, and partly because of their immense overheads in a period of austerity that was to last well into the 1950s. The shift meant that the balance imperceptibly moved in favour of the younger players. The old bandleaders needed their services, fancy ideas or not, and if the youngsters wanted to stretch out, play a little more jazz, then maybe they should be allowed to.

The war slowly turned in the Allies' favour. Those journeys on foot that Tony Crombie and Flash Winston had taken, walking back from the West End clubs in a blazing city, amidst rubble and falling masonry, firemen at the end of their tether, walking where a cab couldn't take you because the roads were impassable, were becoming a dimmer memory. Londoners felt united, and felt the beginnings of optimism too, though not everyone could share it. A local young black woman, Amelia King, from Stepney, was refused entry to the Women's Land Army in 1943 because the farmers objected to her colour. But in general, coming tensions in the nation's life lay mostly dormant beneath the massive duty of the war.

Ronnie Scott's love affair with the music business grew. It wasn't simply the music alone, the seductiveness of what it might be like to unpack the Pennsylvania on the bandstand in front of an expectant audience, warm it up, adjust the reed, run effortlessly through the hits; it was the atmosphere, too, and the people.

Ronnie Scott ran into Krahmer again in 1943. The bandleader had remembered. He recalled that kid with the big sound, quick on the uptake, the raw, enthusiastic recruit awkwardly but determinedly borrowing whatever he could from all the tenorists he heard. Krahmer was running the house band at the Jamboree (later to become the Flamingo) in Wardour Street. His six-piece was short of a saxophonist for a fortnight, a delay in the arrival of the replacement.

'Would you like the gig?' Krahmer asked the young Ronnie Scott. The boy enthusiastically accepted but told the older man that his playing wasn't ready. He didn't know the tunes, he wasn't familiar with his horn in all the keys, he was certain he'd be lost at the first chorus.

Krahmer wasn't bothered. He liked Ronnie, and could see something of Jock Scott, whom he knew slightly, in the young man. 'All you've got to do is sit there with the saxophone,' Krahmer said.

The first night at the Jamboree was a dream come true. The atmosphere was like perfume. When he had to play, it was only to busk his way through 'Don't Be That Way' or 'Tea For Two', bits of blues. Much of the time, when players who really knew what they were doing would arrive to sit in, Ronnie Scott would get off the bandstand and listen, fascinated. Since Carlo Krahmer was a devotee of jazz and knew the music well, to be in his band and to hear him talk was to make contact with what this unruly and spontaneous music was really all about. But what counted most was that for a fortnight, at sixteen years old, having played his horn for only eighteen months, Ronnie Scott knew what it was like to be a professional, in a professional's band, working in a West End club.

He went back to Edgware and told Sol and Cissie all about it. He was in the music business. He was following Jock. Cissie knew that her handsome, humorous, strong-minded boy was beginning to resemble the father he could barely remember. She also knew that, one day, she'd have to bring them together.

# 2

# Sweet Bird

A MONDAY AFTERNOON in Archer Street. At the height of business you couldn't see a square yard of pavement between the elbowing, badgering, gossiping men. Newcomers mingled, carrying instrument cases to demonstrate their speciality. It wasn't unheard of for drummers to be found edging anxiously around the pavements with a snare tucked awkwardly under one arm. Interrogations, investigations and pleasantries were indistinguishable – 'What are you doing?' . . . 'Where are you working?' The hairdresser, reared on the Rag-Time Bob, was shortly to have to reconstruct his business to accommodate the 'Rebop' cut. Relaxation meant the pin-table in the tobacconist's, the one where the 'gig king' (master-fixers of the one-night stand) took up office in the doorway. In the café, the proprietor would watch his more expansive customers miming solos, teacups loosely swinging from flying fingers.

From the Archer Street newspaper shop, *Melody Maker*'s best sales outlet, men in box-shouldered, double-breasted suits would crane for a glimpse of a Windmill Girl in the dressing rooms across the street, until shooed away by the white-haired old lady whose premises were ritually put to the purpose. Sharp operators had codes to economise on the inexperienced and avoid rocking the boat with the regulars: 'It's worth two' they would say if an inexperienced player willing to work under the rate was in earshot, but the three fingers spread on the thumbed lapel of those double-breasted jackets told the real story. It was a world of commerce, not art. It was the nerve-centre of a service industry.

Some time in 1943, Ronnie Scott heard of the departure of a tenorist from the house-band at the Bouillabaisse. The bandleader there was Clarry Wears, a rumba-king in the West Indian community, and Tony Crombie was already a drummer at the club. Ronnie Scott got the job. The club was run by a man called Bah, an athletic-looking black man who had lost half an ear in a fight. Many of the young white musical community played there, including the trumpeter and pianist Denis Rose, an artist sophisticated beyond his years, musically immensely knowledgeable and an acquaintance of Crombie's from Sundays spent in Petticoat Lane, listening to the latest American imports on the record stall. The music didn't require jazz, merely the current dance tunes played hard and loud, but Ronnie Scott's powerful sound suited the repertoire. And, from Rose, he began to appreciate subtleties of construction in music that he had never known existed.

Rose had drawn his friend Tony Crombie into clubland, transcribed the 'V-discs' taken from American broadcasts and reduced them to simple principles that his less sophisticated colleagues could make sense of. A tall, cadaverous figure with enormous bush-baby eyes in a bony face, he looked an artist from the crown of his Homburg to the tips of his two-tone shoes. He was a sharp operator, too, like a cross between an imperious Fred Astaire and an extra from a Hollywood gangster movie. Rose was the total jazz musician in a jazz world so short of real resources and insight. But he was a West End lad too, a survivor, at ease with the criminal fraternity, an inspired teacher, a listener to anything and everything and consistently and helplessly himself. Musically he had a mixture of intuition and natural comfort with structure, and a fund of knowledge culled from hour after hour spent in the Keith Prowse record shop, from opening time to closing time playing disc after disc, making notes.

But the Bouillabaisse didn't last, closing down and then reopening as the Fullado, another black club that encouraged jamming and a loose interplay of musicians. Crombie continued to be house drummer and Ronnie Scott took to visiting Archer Street regularly. When he was seventeen, and in the midst of debating with himself the pros and cons of a dance band job at a local venue, the Cricklewood Palais, Cissie at last arranged a meeting for Ronnie and Jock in an Archer Street café. The passing years had deadened much of Cissie's resentment and her desire to encourage her son, the musician, overcame what remained. Jock was respected in the business and well connected. He might be able to help.

Ronnie was initially shy at the meeting with Jock, who turned out to be exactly as he had imagined him – dapper, sharp, sussed and funny. Jock could see a headstrong quality in his son, the characteristics of a natural musical leader that might emerge too soon for his own good. 'Just read the parts,' Jock urged Ronnie, as he explained about the Cricklewood offer. 'Don't try to lead the saxophone section.' Jock was convinced Ronnie was running before he could walk, but the boy found his father's worries ironic, since as yet he could barely read music, let alone run anybody's show.

The scene was full of heroes, people you could look up to, borrow from, model a phrase or a walk or a gesture on. At the Potomac in Piccadilly and the Princes in Jermyn Street – both plush West End restaurants for those on a lot more than infantry pay – two bands alternated the sets since the establishments backed on to each other. One was run by the Belgian trumpeter Johnny Claes, the other by a glamorous local tenorist called Reggie Dare. Dare was everybody's idea of the romantic dance band musician. He was tall, blond, faintly eccentric (he gesticulated like a windmill in the most casual conversation, and had a neat sideline in conjuring tricks), with a lush, sensuous sound on ballads, a swaggering, grandiloquent manner of delivery and considerable popularity with women – which reputation, in those days, led to idle speculation about aspects of his expertise he couldn't display on the bandstand. Dare seemed everything a musician ought to be. What was also striking was that the tenorist allowed the musical fortunes to rest heavily on his own shoulders – at the time it was unusual for a saxophonist to work simply with a piano trio, since saxophone solos were still regarded in dance band circles as attractive as long as they were brief. Dare had a big influence on Ronnie Scott.

Johnny Claes was a different kind. He had a powerful trumpet sound, fierce and vigorous, not unlike Roy Eldridge. But a combination of musical farsightedness and all-round adventurousness made his band a suitable receptacle for transfusions from the emerging revolutionary jazz on the other side of the Atlantic. For a start it was a nine-piece – a remarkably flexible unit within which to combine the colourful harmonic possibilities of whittled-down big band arrangements with the alertness and manoeuvrability of a small group capable of highlighting soloists. When the Potomac opened, Ronnie Scott went to audition for Claes. The Belgian made as striking an impression as Reggie Dare had done. He drove fast cars (he was later to drive at Le Mans), he went to Jermyn Street for his haircuts, had family money and believed that the band's image was half the battle. This last axiom powerfully influenced Ronnie ten years on when he was a bandleader himself.

The Belgian was friendly, and liked the young man's sound. But, as with Krahmer before, to move from an orthodox dance band setting to one in which at least some experimenting with improvisation was possible, was a big step. Ronnie Scott continued to be unsure of the materials, couldn't read the scores and was trying to get by on sheer instinct and whatever devices used by the professionals he had been able to pick up.

It wasn't long before the chickens came home to roost. Claes invited Ronnie Scott to sit in at the Potomac for one night, get the feel of the band.

The experience shattered the young man's confidence. The music was too complicated and busking couldn't carry him through it. Claes gave him every chance but knew it was too soon. 'Look, son,' the Belgian said, 'you sound fine, but we really need someone who can read.' It was a disappointment but Ronnie knew that he was right, felt that if anything he was being let down gently. To escape from the club that night was a profound relief.

There was always the dance band world to fall back on. He took a job at the Royal, Tottenham, in a band led by Les Ayling in which Diana Coupland – later to move into acting – was the vocalist. Ronnie Scott hated the work because the band wore the kind of little grey bolero jackets he knew Crombie and Rose would crack up at the first sight of. He kept his connections with the East End.

A continual problem on the British jazz scene was the lack of inspiring models other than on disc. Since the end of the 1930s, the opportunity to hear Americans live in Britain had disappeared because of a Musicians' Union ban, a state of affairs that lasted well into the 1950s and which was the subject of considerable dispute in the music business. The diverting of shellac into the war effort similarly meant that the release of new records was all but drying up by 1944. The effect of these obstacles, though, was to make the mystique of the American music scene all the more irresistible. In that year, Scott and Crombie went to Levy's record store where there was a tiny recording studio. An ad hoc assembly of unevenly talented friends recorded 'My Blue Heaven' and 'Blues in C *Sharp* Minor' on an acetate. The second side was actually a blues in C minor but Harry Morris – the garrulous, wisecracking street-hustler who never played an instrument but loved the company of those who did – preferred being able to hear himself announce in a mid-Atlantic accent: 'From one kind of blues to another, "Blues in C *Shorp* Minor".'

The next year, a chance with Johnny Claes came again. The band was leaving the West End residencies and going on the road; it needed a new tenor player. Ronnie Scott was now faster, more familiar with the repertoire, more flexible between the keys. Claes was impressed and took him on. The alto player Jerry Alvarez took the young man aside. 'You'll learn a lot from Johnny,' Alvarez said. It had been his recommendation that had persuaded the Belgian to listen to Ronnie Scott a second time. Denis Rose, also in the group, made the finishing school all the more complete.

The band was sought after by the deprived British jazz fans. Not least because of its drummer Freddie Crump, an extraordinary black vaudeville performer from Richmond, Virginia, who had come from the States with the Blackbirds show in the early 1930s and stayed on. The possessor of an elephantine drumkit unplayable by any of his contemporaries, hand painted in white with black diamonds on the bass drum, the perspective entirely out of joint, Crump's antics were showstoppers. He could produce a deafening, monsoon-like noise from massively overweight cymbals that other musicians swore were made from the conning towers of submarines. He could play the kit as well with his back to it as facing it, his heel producing a thunderous barrage from the bass drum. He could also produce percussion sounds from his teeth and from just about any resonant object in the possession of nearby members of the audience, and he would sign off what he called his 'ack' by skidding across the stage on his stomach, diving into the orchestra pit and emitting one last celebratory crash on the pit-drummer's cymbal.

Though a minute figure of slender build, Crump could generate the sheer volume of a man twice his size, and he delivered it all with an unflagging affability. Tony Crombie was astonished by him. He never revised his original opinion that Freddie Crump was one of the most startling drummers he ever heard anywhere, including Buddy Rich.

But, strong as the musical impression of Claes' Claepigeons was, the impression of life on the road for a seventeen-year-old was stronger. Ronnie Scott had never left home for long periods before, and that first tour was one of the most exciting episodes of his young life. Road life for bands involved hours spent in buses and trains, on journeys made harder by the war years, but the circuit of tatty hotels and digs run by landladies who had in many cases been looking after touring musicians for years was new and full of promise to a young player.

On a stopover in Middlesbrough, Ronnie discovered with the local landlady's daughter just what it was that the older musicians had joked about and sometimes been anguished, chastened, maudlin about. In the front room, by the coal fire, Ronnie Scott discovered another compulsion, a pursuit in life that would be as exhilarating, treacherous, revealing and unpredictable as the affair with the Pennsylvania saxophone. Denis Rose was practising Harry James licks in the next room, his face contorted with the effort of playing James' vibrato. As the fire died down, Rose quietly played 'You're A Long Long Way From Home'.

The Claepigeons featured several of the sharpest and most inventive young players on the local scene, many of whom had heard enough of what was going on across the Atlantic to be certain that the musical future for the palais bands would offer them little. Claes operated more of a jazz policy than was commercially sensible at the time, but he would experiment endlessly with new ways of selling it, through stunts with lighting, novelty routines, anything that would make the band stand out.

But though Claes was a man with a feeling for the future, he could not visualise it as clearly, nor understand the forces at work in it as instinctively as the second trumpet player, the downbeat shepherd with a growing flock, Denis Rose. Rose's crucial role in the development of modern jazz in Britain is impossible to overestimate.

Rose had been called up for the Medical Corps late in the war, but had deserted and hid out in Soho. Though the war was winding down, the German Army had saved its energies for a last counter-punch in the winter of 1944. The setback occasioned a demoralising new call-up. The newspapers were once again full of tales of survival and of the not-so-fortunate being pulled from prim terraces in which the V1s and V2s had suddenly and unceremoniously ripped a hole, like an abruptly extracted tooth. A musical hero who had left a resounding impression in London during his work in Britain with forces' bands, Glenn Miller, went missing in an aeroplane during this time, and was never found.

But the following year seemed to herald that long-imagined deliverance and both citizens and soldiers could only hope – in the offhand manner of those for whom risk had become a daily condition of life – that fate wouldn't deal them a bad card so near the end of the game. For Ronnie Scott, Denis Rose and the young London jazz musicians in search of inspiration, the closing months of the war found them thrown ever more closely into the company of the visiting Americans in the forces' bands, which were exempt from a Ministry of Labour ban that otherwise prohibited American entertainers. The experience made them all the more curious about the culture that fuelled their dreams.

The Americans were only too aware of their impact. If the Benny Goodman band had included even half of the Americans who came through London during the war years claiming to have played with it, it would have been big enough to perform a Mahler opera. But the Sam Donahue band – an American forces unit under the direction of a hardened pro – was the real thing all right. Donahue and his musicians would congregate at a Soho club called the Nuthouse, where Carlo Krahmer had a band.

Sam Koontz Donahue was a tenor saxophonist and occasional trumpeter from Detroit, a man four-square in the tradition of big-band swing who was later to front a recreation of the Tommy Dorsey band in the early 1960s after the trombonist had died. Donahue never went down in the record books as a giant on his instrument, but in the small hours at the Nuthouse, to an audience unfamiliar with the finer points of jazz, in an ambiance of servicemen, good-timers, musicians and hookers stumbling on doctored whisky, the American could unleash the first romantic surf-rolls of 'Body and Soul' and the club would fall to reverential silence. The Donahue sidemen, a long way from home, finding music an invaluable calling-card and the status of their homeland a passport, were heroes. Denis Rose, Ronnie Scott, pianist Tommy Pollard and guitarist Pete Chilver would congregate at the all-night Lyons Corner House in Coventry Street, meet the Americans there, learn ideas from them.

One London club that became a magnet for the musicans among the American population was the Feldman – later to become The 100 – in Oxford Street, an establishment opened by a wealthy businessman for the benefit of his sons, familiar to Ronnie from the streets of Edgware, where they were already part of local folklore. Victor Feldman – nicknamed 'Kid Krupa' – was playing the drums with professionals when he was only seven, and the club was frequently a showcase for his remarkable talents. The club also attracted Americans on tour like Art Pepper, then an unwilling military policeman, a clean-cut, Italian-looking twenty-year-old and a gifted and precociously experienced saxophonist who had already learned the ropes in Benny Carter's band and still in his mid-teens had worked with legendary figures like Dexter Gordon.

Pepper had been playing in a military band at a convalescent centre for injured servicemen on their way back to the States or back into the war. He was the epitome of what all the London musicians wanted to be, a sophisticated messenger from the music's homeland, and his poise and fluency on the alto astounded Scott, who one night made a point of congratulating the young Californian on his artistry. Pepper simply said, 'If you liked that, you should hear Charlie Parker.' As yet, the name didn't mean a thing.

In the late spring of 1945, the press carried two items of information that were of particular interest to Ronnie, Sol and Cissie. In April, *Melody Maker* ran an item on the Claes band that concluded, 'Scott is undoubtedly one of the tenormen of the future.' And the following month, the same paper, under the headline 'Ring Dem Bells', elaborately announced: 'In this great symphony of discord VE day is the coda. Soon, the drums of war throughout the world will be stilled and the calm fluting of a peaceful theme will be stated for the world orchestra to play. May it be in full harmony.' The Second World War was over.

Cissie had shaken Ronnie awake on the morning the news broke. 'Wake up, wake up, it's VE Day!' It was a public holiday, everyone was heading into town to celebrate. Ronnie had marched around Trafalgar Square with his saxophone, Denis Rose accompanying with the trumpet. Then the two of them had gone to the East End, which had taken a fearful hammering during the war. Relief would be sweeter there than anywhere else in town. In Petticoat Lane a piano was wheeled on to the street. Ronnie Scott and Denis Rose performed with it while Flash Winston played the drums and the locals danced. The Royal Family visited the East End to pay its respects.

London had turned into one gigantic party. Outside Buckingham Palace and in Downing Street they thronged in their thousands. A West London magistrate declared: 'It goes against the grain to send anyone to prison today.' Londoners slept in the parks that night, or danced home to the suburbs in the early hours.

Through the war, people had grown used to hearing music brought to them – in the factories, in the forces, at public concerts. These changed expectations brought a boom in the dance halls. And after the invasion of American culture that had hit the nation in 1942 young people wanted jazz.

Of all the younger bandleaders likely to benefit from the emergence of a new and more demanding audience, the best equipped was undoubtedly Ted Heath, a trombonist who had made his mark with the outfit of the dance band specialist Geraldo but had broken away when offered the chance of a series of BBC broadcasts with a band of his own. He soon proved he was capable of fronting a highly commercial blend of the power, noise and drive of the thirties swing orchestras, but by adopting a policy of hiring front-line instrumentalists with a leaning toward modernism, his band had a compelling contemporary edge.

Ronnie Scott was keen for a change. On his nineteenth birthday he found himself already respected in his profession – making money, the apple of Sol and Cissie's eye, and still living in that tiny bedroom overlooking the garden in Edgware. But he was pulled between the conflicting demands of the showbiz appeal of making it big and the knowledge that there was so much to do on the saxophone that he had hardly yet begun. In Heath's band there were two musicians who knew Ronnie Scott's playing and understood his potential. One was Jack 'The Beat' Parnell, a spectacular young big-band drummer and the nephew of impresario Val Parnell (the music press of the day would describe him in such terms as 'ace high drum stylist') whose party-piece solos were a climax of the Heath act. The other was Dave Goldberg, a Scottish guitarist growing increasingly fascinated by the sporadic news of jazz revolutions taking place in the States. Both men recommended Ronnie Scott to Heath, and the young tenorist auditioned for the band at the BBC's Aeolian Hall.

Ronnie Scott was still convinced he didn't know enough – a conviction he was to sustain for a lifetime, but at this stage in his career it was probably true. He had learned by making instinctive connections, a facility born of a good ear and feel. But he was not a fast reader of music, and he had an appetite for personal embellishments that might not endear itself to a man as preoccupied with the finished product as Heath clearly was.

But on this day the fates were with him. He handled Heath's brash, pumping arrangements comfortably and the bandleader's lead altoist Les Gilbert had no hesitation in going over to his boss and giving the young contender the nod. Ronnie Scott found this acceptance hard to believe. Even more unexpected was Heath's offer when he went to the band's Albermarle Street office to sign up. 'The money will vary from week to week,' Heath began ominously. 'But you'll never earn less than £20 a week.' In 1946 that was a fortune. And since the band was in growing demand throughout that year, often they earned much more. They performed for a movie, *London Town*, with Kay Kendall. They did a Scandinavian tour, the first time Ronnie Scott had ever been out of austerity-hit England – breakfast on a continental railway, unlimited supplies of eggs, butter, three different kinds of bread. Being a snappy dresser in a business where appearances counted for a lot, Ronnie Scott took to spending much of his new-found wealth on made-to-measure suits in the latest square-shouldered American styles and bought his shirts from musicians coming off the transatlantic liners. More conservative columnists on *Melody Maker* bewailed the takeover of the music business by 'rainbow-tied, over-dressed, super-padded, loud-talking and queerly tonsured youths'.

If the war had changed the music that people wanted to hear, and the places they wanted to hear it in, it had also changed the way musicians wanted to conduct their business, causing a controversy that would affect the way Ronnie Scott himself would work only a few years later. The brilliant young trombonist George Chisholm had written in *Melody Maker* towards the end of 1945 that the days when the maestro was entitled to expect unquestioning obedience from musicians was passing. The music business would have to accept the fact that more and more young players would want real participation in the policies of the bands they played in, or they would break away and run co-operative bands from scratch. Ted Heath had replied to Chisholm in December 1945, saying that he believed in consultation with musicians but insisted on the right to run his own show.

It was a sign of the times. The Labour government, that had unexpectedly come to power in 1945, had been carried in by an awakened hope that the loosening of British class divisions glimpsed during the war years could be legislated out of existence in peacetime. Growing restlessness among young musicians was merely a reflection of the mood of the times, recognition that they were in an industry like any other and helping to make their employers rich. And as they hung out together in the corner-houses and after-hours joints, listening to records at Carlo Krahmer's flat in Bedford Court Mansions, the germ of independence took root.

But the war still had a trick to play. Early in Ronnie Scott's stint with the Heath orchestra, he got his call-up papers for the Army. By this time, any appeal the invitation might have had – the opportunity for adventure, to leave home, to strike out in the company of kids his own age – had been replaced by the excitement of his growing prospects as a professional musician. But the music business had its ways around official requests. The Heath musicians knew a doctor in west London who could take care of such eventualities. For £20, the physician – a shambolic figure with a fastidious Alec Guinness voice, horn-rimmed glasses, cigarette ash covering his lapels – would steadfastly maintain that a patient he had only just met had been known to him for years, and was moreover clearly unfit to travel on account of nervous stress or persistent headaches. Schooled by an expert, Ronnie Scott went to an RAF medical examination at Uxbridge, wearing Dave Goldberg's enormous overcoat down to his feet, unshaven, speeding on benzedrine. The medics knew plenty like this, but they bought the story. Now that the war was over, the really dedicated layabouts were more trouble to the forces than they were worth.

Ted Heath's music didn't particularly appeal to the young saxophonist, but he felt at home with the company. The lifestyle was seductive and players like Goldberg and Parnell were obviously interested in experimentation too.

Moreover, Ronnie Scott was in love.

He had met a girl called Joan Crewe, the pretty, dark and unassuming daughter of a Caledonian Road builder, at the Hammersmith Palais. She was sixteen, he dance band star, and he became Joan Crewe's first lover. Soon they were inseparable.

She joined the jazzmen's circle, as anyone in a relationship with one of them was more or less obliged to do, trying as best she could to keep up with the relentless nightlife, the long hours in the all-night cafés, and still get to work the next morning. She taught Ronnie Scott to dance, amazed that someone who could play music so naturally hadn't a clue about where to put his feet. They would practise jiving, Ronnie stopping and starting in unexpected places and insisting in response to Joan's perplexed look, 'There's two more beats yet before the end of the bar'; her laughing and saying, 'We're just dancing. Beats in the bar have got nothing to do with it.'

Though Cissie didn't make as much of an issue of it as some Jewish mothers, Ronnie knew she still wanted him to marry a 'nice Jewish girl'. But Joan's parents liked Ronnie, found him funny and charming and were impressed by such early success. They wanted the couple to marry too, couldn't really see, as the relationship grew and was clearly the most serious partnership either of them had known, why they didn't make their commitment to each other official. Ronnie had money and prospects, Joan had been at work from the age of fourteen; they were obviously in love.

But Ronnie distrusted marriage, a throwback to the elusive Jock, who wasn't cut out for it but did it anyway. When Joan became pregnant they chose a termination. 'I didn't regret it,' Joan would say later. 'It takes two to tango. But I knew I couldn't go on like that for ever.' The affair lasted for most of the next decade, though its conclusion would be stormy, and for the first time in his life break Ronnie Scott's confidence in the certainty that things would always pan out all right. Nothing that ever happened in the household under the care of Cissie and Nana Becky had ever made him doubt it.

The Heath band used to play Monday nights at the Hammersmith Palais, Ronnie Scott getting the spotlight on a solo rendition of 'I Surrender Dear', played in a hybrid style of the broad brush-strokes of the swing-era tenorists and the more complex and ambiguous variations of the modernists. This was a method much used by popular American saxophonists like Charlie Ventura. Parnell had frequently talked about forming a breakaway band of his own, and one night at the Palais Heath asked Scott if he had been invited to join – and if so, what his answer would be. The young man said he would go if Parnell wanted him, and then bit his lip. Heath was not really the kind of man to whom you could make such casual declarations. The bandleader looked momentarily aggrieved, but didn't pick it up.

It was risky to consider such a gamble. Over half the Musicians' Union's 4000 members had no regular employment at the time, and certainly wouldn't consider lightly relinquishing such a prestigious job as Heath's. But for the moment Heath bided his time.

Dave Goldberg shared a flat with fellow-guitarist Pete Chilver in Phoenix House, a rabbit warren of tiny apartments above the Phoenix Theatre in Charing Cross Road. The two men had become obsessed with the fragments of material that had been finding their way out of America, and Chilver in particular was investigating the flowing guitar style of Charlie Christian – a young swing-band musician who had been a star soloist with the Benny Goodman orchestra, pioneered revolutionary techniques for the new electrically amplified guitar, played rapid single-note solos like a saxophonist and made sensational use of fast chord changes to add rhythmic drive to the band. Christian had died of tuberculosis five years previously and had barely recorded, but the work of the young New York musicians developing an alternative to the set-pieces of the swing orchestras that dominated the labour market rang a bell with British players resigned to doing exactly the same.

Goldberg and Chilver made friends with two black American artists – L. D. Jackson and Cornell Lyons, 'The Businessmen of Rhythm', then performing a song-and-dance act at the London Palladium who had brought over with them some of the latest American recordings. From Jackson and Lyons, they heard stories of the 52nd Street nightclubs. London had been lively during the war years, but nothing like this.

One January Sunday in 1947, Ronnie Scott, Tony Crombie and Pete Chilver, with the bassist Lennie Bush and Laurie Morgan (a fast-developing young drummer who had first met Ronnie in the Fullado Club during the war) were at Carlo Krahmer's Bloomsbury flat for one of his informal record sessions. Art Pepper's hint to Ronnie Scott two years before that there was a musician at work in the States who had magically made sense of all the half-grasped visions and dammed-up energies of the dance band players had been pushed to the back of his mind by the excitements of life with Claes and Heath in those crowded years. This particular day rekindled it.

One record in particular was to be the focus of the afternoon's listening. But its impact, as it emerged from its featureless brown-paper sleeve outlasted an afternoon, in Ronnie Scott's case filled a lifetime. Out of the crackle and hiss came a sudden unison chorus. The tune seemed familiar, though far more urgent and driving than the idiom from which it had been borrowed and reforged. It swung easily, with that arrogant relaxation Ronnie Scott already knew as a trademark of American jazz. And at the end of the ensemble introduction arose something utterly different, a sound so bursting with life and tumultuous harmonic complexity as to be unlike any kind of saxophone playing Ronnie Scott had ever heard. It was a seamless flow of variations on the chords that never faltered, never repeated, that were perfectly shaped, shot through with the blues, and which would clearly have swung irresistibly even if all the soloist's colleagues had never shown up. The tune was 'Red Cross', a Savoy release of a last-minute adaptation of the chords of 'I Got Rhythm', cut to fill out the closing minutes of a three-hour recording session intended to be a vehicle for the unspectacular vocal talents of Art Tatum's guitarist Tiny Grimes.

The alto saxophonist was Charlie Parker.

# 3

# Hip

'The history of jazz can be told in four words. Louis Armstrong, Charlie Parker.'
(Miles Davis)

'Bird was like the sun giving off the energy we drew from.'
(Max Roach)

OVERNIGHT, LIFE WITH the Ted Heath orchestra felt like marking time. The word was out. Musicians of Charlie Parker's generation reported that hearing Bird – or 'Yardbird' – for the first time was like suddenly being able to recollect a dream, being able to see the clinching move in a game of chess, unexpectedly finding a locked door swing open before you. It was the solution to a problem that most young commercial musicians had only been able to experience as restlessness and frustration. It was not the music of the future, it was the music of its time, and when Ronnie Scott heard it he knew it was the only way to play.

He began, tentatively, to introduce as much of Parker's approach as he could understand into his own work. Denis Rose continued to dissect the mysteries of the American's transformation of chord patterns, transcribing the music of the new idiom from discs. Frequently the basic shapes of the old swing-era hits were used – 'I Got Rhythm', the underpinning of 'Red Cross', was a favourite. Another Parker composition 'Scrapple from the Apple' was the same tune, but with a counter-melody, taken from 'Honeysuckle Rose'. The music was a remoulding of everyday tools of the trade, but it had a sardonic edge too, a way of saying to the old bandleaders: 'You think you know this, but you don't.' Where the most basic chord structures would have sufficed for bar after bar of a dance tune, the revolutionaries would substitute new and complex variations that would add subtle colourings to the harmony even though not departing from the same roots.

A name evolved for this new music. It was a piece of onomatopoeia taken from its jittery, headlong momentum. It came to be known as bebop, or rebop. The latter version was the one in widespread use at the end of the 1940s.

In the winter of 1947, soon after that astonishing day at Carlo Krahmer's, Ronnie Scott's new inspiration led him to try one of Parker's most conspicuous devices on the Heath orchestra's version of 'Stars Fell On Alabama'. He played part of the solo in double-time, not entirely sure of the technicalities but carried ahead by sheer exhilaration, the notes flying and ricocheting over Parnell's steady swing. Heath didn't like it, but kept his objections to himself at first.

A little later, Ronnie Scott committed the musicians' cardinal sin of missing a gig. The band had been playing in Liverpool, and took the night train back to London for the following day's show. But Ronnie Scott was in adventurous mood. He had never been in a plane, suddenly fancied the idea, and booked into a Liverpool hotel overnight, planning to come back in style the next day. But snowstorms closed the airport, and the twenty-year-old Scots tenorist Tommy Whittle was quickly brought in to take the missing saxophonist's place. Shortly after, Scott received a brief note from his employer, informing him: 'Your services are no longer required.'

Whittle took Ronnie Scott's place. *Melody Maker*'s report on 22 February 1947 ran: 'Scheduled to join Ted Heath on Monday next is atomic tenor-stylist Tommy Whittle. He takes the place of the outstanding young tenorist Ronnie Scott who leaves Heath this week.' But alternative work, at least of the bread-and-butter kind, wasn't hard to come by. The same paper was soon announcing Ronnie Scott's arrival in the band of trumpeter (and later DJ) Jack Jackson at Churchill's, a West End restaurant. 'He is now in the kind of environment where he can take all the solos he wants' ran the story.

This wasn't strictly true. Pete Chilver and Laurie Morgan were in the band, and the musical direction was more chaotic than open-minded. Jackson was something of an old-style bandleader, as was his co-leader and pianist Hamish Menzies, and disliked the tendency of bop-influenced play-ers to go on playing solos that seemed to last half the night. Jackson and Menzies were also frequently fatigued by the resources of Churchill's bar, and would on occasions be simultaneously instructing the band to play completely different tunes.

Scott and his friends also played with pianist Jack Nathan's band at the

Coconut Grove (they inevitably redubbed it 'the Coconut Grave') in Regent Street, but the work was mostly dull and enlivened only by whatever attempts they could make to live it up in the West End. They broke the monotony by taking it in turns to ride Ronnie Scott's Triumph Tiger 100 motorbike around the backstreets during the intervals. There were a lot of biking fans amongst them – bassist Joe Muddell, saxophonist Harry Klein, and Ronnie himself, who would head the Tiger 100 home to Edgware in the small hours, often sitting on the pillion so that he could lie flat towards the handlebars like a racer. Ronnie Scott and the young altoist John Dankworth would also regularly visit the White City to watch the speedway, and even once visited a speedway school, an expedition they drew to a prudent close when they saw one of the riders fall off.

Dankworth was already recognised as a prodigy, and was to become as significant a bandleader in post-war British jazz as Ronnie Scott. Dankworth was from Highams Park in Essex, an enthusiastic music student who had begun as a classically trained clarinettist, developed an interest in jazz and impressed Art Pepper as one of the most promising musicians emerging in Britain on those nights at the Feldman Club in the last year of the war. Dankworth took to the alto after hearing Charlie Parker's 'Cherokee' on the BBC's *Radio Rhythm Club* and had quickly made a reputation for himself on the unfamiliar instrument.

But the young pioneers knew that they were wasting time. All that they could make of the new American genre was a rough approximation of its superficial qualities. They knew little of the culture from which it had come, little of the cities that had become its bases and whose vibrations it apparently reflected, and the union ban meant that there was little prospect of hearing its high priests anywhere in Britain.

The Londoners knew that there was a shot in the arm to be had for their condition, just a plane ride away. They were all out there, on every street, in every club. Dizzy Gillespie, Charlie Parker, Lester Young and Coleman Hawkins, back to back, side by side in the basements of brownstones in the heart of non-austerity, unrationed, superhip New York.

Laurie Morgan chatted it over with Chilver one night in the bandroom at Churchill's. Chilver said, 'Let's go over there, see what it's all about.' Morgan was so keen he sold his car and his drumkit to raise the fare. He already had some contacts in the States – a woman he'd known in London had married a GI and left with an open invitation for him to visit the West Coast, and Americans he'd met on tours of the airforce bases had promised the same. Tony Crombie and Ronnie Scott decided to go under their own steam and Crombie got in touch with the editor of the *Musical Express and*

*Accordion Times* (a forerunner of the *NME*) to see if the sale of some articles on the New York scene might help to subsidise the journey, and arrange some accreditation that might help with reluctant club managements into the bargain. The paper accepted, but Ronnie Scott hadn't saved much of the proceeds of his prosperous year with Heath, so the journey's overheads had to be pared to the bone. The cheapest flight to New York was by Icelandic Airways – a method that took the best part of twenty-four hours.

But New York dispelled all that. It was an experience as different from everyday life as arrival on another planet. New York was just the way it had been described those nights in the Coventry Street corner-house and the Feldman Club, but bigger, faster, noisier, wilder. Hershey bars, pineapple drinks, butter, modern shirts, ties. The 52nd Street buildings frequented by 'studios for sign painters and silkscreen operators, mail order drops, import export concerns run out of a hat, offices for private detectives and teachers of the piano and saxophone, darkrooms shared by photographers who prowled Broadway nightclubs with Speed Graphics,' as Ross Russell described in his biography of Charlie Parker. Scott and Crombie took a cab, dumped their luggage at a rundown Greenwich Village hotel called the Marlton on West Eighth Street and took off into town.

They discovered in the days that followed that the tensions and euphoria of New York were much bigger than getting a three-inch down-page write up in *Melody Maker*. If they weren't playing they were listening or arguing or shouting, going around in bunches singing riffs and licks.

They found that Bird was the Messiah. People would turn in jobs to follow him around the country. They recognised that Bird's sound – quite apart from his lightning fingering and tumbling phrasing – lay in gospel music and the blues, though much of its sophistication was drawn from that musical genius's absorption of European orthodox devices too. It seemed to be the voice of an emerging consciousness in post-war youth. But above all, it was the sound of America. The sound, the hum, the background noise of Edgware or Stepney, or even Archer Street, was not the same. As the older generation had always said, New York seemed like a place with no traditions and no respect. But it was a place where, over the preceding century, the blood vessels of many cultures joined. The result seemed to course with more feverish heat than anything the visitors had encountered before.

The New York jazz clubs mostly occupied basements or abandoned ground floors of the brownstones. They were popular and made money through fast turnover. Many would be cleared of punters every half hour or so and a fresh audience brought in. Of all the 52nd Street joints, it was The

Three Deuces that impressed Ronnie Scott the most. This was a cramped establishment at the Sixth Avenue end of the block, run by a young Jewish jazz fan called Sammy Kaye. Three cards spread in a poker hand was its emblem, which adorned the entrance. The doorman was a man called Pinkus, who wore a commissionaire's peaked cap and an overcoat, and always smoked a cigar. 'Come on in, folks. You're just in time for the complete performance,' he would say to all and sundry, regardless of what stage the performance had actually reached. When Ronnie Scott met Pinkus years later he was still doing the same job. He insisted: 'I'm the happiest man in New York.'

Charlie Ventura's band was in residence on the Londoners' first trip, featuring the idiosyncratic trombone-playing of a regular Woody Herman sideman, Bill Harris. Ventura, a white swing saxophonist in the style of Chu Berry, had found a modern context for the idiom in a music halfway between swing-band sensationalism and bebop. Harris's trombone and the crackling drumming of Dave Tough were enough to convince Scott and Crombie that they were in the right town. But it wasn't simply the music, it was the venue, and the street. Even in the war years, when Sam Donahue had entranced the regulars at the Nuthouse, London had never supported such establishments dedicated to music lovers such as these.

Scott and Crombie went everywhere in pursuit of music. They heard Duke Ellington's orchestra playing the interval show at a Broadway cinema, and Lionel Hampton's band at the Apollo Theatre in Harlem, where they were the only whites in the crowd. They got themselves photographed on the balcony of the Roseland Ballroom, looking like a couple of apprentice Mafia hitmen. They heard the full impact of the new vocabulary of jive-talk, a language developed to shut intruders out, just as the growing fashion for wearing dark glasses at all times of the day or night was designed to do. To be hip, or not, that was the question. If you could dig the music, you were probably not a 'square'. If it was a 'knock-out', or even a 'gas', you were halfway there. A mystifying catchphrase was a useful hipster prop. 'Steady, Waldo,' Laurie Morgan would insist, to no one and for no reason in particular.

Morgan and his non-playing partner Harry Morris (who had a photography arcade in Soho, looking like Chico Marx behind the unwieldy 1940s cameras) had gone out to the West Coast and Morgan remained there for months, much of the time at the Westlake Music College. He met Bird fans there, played the records long into the night with them, discs on which the Parker solos were worn out with repeated listening. Scott and Crombie, meanwhile, were running out of funds. A visit to Ronnie Scott's Uncle Phil,

33

one of Jock's brothers who worked at a tailoring establishment called Bond Menswear on Times Square, won them an evening of elaborate tales of the money he made as a gambler, but no hard cash. They had an open ticket back by sea, but the Cunard office told them that the boats were booked, that they would have to wait at least ten days. The two lived on coffee and doughnuts for the rest of their stay, came back broke, sleeping rough on a shabby vessel called the *Ernie Pyle*. But it couldn't take away the taste that New York had given them. They couldn't wait to go back.

When Ronnie Scott returned to London, in the midsummer of 1947, it was to find that *Melody Maker* was sponsoring a public recording session at the EMI studios on Sunday 29 June, and that 128 British musicians had been given the job of choosing a series of pick-up bands made up of what they thought were the leading musicians of the day. The tenors were Ronnie Scott, Reggie Dare and Tommy Whittle. Ronnie Scott performed with Woolf Phillips on trombone, Pete Chilver on guitar and the lyrical blind piano player George Shearing, later to become an expatriate to the States and an international jazz star with his composition 'Lullaby of Birdland', inspired by the same wondrous exposure to 52nd Street. *Melody Maker* recorded that Scott wore red, white and blue socks (which it took to be a patriotic gesture following his absence abroad) and played an elegant rendition of 'Blue Moon'. He also performed alongside Dare, his old hero.

Only five years had passed since the days when he would have found this company awe-inspiring, but America had changed all the young players who had made the trip, and many more were shortly to follow. For Ronnie Scott, absorption of new influences was happening so fast that it was in danger of swamping the musician he might uniquely be. America had been the experience that completed his transition into a natural front man for his musical generation. It was a role he would always deflect himself but which was increasingly acknowledged by those who came into contact with him. It could only be a matter of time before he would lead a band of his own. Jock Scott's cautionary advice that he shouldn't try to run the show had applied to young men of an era gone by. The war had taken care of that.

Opportunities quickly came, sooner than Scott could have anticipated. The *Queen Mary*, refitted after its emergency service as a troop-ship, was due for its second honeymoon on the transatlantic run and needed musicians to make up the several bands booked for the voyage. Drummer Bobby Kevin was forming one that Scott was invited to join, with John Dankworth as its alto player.

Playing dance-tunes for the revellers on the *Queen Mary* was a small price to pay for the trip. When the boat docked in New York there was a celebration to herald the return of transatlantic business-as-usual, but the musicians had other celebrations in mind, a return to the fountainhead of the music that obsessed them. Laurie Morgan, still in the States, knew they were coming. He knew better than to bother to welcome them at the quayside. He went instead to 52nd Street, stood outside The Three Deuces and waited. Within an hour, the Englishmen rounded the corner. Scott, Dankworth and their friends were breathless for another tour of their wonderland. Kansas Fields, a drummer who had befriended Morgan, took them into Harlem. It was as if Ronnie Scott had never been away and England seemed like a country you could hold in the palm of your hand. They were green but even the stings didn't hurt them. Dankworth offered his cab driver a twenty-dollar bill for a two-dollar fare, and the driver gratefully vanished in a cloud of dust. Saxophonist Harry Klein ecstatically proclaimed to Charlie Parker, 'That's the best music I ever heard.' 'Lend me twent dollars,' said the great man. Klein didn't hesitate.

Ronnie Scott did half a dozen trips on the *Queen Mary* during the following year. One night at The Three Deuces, Miles Davis and Charlie Parker were together, the young trumpeter nothing like the faltering and hesitant newcomer of the recordings of the period. But it was still a one-way traffic. The impasse remained and back in Britain the union ban still held out. Dizzy Gillespie's Orchestra was due to visit at Ted Heath's invitation in March 1948 but Ministry of Labour rules didn't allow it to play. Music press headlines from the band's gig in Copenhagen declared: 'Tense, neurotic – but it's DYNAMITE!'

Early in 1948, Denis Rose and Harry Morris opened a short-lived club called the Metropolitan Bopera House and Rose led a sextet there with Ronnie, Dankworth, Tommy Pollard, Lennie Bush and Tony Crombie. For Ronnie Scott, it was now one of a host of opportunities. Whatever the circumstance he was always bursting to play, and would frequently appear as a guest soloist with local rhythm sections as well.

There was a refuge for converts to the bop school such as Ronnie. From October 1947 he had become a regular performer in the band led by Tito Burns, who had made an unusual mark as a bebop accordion player. Pete Chilver and Denis Rose were in it and the band was a convenient hiding-place for them. Burns was a bebop fan at the time but later lost confidence in being able to make the music commercial. Stoke Newington town hall was one of the band's ports of call. In Jack Oliver's semi-pro band, which played there too, was a stocky, humorous, easy-going young tenorist called Pete King. It was a short meeting, but led to a lifelong friendship.

When the young players came back off the boats they were, as Laurie

Morgan would later put it, 'boiling with music'. The problem was that there weren't many places to let off steam and if you did it on somebody else's time you weren't likely to be asked back.

One solution to the problem was a tatty basement called Mac's Rehearsal Rooms in Windmill Street, opposite the Windmill Theatre. Since it was so close to Archer Street, the young boppers would book the room on Monday afternoons and pass the word – surreptitiously – that playing would be going on there for anyone who fancied a little animated relaxation. Regulars were Scott and Dankworth, Tony Crombie, Laurie Morgan, trumpeters Hank Shaw and Leon Calvert, bassists Lennie Bush and Joe Muddell, pianists Tommy Pollard and Bernie Fenton, altoist Johnny Rogers, with occasional visits from Denis Rose. It rapidly became a focus for jam sessions, and it caused a stir in Archer Street. Laurie Morgan would keep his drumkit in the Piccadilly left-luggage office, available for use at the drop of a hat. Secret messages would be passed. And when they played, curious faces would pop round the door, anxious to listen or blow.

So much curiosity was aroused that the ever-vigilant Harry Morris convinced the others that a golden opportunity was being missed by neglecting to charge the listeners for the privilege. Events at Mac's Rehearsal Rooms became more frequent. Both Dankworth and Crombie led bands there, augmented from time to time by visitors. And because there were ten musical 'regulars' plus Morris, who became the unofficial manager and doorman, the establishment was dubbed the Club Eleven on its opening night of 11 December 1948. It was the first club in Britain to present an all-jazz repertoire, with a policy devised entirely by a co-operative who were also practitioners themselves.

At night, life in the club was the perfect definition of bop style and exclusivity. Much of the dress was American derived, for those who could afford it. There were the drape-back jackets with aggressive shoulders, pegged cuffs, Billy Eckstine shirts, lurid ties with a big knot. Cecil Gee's was the outfitter that specialised in the genre. Detractors of the lifestyle – and that was almost everybody not intimately involved with it, in particular the adherents of the new cult of traditional New Orleans jazz that was gathering steam in south London and Kent – spoke disparagingly of it all, sardonically dismissing the hipsters and their 'fruit salad' ties.

There were plenty of other variations. Corduroy bags were popular, prismatic sweaters, waistcoats. Thelonious Monk's polka-dot bow-tie was also much imitated (the two bands at the Club Eleven had red and blue ones respectively) and so were cravats. Music was for a more sophisticated young clientele – taking unwitting advantage of the fact that the university population at the end of the 1940s had reached an all-time high, partly due to the return to studies of forces personnel back from the war.

There was nothing prepossessing about the Club Eleven in those days. Visitors descended the wooden staircase opposite the Windmill to find themselves in a cramped, low-ceilinged room with a bandstand at one end dimly lit by bare bulbs. A few battered sofas passed for the soft furnishings. But on a good night the Club Eleven could be the wildest place in town. Young women who became regulars at the club developed their own half-speed dancing momentum to cope with the breakneck tempos of bop, dirndl skirts elegantly twirling, backs straight, cooler and more distant than the jitterbuggers that had preceded them.

Other implications of bebop were emerging on either side of the Atlantic. For Louis Armstrong's generation, a white-run entertainment industry, frequently racist, demanding everyday humiliations and compromises, none the less seemed an inevitable world of work. In the generation that followed, Lester Young symbolised a Bohemian retreat into another world with its own language; its own ethics, its own mode of dress – the beginnings of hipsterism. But though the beboppers idolised Young, they were different. The sound of the music was fierce, urgent, where Young was a pretty, mellifluous storyteller. Pioneered by Kenny Clarke, bop drumming took the beat from the bass drum to the top cymbal (a more varied, flowing and sensuous approach) and left the bass, tom toms and snare for accents. The metronomic quality of the swing bands was thus disrupted at a stroke. Thelonious Monk, an unorthodox and untrained pianist immersed in church music and hymns, played percussively with his fingers splayed, used unconventional chords, and welcomed bop as a way of freezing out strangers, musicians who, by his standards, weren't really serious.

In early 1949 Ronnie Scott and Johnny Dankworth got a chance to sample Parker's work at even closer range. They were invited to the Paris Jazz Festival, where many of the heroes were scheduled to appear. Scott nearly didn't make it at all because whilst waiting at the airport to leave he discovered that his passport was out of date: 'We can let you through,' said the customs officer to Ronnie Scott's frantic pleading. 'But you'll never get off at the other end.' As with the invitation to join the Army, official obstacles were not always impenetrable to musicians who knew the ropes. In an unstable post-war world, it was often only necessary to know the right phone number. Scott eventually tracked down a passport official after hours, and it took a fiver to get the passport problem fixed. The delay made him a day late, and put him on to a plane heading into the worst storm he was ever unlucky enough to fly through. But by the time Scott, altoist

Johnny Rogers and Dankworth found themselves in a small club in St Germain, busking gently through their semi-bop repertoire, all the effort became worthwhile.

The word came that Charlie Parker was on the way. When he arrived – a large shapeless young man with a fitfully angelic look that dissolved the world-weary impression of his shambling appearance – he was followed by an entourage of acolytes. He joined the band, borrowing Dankworth's alto, roared through an uptempo bebop standard, insisted on playing no more choruses than his fair share – to the chagrin not only of those who had come to watch, but to those other performers on the stand who would have been happy for him to go on all night.

Dankworth discovered, standing next to Bird, that the saxophonist hardly needed a microphone, could – as bandleader Thad Jones once remarked – 'seal every crack in the wall' with his sound. Ideas tumbled from him, even when he was exhausted, in bad mental shape, or drunk. Dankworth said later that his alto felt as if it had been transformed by Parker's handling of it, seemed as if it had somehow been 'opened up'. Parker's wind came up from the gut, his stomach muscles could be made so taut that he could resist a full-blown punch in the midriff as if it were a playful tap. Moreover, he had served an apprenticeship with the orchestras, was used to making a big sound in big venues.

This unmistakable craftsmanship, behind the mannerisms of Bohemianism and the language of a new music, helped Jock Scott, who sometimes bumped into his son in Archer Street, to admire the boy's achievements without always understanding them. 'Come down to our club one night,' Ronnie urged him. 'See what it's all about.' 'Maybe I will,' Jock would reply. 'But it's not really my cup of tea.' He never came.

Ronnie Scott's admiration for the long-lost father who had suddenly come back into his life, a man who was widely respected in the same line of business, might have been expected to bring the two closer together. But their pursuit of the same profession made it harder, because they occupied such different parts of it. The difficulties presented by a generation gap that both men could experience musically as well as socially were brought sharply home to both of them over the episode of the *Caronia*.

The *Caronia* was a cruise liner booked for a round-the-world trip in December 1949, starting with a series of journeys between New York and the Caribbean. Jock invited his son to join the band. Ronnie, attracted by the idea of such an exotic journey and by the thought of getting to know his father better, agreed. The ship sailed from Southampton to pick up its passengers, then from New York to the West Indies and back.

They were a long way from home, but some old habits weren't left behind at the docks. On his first night on the *Caronia* the head barman invited Jock to his cabin for an introductory drink. 'What's your name?' the sailor asked. 'Jock Scott.' 'Pleased to meet you. Makes a change from these fucking Yid bandleaders.'

Jock was cut out for this kind of work. He had a remarkable memory for music, and absorbed new pieces fast. But though he was an irrepressible joker, he had his diffident side too, as did his son. The *Caronia* cruise was for millionaires, and there was only one class – first. The sidemen repeatedly asked Jock to make more of an effort to persuade the customers to leave tips – 'They're good bungers, these people,' Jock's partners would say. 'You have to chat them up a bit.' 'I don't want to do that,' Jock said. 'It's not my style.' They talked him into it eventually. When one of the Americans next approached the bandstand to request a tune, the bandleader came straight to the point. 'Do you want the five-dollar version or the twenty-dollar version?' He was reported to the purser for it.

Ronnie got bored. Apart from the band's bassist, Pete Blannin, and Harry Conn, a saxophonist, the other musicians were all of his father's generation. At that time, congenial company to Ronnie Scott meant people to whom you could talk about Bird, and Diz, work out licks and complicated chord substitutions, share a private language. The only virtue of the trip had been the opportunity it afforded to visit the New York clubs once again. Ronnie had sat with Harry Conn one night listening to Charlie Parker and a gentler white West Coast saxophonist, Lee Konitz, and the older man had said of Parker: 'I prefer the other guy.'

'You'll learn,' Ronnie had said pityingly. 'You'll learn.'

But when the *Caronia* docked again at Pier 90 on the return journey from the Caribbean there was a letter from Joan Crewe. She was sick of waiting. Life seemed to amount to little more than waiting for him to come back from one job or another. It was the final straw. Ronnie decided to cut the job short and come back to London. However, technically, the musicians became merchant seamen for the duration of the cruise and were answerable to the purser. Ronnie Scott persuaded his mother to send a wire from London stating, 'Grandmother dangerously ill – come home at once.' He then went across the quays to the *Queen Mary*, which had also docked and was due for its return trip to Southampton. He looked out Ray Feather, the tenorist on the *Mary* and asked: 'How do you feel about going round the world?' Feather accepted. The hard part was then to persuade the officers on both ships. The hardest part of all was telling his father.

Jock didn't believe a word of it. He was furious at what he believed was a combination of deception and ingratitude on the part of his son. They had a heated argument about it and the confrontation exposed the ambivalence of Ronnie's feelings towards his father.

'It's a matter of principle,' the older man insisted.

'You can't tell me about principles!' Ronnie Scott shouted back. 'My mother's told me all about you. You can't have a go at me.' It wasn't even true. Cissie had never spoken disparagingly of Jock. Ronnie regretted the outburst all his life. Jock even wrote a letter to the Musicians' Union in London demanding his son's expulsion from it, but had second thoughts and tore it up. Ronnie went home.

Back in London, Club Eleven continued to be the place to be. It wasn't only a jamming and socialising haunt for local players, it was a refuge for visiting musicians as well. Benny Goodman, Ella Fitzgerald and the composer Tadd Dameron all appeared in the audiences there. Dameron was returning a social call that Scott and bassist Pete Blannin had made to him on the *Caronia*'s stopover – when Miles Davis had arrived in the middle of the evening, taken one look at the two Londoners and growled to Dameron, 'What you doing with these ofay cats?'

Club Eleven was so popular, and yet so poorly endowed, that a move was essential. In April 1950, they took a bold step, shifting the premises to number 50 Carnaby Street, one of the hippest thoroughfares in London, as it was to be again a generation later. The club moved into a disused night-club, as shabby as Mac's, but it was somewhere to take the music to, and somewhere to hang out. The doorman was Charlie Brown, a black ex-boxer and the landlord of 10 Rillington Place, an address that became one of the most famous in English criminal history as the location for a gruesome string of murders. Musicians and fans ate at 50 Carnaby Street, played cards there, drank there, played.

New premises occasioned thoughts of a new policy. It might be worth trying to get some of the passing international celebrities to perform at the club to raise its profile. But the subject was a minefield at the time. The legendary saxophonist Sidney Bechet had illegally played a concert in defiance of the Ministry of Labour's and the Musicians' Union's strictures in November of the previous year and the men who had brought him in were convicted and fined in June 1950. Nevertheless, they figured that if they got a big fish on the hook, they could then argue the pros and cons later.

They sent an invitation to Billie Holiday, the optimistic young proprietors of Club Eleven offering $250 for a week's work and accommodation. They didn't mention the air fare, had no idea they were supposed to. They didn't know the singer's whereabouts either, and sent the request care of the American jazz magazine, *Downbeat*. Knowing Lady Day was involved with drugs, they dropped various hints about being able to meet more exotic requests. But, unsurprisingly, they never got a response.

Ronnie Scott continued to grow as a British musical celebrity. The saxophonist (and subsequently writer) Benny Green later recalled the day at Sherry's Ballroom in Brighton when he was playing his first professional assignment and discovered that Ronnie Scott had arrived on the balcony of the hall. Scott's reputation made the saliva dry up in Green's mouth and he couldn't play a note.

Back in Club Eleven, trouble was brewing. Ever since the war years and the American 'invasion', drugs had been part of the scenery. For those living from day to day in a city under attack, edging along a highwire of nerves, it was bad enough. For musicians in that world, driven moreover by a boiling desire to crash through a sound barrier to the sublime, to play as well as their heroes, to play as well as each other and better, some drugs seemed an aid to stamina and concentration. They could, as Laurie Morgan put it, 'shorten the distance between not knowing and knowing something'.

Most of the problems associated with this centred on the pianist Tommy Pollard, who was one of the first of the circle to become dependent on hard drugs. Pollard was a brilliant musician, who understood the circumlocutions of bebop as well as Rose and was genuinely 'inside' the music rather than simply covering its mannerisms. But he was already a heroin addict and the habit was leading him toward the fringes of the underworld.

The night of 15 April 1950 promised nothing out of the ordinary. Ronnie Scott was playing Parker's 'Now's The Time', with his eyes closed as was his frequent habit. When he opened them he found that the club was teeming with police. A massive uniformed sergeant almost blocked his vision.

The scene was chaotic, close to farce. Ronnie Scott had cocaine in his wallet, and no chance whatsoever of disposing of it. Denis Rose headed frantically for the stairs, hoping to escape from the club's lavatory window. Scott saw him again a few seconds later being carried back down by two policemen, his feet not touching the ground. Rose already knew he was in big trouble, since his unannounced absence from military service wasn't going to go down well, whatever else he might be charged with. Everyone was carted away to Savile Row.

The night in the cells was rescued by the fact that many of the miscreants were jailed together, and that Flash Winston was present, who treated the whole thing as an opportunity for a solo recital. It had been helped on its way by the behaviour of the police themselves, obviously unfamiliar with the intricacies of this kind of arrest. One of the confiscated items was a matchbox used for smoking roaches, with a scorched hole in it where the joint would be inserted. The station sergeant had declared authoritatively to a constable, to the barely concealed hysterics of the accused: 'See that. They sniff it through there.' Mario Fabrizi, the Italian Cockney who was to win fame as Corporal Merryweather in *The Army Game*, was one of those in the cell, and similarly grasped the opportunity to milk the situation. Winston took to crawling across the cell during the night and banging on the door, croaking, 'Water, water!'

It all looked more serious in daylight. The magistrate knew nothing about the jazz life, or about jazz clubs, and seemed to feel that he was standing on the bridge between the nation's moral welfare and the assault of a collection of dangerous Americanised subversives. 'Musicians and Seamen in Early Morning Raid' trumpeted the *Evening News* in alarm. 'Police Swoop on a Soho Bebop Club!'

Sol and Cissie had been petrified by the news. They distrusted the obsession with America and the idols that Ronnie and his friends had chosen to follow, but they still trusted him. They knew he wasn't a drug addict. He had tried heroin and it had made him so sick, vomiting and struggling for breath, that he had thought he was going to die and swore never to touch it again.

For Joan Crewe, it was different. Through the circle of musicians, she had already encountered the drug and took to it, as she later admitted, 'like a duck to water'. It could blind you to feeling, make you indifferent to sadness, preserve the euphoria of the nightlife, the energy of the music, the anarchic originality of the company, long after natural reserves ran out. She had tried to keep it from Ronnie, but it was a hard habit to hide. When he found out, he would repeatedly examine her arms to look for the marks and she would try to cover up by using the same point over and over again. 'Marry me and I'll stop using drugs,' Joan said to Ronnie one day. 'Stop for three months and I will,' was his answer, but there was no opportunity to prove he meant it. Joan didn't and couldn't stop. The habit was so little understood that expert support for withdrawal hardly existed. Ronnie Scott had even gone to the Caledonian Road police station to ask if there was anything the law could do.

Joan came to the court to meet Ronnie and the others after the case. Uncle Mark was waiting there too. He came over to the young woman and asked, 'Are you Joan?'

She nodded.

'Who are you waiting for?'

'I'm waiting for Ronnie.'

Uncle Mark twisted the meaning. 'Don't you think it's time you stopped waiting? He's never going to marry you, you know.'

Joan was still stinging from that barb when Ronnie Scott and the others left the courtroom. She had never wanted to be Jewish so much in her life.

# 4

# It Won't Always Be Like This

'Denis thought it was all childish. As the elder statesman, he always thought we were silly, getting stoned out of our minds, thinking we were God.'

(Laurie Morgan to Kitty Grime, *Jazz At Ronnie Scott's*, Hale, 1979)

'How do we know that Jesus was Jewish? He lived at home until he was thirty. He went into his father's business. His mother thought he was God Almighty. And he thought she was a virgin.'

(Jewish gag)

CLUB ELEVEN'S LANDLORDS were not unfamiliar with the courts. They recommended a lawyer to their tenants, whose case was due to come before Justice Daniel Hopkins at Marlborough Street Court. The rumour that Hopkins suffered from gout came as little consolation. 'Maybe we should fire the lawyer and get a chiropodist,' Flash Winston suggested.

When the case came to sentence, it looked bad. All twelve miscreants convinced themselves that prison was inevitable. The magistrate's position was ambiguous. On the one hand, he was clearly of the view that any form of drug usage was taking its adherents, and anyone who came into contact with it, straight to hell. On the other, he was citing the previous good behaviour of all the young men before him, of their education, of the high standing of some within the music business, of their prospects. London's modern jazz scene was obviously a mystery to him, however.

'What's bebop?' the magistrate enquired of the officers of the law.

'It's a queer form of modern dancing,' Chief Inspector Brandon of Savile Row had replied. 'A negro jive.'

'This sounds a queer sort of place to me,' the magistrate reflected. 'A very rum place.'

In the end they were all heavily fined and told to shape up. But even though nobody went to jail, Club Eleven didn't really recover. The place closed a few months later: somehow, the heart had gone out of it and no one was especially surprised. The explosion of the discovery of bebop was already three years into the past. They had all discovered how much they wanted to play it. But they hadn't yet worked out why.

The players celebrated a hip lifestyle intended to exclude the 'peasants' – everybody else. They withdrew into practised nihilism fuelled by Mum's chicken dinners. They were wild, arrogant, frightening to some in their private languages, hyperactive habits, frequent insensitivity to women who weren't blood relations, and even those that were. Their version of American jazz possessed very little of the sensuous relaxation that some of the originators displayed.

Laurie Morgan and Denis Rose were both unhappy. Morgan thought that there was little romance in it: 'In a jungle,' he would say later, 'you can pick an orchid and another one grows while you're watching. In a greenhouse it's much harder. That was the difference between America and Britain.' Morgan thought there was a religious and spiritual dimension to the black American experience that confounded the most sophisticated grasp of technique. He felt that the players in Britain didn't listen to each other sufficiently and didn't, in the end, support each other. Unhappiness with the inheritance of a borrowed culture almost made him give up the drums.

Rose felt much the same. After years of being a cornerstone in the development of some semblance of credibility for British bop, he became jaundiced with the jostling for music-business work, and the delicate politics of juggling a progressive music policy with the expectations of promoters and dance hall managers.

Some bandleaders grasped the nettle of taking bebop to the dance halls, and generally adopted a conciliatory stance, usually employing a vocalist to sing the hits. Dankworth, Tito Burns, the pianist Ralph Sharon and saxophonist Kenny Graham – a gifted and highly original tenor player and composer – all took bop-oriented bands around the halls, though Burns's heart eventually ceased to be in it and he and his singer wife Terry Devon moved steadily back towards showbiz.

Carlo Krahmer was by now acting as a chronicler of the work of his younger colleagues, having established a record label – Esquire – with his wife Greta and an old friend, drummer Peter Newbrook, who had been his deputy in the wartime days when Krahmer had gigs all over town and frequently double-booked himself. As dedicated collectors, they were convinced that a market existed for the new British jazz and recordings made by the independent American companies – neither of which much interested the existing duopoly of Decca and EMI. Esquire set about recording Ronnie Scott and John Dankworth, Krahmer's old vibraphone pupil Victor Feldman and many other local players – as well as re-pressing foreign recordings. The activity helped bring Charlie Parker, Dizzy Gillespie and Miles Davis to British ears. Esquire even released modern classics by Alban Berg and Arnold Schoenberg. The early Esquire releases were through a mail-order record club that sold ten-inch 78s for ten shillings, twelve-inch ones for fifteen.

Krahmer signed Ronnie Scott to the label at the beginning of 1951, and the tenorist recorded extensively through that year. But anyone who had heard him in the Heath days would have barely recognised his sound now. The muscular swagger of the Ventura influence, compounded by swing players like Flip Phillips and local heroes like Reggie Dare had mostly disappeared. Ronnie's tone was now delicate, muted, fragile as an alto sax instead of a tenor, being played by someone trying not to wake the occupants of an adjoining room.

Though hearing Charlie Parker had been a revelation as a way of approaching jazz, Ronnie Scott had not tried to absorb Bird's technicalities as meticulously as Dankworth. And when a 1948 recording of the Woody Herman band demonstrated to him the utterly different skills of Stan Getz, a white Philadelphia saxophonist of his own age who had derived his style from Lester Young, Ronnie was hooked. Out of the rich, swaying sound of an American big band at the height of its confidence, at the end of sonorous, downward-spiralling reed section passages, the brass elbowing insinuatingly into it, came a sound as delicate as a breeze in branches. It was Getz on the classic 'Early Autumn', playing a brief but gem-like solo ending in a coda like a flurry of falling leaves.

Ronnie Scott was knocked sideways by Stan Getz. He recorded tunes like 'Too Marvellous For Words' and 'September Song' for Krahmer two years later with that light airy sound, the notes blown like bubbles gently propelled into space. Scott absorbed influences fast. As with the uncannily accurate impressions of movie stars of the day with which he entertained his colleagues, he had no trouble mimicking anything he could hear as a player either. He had a feeling for inflection and nuance that in jazz transformed the often rudimentary materials inscribed on a stave into music of vibrant beauty.

The knack won him many things – regular occupancy of the 'top tenor' slot in the music-press polls for being what amounted to Britain's very own stand-in for an American, the admiration of his colleagues and the fans. But profound lapses of confidence would grip him. Coupled with that early ascent to the top of the music-business tree that seemed of such ambiguous appeal to more intractable individuals like Denis Rose and Laurie Morgan, the path to finding an original voice for himself on the instrument was that much harder.

In April 1951, Scott found himself performing, not in the adventurous outfit he had anticipated Jack Parnell leading, but in the pitband of a West End musical, *Fancy Free*, featuring variety stars Tommy Trinder and Pat Kirkwood, at the Prince of Wales Theatre. Considering the number of sophisticated musicians in Parnell's band, the requirements of the assignment were like exercising greyhounds in a telephone box. Apart from Scott, Phil Seamen was in the line-up – a drummer who was to become a legend, both as a player and as a wild and finally tragic eccentric. The repertoire, two shows a night, was cripplingly banal but it was work, and the pay wasn't bad.

Inevitably, the boredom caused chaos. Trumpeter Jimmy Watson took to escaping through the emergency exit into the pub outside the theatre, repeatedly attempting to break a record of his own invention, the ordering and consumption of a pint and return to his seat in the space of a twelve-bar rest. Watson would also declare: 'I'm coming up' in a reverberating stage whisper to his colleagues, make his way on hands and knees to the piano, bite pianist Max Harris firmly in the leg and make his way back. Later in the run, as a variant on the exercise, the saxophone section would block his return as the cue for the brass entry drew ever nearer.

All this horsing about was bound to get its comeuppance. The brass section had taken to firing paper pellets at each other from the mouthpieces of their instruments, Seamen responding by upping the stakes to a catapult. One night Trinder bounded blithely onstage for his solo spot, a mixture of gags and song and dance routines that had been his trademark from vaudeville days. On the cue of his catch phrase 'You lucky people' he was forcibly struck by a missile from the orchestra, and took it personally. The musicians kept their jobs, but only just.

The show ran for over a year before the Parnell band finally did what its members had been hoping for – it went out on the road. The highlight of the new show was the drum duet between Parnell and Seamen. It was on this tour that the real quality of the band for which Parnell had left the lucrative Heath job could really be heard. Seamen, Humble, Scott and Parnell himself were clearly not simply imitators alone, and ecstatic crowds sensed it.

High regard for Parnell's outfit won it some prestigious and lucrative work, including acting as Lena Horne's backing ensemble on the singer's tour of Britain in 1952. American singers were not uncommon on the circuit in Britain in the fifties, because they were not covered by the terms of the Ministry of Labour/Musicians' Union embargo. Ms Horne brought with her a pianist, Arnold Ross, who fitted in comfortably with the Parnell musicians both professionally and socially. Scott and Derek Humble were already enthusiastic gamblers, in the former's case an inheritance from the East End legacy of Uncle Mark, Uncle Rafie and Jock himself. They introduced Ross to the gambling scene. This was the era preceding legalised betting shops, and the country was riddled with illegal ones, some of which nevertheless had convenient arrangements with the authorities which would often result in a diplomatic warning phone call from the local police before the arrival of periodic token raids.

Whilst in Glasgow on the northern leg of the tour, they took Ross to Billy Bell's betting shop in the basement of a forbidding tenement building. Ross won a comfortable sum backing a horse with the same name as his mother, after which one of the establishment's minders visited the party of musicians and persuasively insisted they should 'come up and see the boss'. They were convinced that the Billy Bell gambling emporium was going to get out of the bill by the simple expedient of killing the creditors. But when they got to the proprietor's office, he turned out to be a jazz fan and an ex-saxophone player who just wanted to talk music. For the rest of the season in Glasgow, 'the boss' arranged for the band's more energetic members to be picked up from the hotel in the mornings and taken to his golf club. Gamblers and jazz musicians, united by uncertainties and the haziest of career prospects, frequently felt as if they were related.

But the only way to get one-night stands into the engagement book was to get yourself heard around the country. That meant radio broadcasts. And the route to radio was commerciality. Radio music was flooding uninvited into people's homes and there had to be something to mark you out.

There were two ways to be commercial. One was to play the hits of the dance band circuits, since an entirely home-grown repertoire wouldn't work with fans convinced popular music was by definition American. The other was to use a vocalist, preferably one that sounded good and looked good too. Most of the band singers were women, though not all, and it was the palais band singers of the early 1950s who made it in the early Hit Parades before the coming of rock 'n' roll. Parnell's choice for a singer was Marian Keene. But Marian was married to a tenor saxophonist, Ronnie Keene, and the price of her services was a job for both of them. Parnell got round the problem by firing his second tenorist, Pete King. The resulting row altered

King's career. And though he had by this time left Parnell's band to return to the life of a tenor soloist, it changed Ronnie Scott's too.

King was a laconic, squat, deceptively laid-back man with the demeanour of a fight referee, who had come up in semi-pro bands in Stoke Newington, and first encountered Ronnie Scott as a guest soloist on one-night stands. King had later turned pro, played in the outfits of the popular black bandleader Jiver Hutchinson, British swing veteran Bert Ambrose and the rising young saxophone star Kathy Stobart. He was popular and his treatment at Parnell's hands – even though the bandleader had shrugged, 'There's nothing I can do' – rankled with his partners. On the coach back from King's last gig with Parnell at the Colston Hall in Bristol, saxophonists Derek Humble and Kenny Graham, Phil Seamen and trombonists Ken Wray and Mac Minshull had gone to Parnell, sitting in the front seat of the coach as the bandleaders always did, and handed in their notice. By the time the bus arrived at Alsop Place, Baker Street, the Parnell band was in tatters. King was profoundly moved, and said as much to the press.

January 1953. 'What the fuck are we going to do?' was the question that opened the New Year for the ex-Parnell musicians. A group of them were sitting in an Archer Street café called the Harmony Inn. It was a popular refuge, particularly when it rained, at which time every musician in the vicinity would try to squeeze in. Run by a Czech by the name of George Siptac (all the musicians remembered it because it was 'cat piss' spelt backwards, more or less) a man who knew little enough about jazz but recognised the market value of all his regulars. Siptac knew that Ronnie was a rising star. He regarded himself as something of a social service to musicians, and it wasn't uncommon for him to put meals on a slate that he knew would never be settled for those who were in bad trouble.

The musicians were friends, much of the same age, jazz lovers who had had too few opportunities to present their enthusiasms to the public in suitable surroundings, and they were open to any suggestion. Ronnie Scott had left Parnell before the row, and was playing in a quartet in which Tony Crombie was the drummer and Lennie Bush the bassist. A combination of that band and some of the ex-Parnell men had possibilities. Co-operative bands were a big discussion point in the music press. Nobody was rich, but nobody's needs seemed that much greater than anybody else's. They could share and share alike. Scott recalled Johnny Claes's band, how the front line had been so flexible but could sound like a much larger outfit than it really was. But he liked the idea of a baritone saxophone to deepen the sound, Gerry Mulligan's baritone being a prominent feature of the popular 'cool school' jazz from America's West Coast.

Unexpectedly Ronnie Scott invited Benny Green, a musician he had met the previous year on a one-night stand at a Manor House club. Green, another veteran of the wedding and barmitzvah circuit, wrote later that to the average dance band musician this outfit 'smacked strongly of syncopated Marxism' because of the unconventional way it was run. It was a dance band but a dance band charged with new jazz, which made it saleable to a younger audience, sometimes to the chagrin of older professionals. Trumpeter Jimmy Deuchar had written many of the arrangements, highly original adaptions of bop phraseology into the smoother lusher sounds of the dance floor.

Jock Scott was now unreservedly proud of his son. Sol and Cissie were ecstatic. After all, the band were a smart bunch: they wore blue suits with check waistcoats, which Sol – whose textile business was now flourishing – had made for them as a gift at his Petticoat Lane premises. Blue plexiglass music stands with their names inscribed were intended to glow romantically in the backlighting. Ronnie Scott, who was unchallenged in the leadership of the outfit despite its egalitarian constitution, was businesslike in the public relations. He told *Melody Maker*, 'This is first and foremost a commercial band.' He was nervous of any arty label, knowing Tito Burns had regretfully concluded in 1948 that the public for a purist contemporary band couldn't keep the wolf from the door. 'Idealistic thoughts of playing jazz only are out. The formula will be pop tunes with the melody predominant.' 'I have the last word on musical policy,' Ronnie additionally informed the paper's correspondent, Max Jones.

But before the band was ever really tested on the road, a unique opportunity materialised, an event whose significance would be hard to imagine just a few years later, when after the coming of rock 'n' roll a jazz story could no longer be guaranteed front page space in the music press. Though the Musicians' Union and the Ministry of Labour still held their old line about American imports, fate took a hand that broke the spell.

The winter of 1952/3 brought widespread flooding to Britain, a major disaster on top of post-war repairs. American impresario Norman Granz, a tireless promoter of a frequently sensationalised jazz that nevertheless employed some of the music's greatest originals and provided the world with an opportunity to hear them at first hand, offered his 'Jazz At The Philharmonic' roadshow to Britain as a fundraiser for the recovery effort, in which respect the show would be exempt from the ban.

Granz's tours were known to gross $5 million at times even in the 1950s. He also paid well, insisted on a racial mix wherever he played and was utterly professional, even down to handling much of the dogwork of administration himself. A star-studded gig was planned for the Gaumont, Kilburn, on 8 March 1953. The Musicians' Union and the Ministry of Labour concurred, as long as the visitors would undertake not to play any other engagements. The Ministry would not issue work permits, so concerned were they to emphasise the once-only status of the concession, but what they called 'entry notes'. Ronnie Scott was booked to play on the first half of each of two concerts on that Sunday, the day after the nine-piece was due to make its debut on a series of Manchester warm-up gigs, at venues with names like the High Street Baths Ballroom and the Lido Palais de Danse. He would thus find himself playing opposite artists like Lester Young, Oscar Peterson and Ella Fitzgerald, illustrious liaisons not experienced by Britons since those distant, dangerous, glamorous days of the bottle party clubs and the Coventry Street Lyons Corner House meetings of the small hours.

In the music world, the visit of Granz's musicians took precedence over everything else. Both concerts sold out, and the gigs raised £4000 for the Flood Relief fund. Fans queued for hours for tickets outside the Gaumont State, whose manager declared: 'In twenty-six years in showbusiness I've never seen anything like it.' A young fan from Willesden, queueing in the early hours, said to a reporter, 'I want to see American jazzmen. I'm mad at the Ministry of Labour for banning them. '

Jazz at The Phil gigs in those days were fast, loud and aggressive. A Ronnie Scott sextet – not the full nine-piece that was then in rehearsal – with three other local ensembles, warmed up the show, Scott himself playing at the top of his form, energised by the occasion. Then the Americans began with a slamming version of 'C Jam Blues', set rolling by a furious, thumping beat from Oscar Peterson's piano. From Peterson's first tumultuous chords, Benny Green recalled that the entire mysterious world of jazz that beckoned from across the Atlantic and which was denied local musicians and fans alike was suddenly revealed to him. He realised exactly what the ban on American players had really meant to the developing sensibilities of the British jazz players, how the conceptual difference was a gigantic chasm no amount of absorption of tutors or transcription from discs could bridge.

It was a sweating, relentless and breathless show, in the barnstorming Philharmonic tradition. Flip Phillips, a fast and boisterous swing tenorist made a powerful impression, at the expense of Lester Young, the real legend, who was by 1953 in decline. Journalists were merciless about Young's performance, notably Mike Nevard in *Melody Maker*, who called the saxophonist's playing 'a pathetic parody . . . an empty shell of a man . . . a whisky drinker who makes a lot of witty remarks.' Young had been in low spirits throughout the visit, maintaining his distance, playing below his sublime best, but still the object of immense affection from the British fans and musicians, who besieged his dressing room.

'How's Billie Holiday?' Young would be asked by the glowing visitors.

'Lady Day?' Young would struggle to remember. 'Many moons, no see. Still nice!'

'Hope you'll be back soon,' somebody said.

'I don't think so,' Young prophetically replied. 'Man, I'm so tired.'

Whatever his shortcomings on the show, Young impressed himself on Scott and Crombie. He was gentle, softly spoken, had a melancholy, spaniel-like face and a strange way of carrying his saxophone while playing, holding it to one side as if trying to hide it – the legacy, it was said, of playing in cramped Kansas City clubs where the audience was so close they didn't give you space to hold the horn out in front of you. When he played, his sound was a delicate, mournful, plaintive tremor – though never sentimental or maudlin; it frequently resembled a voice about to break down in tears.

Scott went to Young's dressing room where the American demonstrated to him the mysteries of 'false fingering', whereby the same note could be created at different positions on the horn, with subtle variations of tonality in each. He opened a pewter pot, the one that had appeared in so many photographs in his company, usually described as containing beer, muttering 'Bells'. Like snakes in a basket, a cluster of joints nestled in the bottom. Ronnie Scott and his friends had come to hear Young first and foremost, still an improvisor on a largely grandstanding show.

The American was hardly into his mid-forties at the time but was in a bad way. His experience of being precipitately drafted into the Army (he was held in Army detention on drugs charges for a year) was a period of utter misery for him. It was also troubling him that the group of white players – led by the young Stan Getz – from the Woody Herman band who had so idolised Young as to attempt to replicate his every breath and nuance were becoming increasingly successful at selling a style that he, as the pioneer, was finding it harder and harder to perform the way he heard it. Young died six years later, returning from his self-imposed exile in Paris to New York for his last months. Ronnie Scott had found Lester Young a 'beautiful man', and knew him to be one of the most innovative and poetic saxophonists in all the music too.

In some ways the Philharmonic performance came as a shock to British musicians and to their fans. Correspondents wrote to the music papers with varying degrees of disenchantment with their local heroes. 'How my British idols have crumbled' wrote one to *Melody Maker*. Another declared:

> Three facts stand out. (1) That English musicians should return to their elementary text books and check up on the meaning of the word 'dynamics'. (2) That Ronnie Scott held his own with both of the American tenor players. (3) That at last I know what the critics mean when they say that we do not possess one real rhythm section in this country.

Granz himself said after the performance, 'A lot of your musicians said at our concerts that they could do better musically. Maybe. I didn't hear much of them. I heard some warmed-up Getz and Shearing.'

None the less Ronnie Scott went back, elated by the experience, to preparing his new band for road life. It had been an exciting week for him. In addition to the Philharmonic show and the debut of his band, he had also won the *Melody Maker* tenor saxophone poll for the fourth time since 1949, clocking up 1596 votes against his nearest rival, Tommy Whittle, with 472.

But Ronnie Scott was sure musicianship alone wasn't enough, and had learned some useful lessons already. Johnny Claes had been convinced that the right presentation was essential to break the ice of an uncommercial sound. Freddie Crump had been a one-man icebreaker all on his own. And wartime entertainment had thrown up other inspirations. The world of Archer Street, so close to the Windmill Theatre, was where budding comics like Peter Sellers, Spike Milligan, Alfred Marks and Michael Bentine went – all fresh out of the forces, their sense of humour honed on a mixture of pre-war music-hall routines and the anarchic vision of those who had experienced that mind-warping mixture of absurdity, jingoism, ideals and death in the battlefields. Ronnie Scott therefore borrowed something from all of them, including the part of Dizzy Gillespie's act in which he announced his intention to introduce the members of the band and then proceeded to introduce them to each other. He would stumble around a darkened stage with a cigarette lighter to recreate the blackout, and declare: 'And now, an unexpected appearance by Toulouse Lautrec,' lowering the mike three feet and abandoning the stage. It all helped to make the nine-piece band take off.

'Ronnie had a lot going for him,' Pete King reflected later. 'He was young, good-looking, bright; he had a good dress sense. He was made to be a bandleader.' After the Manchester tour, the band began to travel the country in a rundown bus without a heater or radio, bought from British European Airways and driven by an ex-boxer called Les Bristow. Bristow's antecedents didn't bear too much going into, but the fact that he had been a serious contender for the southern area light heavyweight title had endeared him to Ronnie Scott, a keen follower of boxing as most East End boys were, when Bristow came to the Wimbledon Palais to ask the band-leader for a job as a roadie in the opening weeks.

Bristow thought the musicians were soft and tried to instil in them a concern for their physiques, at one stage even attempting to get them to run behind the bus in quiet country lanes. The road manager's ringcraft was firmly brought home to Derek Humble, a clown who didn't always know where to stop. Humble's face sustained something to remember from Bristow one day, revenge for the saxophonist's terrifying habit of pulling an overcoat over the head of the driver as he was piloting his charges at full belt through the hedgerows.

The boredom of road life was the enemy. With Bristow's encourage-ment, they took to carrying cricket equipment, and Blackheath was a favourite stopping point in the summer months to pursue their inelegant version of the elegant game, though Derek Humble quickly gained a repu-tation as a demon fast bowler.

Scott found his gambling to be a handy pastime as well. He would always maintain to the others that it wasn't an obsession for him the way it was to some of his relatives, but it was a serious preoccupation, as members of the band discovered whenever the coach was in the vicinity of an appro-priate venue, such as Doncaster. Bandwagon time was also a dimension measured partly by the invention of new vocabularies. Like the recently demobbed comics working at the Windmill, much of the raw material of the day, extensively drawn from forces humour, was unsurprisingly based on gags about other races, mingled with as much New York jive-language as the players could remember and a good deal of all-round surrealism culled from Marx Brothers movies. Those movies portrayed a world that appeared to function exactly in the way that the musicians perceived theirs – where a small group of sharp operators moved through life like quick-silver while 'normal' people just stood round scratching their heads.

Jimmy Deuchar, the quiet Glaswegian trumpeter, was famed for being able to draft out the charts for all the members of the band on a new addi-tion to the repertoire simply in the time between the outfit's departure from London at nine in the morning and arrival at the venue, and irrespective of whatever mayhem was going on in the bus throughout the journey.

Deuchar's ear was such that he would be able to write out the individual parts for the players without scoring the overall arrangement first. They had absorbed both the skills of the Archer Street professionals and at least some of the more iconoclastic inclinations of the American boppers, and they quickly began to be a hit with the public.

The solace of the Edgware house remained in the background. The band could sense how much it meant to Ronnie. There was always the comfortable figure of Nana Becky, whenever the young bandleader or any of his partners just happened to drop by, always anxious to make them feel at home. 'I just made this cheesecake specially for you, lads,' she would say, even when faced with the most unexpected visit. 'Come right in and have some.' Her grandson was doing well. That was all that mattered.

But it wasn't exactly the kind of success you could contemplate retirement on. Scott brought his old enthusiasm to Benny Green's attention one night in 1953 at the Orchid Ballroom, Purley, in response to an unquestionably modest return for a night's work. The two men were engaged in trying to divide nine into £14.6/5d. Scott announced that he was planning on investing his share of the nine-piece's overall profits in the launch of a jazz club.

'What profits?' Green enquired.

'It won't always be like this,' Scott replied. 'Not every date will turn out to be like this one.'

Green mercilessly recorded that, in a sense, Scott was right – at the following week's gig, at Acton Town Hall, they received £12.10/6d. 'It is not really surprising that it took Scott another six years to realise his ambition,' Green wrote many years later.

This was not, however, a status that was obvious to the BBC, an organisation to which all new bands were beholden for the exposure air-time brought. The BBC auditioned the Scott nine-piece in the summer of 1953 and turned it down flat. There was uproar in the music press. In truth the Corporation just didn't like modern jazz and was doing its best to keep it away from the public. The band, however, was now too good for this to be much more than a temporary setback.

Though the momentum of the Ronnie Scott Band was impelled by music and youth, it had an enthusiast behind it who understood the hard realities of the music business far better than the performers, however worldly they might imagine themselves to be. The enthusiast was Harold Davison, a music business entrepreneur who had come out of the RAF with a passion for jazz and a conviction that with proper attention to details and some serious professionalism there was no reason why some money shouldn't accrue from it. Davison had started his business as the manager of a popular swing and jump band led by a guitarist, Vic Lewis. He had served with Lewis in the air force and had subsequently taken John Dankworth under his wing as well.

Pete King had begun working with Davison during the latter's association with the Jack Parnell band and had even been on a scouting expedition for the manager when *Fancy Free* was being run in in Birmingham, checking on the first appearance with the Dankworth band of a spirited young singer called Cleo Laine. Despite the Parnell bust-up, the splinter group nevertheless had no hesitation about asking Davison if he would represent them as well. He lent them the money to buy their bus, and was an endless source of advice, encouragement, and frequently hard cash over the years to come.

It was sometimes a confusing relationship for an agent, even though he was not much older than his charges. All the unruly energies exhibited by young men and women in the front line of the music of the moment could be difficult to square with the philosophy that the customer, if not always right, has at least got the option to take it or leave it. Davison, like most managers likely to succeed, therefore spent a lot of time trying to keep his artists in line. When the offer came for the nine-piece to perform at the Sculthorpe American forces base it seemed like a great opportunity since British groups rarely got the chance to play such venues. Since they were also technically performing on American territory and thus outside the reach of the imported-players ban, Davison also scented an opportunity to make ground for himself and his organisation for the days when the blackout would finally be lifted.

He was convinced that the squeeze couldn't last for ever. After all, that very summer James C. 'Little Caesar' Petrillo, the American musicians' union leader, had proposed an experimental trial period of twelve months in which there would be a free exchange of British and American players. Hardie Ratcliffe of the British Musicians' Union turned it down, arguing that there was no such thing as a free exchange when American musicians were so much more popular in Britain than British players could possibly be in the States. But a dialogue had been opened.

Davison's status didn't protect him from the young musicians' inexhaustible enthusiasm for mockery. Since forces bases did not provide the luxury of dressing rooms for visiting performers, on its arrival at Sculthorpe the band was obliged to change in the offices, where Benny

Green discovered a supply of the unit's headed notepaper. He and Scott devised a letter to be delivered to the luckless Davison, purporting to come from the unit's commanding officer. It accused Scott's band of every variation of unprofessionalism and offensive behaviour in the book. The musicians, the letter protested, went in for fraud, larceny and even unwelcome suggestions to an officer's wife. It was hardly the kind of behaviour that a host country might be expected to display to its guests and what was the management's opinion of it? They posted the letter on the base that night and went on with the week's work. But Pete King got an urgent call to visit Davison's office and found him with the letter trembling in his hand. Putting things right wasn't the easiest thing that King had ever attempted.

Nevertheless, Davison's instinct to use the forces gigs as an ice-breaker in the transatlantic impasse made sense. Useful connections were made then – particularly with the visiting band of Woody Herman. Herman was impressed with Scott and Victor Feldman, going as far as to say to them, 'If you ever want to come over to the States and join the band, it would be nice to have you.' Feldman took up Herman's offer two years later.

Then one night at the Folkestone Leas' Cliff Hall the band discovered Art Baxter.

Scott had experimented with a number of vocalists, including Barbara Jay, a lively and flexible performer who was later to marry the tenorist Tommy Whittle; and Johnny Grant, a relaxed, Perry Como-like singer. For Barbara Jay, who was with the band for the longest stint of all its female singers, it wasn't an entirely happy occasion. Members of the band admitted that the outfit once went through an entire day's auditions of entirely unsuitable girl singers just to get a laugh out of their embarrassment. Barbara Jay knew that in their minds she really had no role to play. All the young men in the outfit wanted to play jazz; and they weren't overly respectful of womankind either. A singer was only necessary for the commercial dance tunes they played as their passport to the circuit, and as such was generally undervalued. Girl singers were often dismissively referred to. Barbara Jay later acknowledged that she had sometimes had to conceal the tears of her isolation in the back of the bus.

Art Baxter found it easier to cope with. He was singing in Folkestone with the Jan Ralfini Orchestra, the outfit that Cissie had taken Ronnie to see all those years ago when Jock was in the line-up. Baxter had a good voice, an extravagant and mildly camp stage presence, and an attractive informality in his presentation – he would sit on the edge of the stage and take the audience into his confidence in a manner that was rare at the time.

Moreover, he was a hilarious and outrageous companion, which quickly endeared him to the Scott men. His finale was the song 'Somebody Loves Me', which he delivered with as much indignation as coyness on occasions – if the audience didn't like him, he'd leave the stage directing V-signs at it. When he unexpectedly cropped his hair during a tour, the band thenceforth referred to him as the 'Singing Coconut'.

Baxter, who was later to make occasional unscheduled appearances at what became Ronnie Scott's Club wearing such unconventional attire as a ballerina's costume, and from time to time with equally unconventional adornments – such as Coca Cola bottles – attached to his genitalia, was nevertheless, for all his expansiveness, a man of deep insecurities. When the opportunity came to play a pollwinner's concert at the Albert Hall opposite the Heath Orchestra, the Jack Parnell band and others, Baxter didn't show for the sound check or the rehearsal, and eventually a telegram arrived for Ronnie Scott: 'BAXTER NEEDS COMPLETE REST BACK AUG 11.' It purported to come from a doctor, but everybody knew it was from the singer himself. One night at the Palladium Baxter had been so paralysed with fear in the wings before his entrance that he only got on stage as a result of being hurled into the spotlight by Les Bristow.

But if the ups and downs were the fuel for endless after-hours anecdotes, they could create havoc on the road, and Scott himself later came to believe that most bands would have a year of vitality, a year of levelling out and a year of deterioration. The course of the small band went pretty much that way. Touring would force changes, it was unavoidable. The boy on the tricycle from the Edgware streets, the multi-instrumentalist prodigy Victor Feldman, replaced Norman Stenfalt on piano, and Feldman's arrival also made possible a drum routine between himself and Tony Crombie that had shades of the two-drummer routines that Ronnie Scott had witnessed in New York's Apollo Ballroom. Then Crombie left to start his own band and Phil Seamen replaced him.

Like Crombie, Seamen was that rare thing, a British drummer who had an instinctive and sympathetic grasp of what swing really meant, and a warmth in his playing rare on the instrument – an effect partly gained by a subordination of technique to the musical atmosphere. Seamen's talent was such that he could have dominated the British jazz world for the next three decades, but alcohol and narcotics prevented it, and his unreliability throughout the 1960s lost him high-profile opportunities. However he remained one of the best-loved and, in his way, most respected of local percussionists. In the early 1970s, not long before his death, at a drum convention in London, Buddy Rich paid just such a tribute to Seamen. Though the drummer had a hard time struggling to his feet to acknowledge Rich's gesture – not a man given to casual praise – the audience of hundreds of drummers cheered him loud and long.

In the summer of 1955 the nine-piece broke up. It made its last recording on 13 April of that year with a disc that featured 'S'il Vous Plait', 'Pearl', 'This Heart of Mine' and 'Jordu', the last a nod in the direction of the cloistered but glowing chamber-jazz sound of the Miles Davis band that had so affected John Dankworth's development as a composer. That cool sound had a special appeal for Europeans – it could somehow be both adventurous and yet not upset your parents. Some would later say this was the problem for many of the young British jazz artists of the day, and of later days. You could be a day-tripper into rebelliousness in Britain in the 1950s. You could smoke a joint, and go home to mum for supper, just the same as you could grow your hair long and cut it when the going got tough in the Britain of a decade later. Many black Americans, most notably Charlie Parker, never had that choice. Maybe real artistic growth needed to be more than a fling of youth.

For Ronnie Scott, 1955 was also the year of another kind of parting of the ways. Joan Crewe abruptly left for the United States, in the tenth year of that relationship which had begun as a teenage romance at the Hammersmith Palais as London returned to peace. Work on the road with the nine-piece had taken Ronnie Scott away from Joan a lot, and she had become seriously dependent on heroin, and drawn to the company of those who used it and who knew where to get it. Her ignorance of the damage it did was shared by almost all of those experimenting with it at the time. Scott was grateful that his own flirtations with it had proved so completely unappetising.

Joan was also coming round to the conclusion that Ronnie Scott would never marry her. Uncle Mark had been harsh but right that day after the Club Eleven court case. She also felt that he made her carry all the responsibility for the nature of the relationship. 'Don't force me to marry you, Joan,' Ronnie had said to her once. Her mother had even had the banns read in church. Ronnie Scott wanted a boy-meets-girl encounter to last indefinitely. Joan met a young American saxophonist, Spencer Sinatra, in Britain with the Stan Kenton orchestra. Sinatra was also an addict, which drew him and Joan together, and while the nine-piece was touring, they began an affair.

When he discovered it, Ronnie was frantic. At twenty-seven, it was the first time anything like this had ever happened to him. Rational thought fled. He rang Kenton, Sinatra's boss, and told him that the saxophonist was a junkie, not particularly to Kenton's surprise. He heard of a flat in the suburbs of London where the couple were meeting, went there one night in a rage and confronted them both, ending up struggling noisily but without much impact with Sinatra on the floor. 'We could neither of us punch our way out of a paper bag,' Scott recalled later. Sinatra returned early to the States, maybe because of Scott's complaint to Kenton. But Joan Crewe followed him.

Ostensibly it was for a holiday, to see what America offered and maybe consider a new start. When Sinatra met her in New York he proposed that they should marry at the end of that week. Joan was surprised by the rush. 'You didn't come all this way just to see the sights, did you?' Sinatra asked her. So far from home, and so close to the American's insistence, she didn't refuse.

Until Joan was gone, Ronnie Scott had not considered what life might be like without her. He sold everything he could to raise the fare to the States. Since the Club Eleven raid, he had always considered that association with drugs would make it hard to get an American visa, but five years after the event seemed a sufficiently long period of atonement and the Embassy came through. When he got to New York he had no idea where Joan and Sinatra had gone. He was able to trace the saxophonist to an accompanist's gig in a strip club, followed him from work, got on the same bus and sat at the back, anxiously rehearsing what he would say, whether there would be a scene or another fight, whether he would be able to talk Joan into coming back with him.

Sinatra went to an all-night restaurant and met Joan there. They were sitting chatting at a table as Scott approached. He had no idea what he would say, but was surprised that much of the fury died down in him. They seemed a couple now, as if they'd been sitting there for ever. Life had moved on. In the end, they hardly spoke at all. 'I hope you'll be very happy together,' he eventually said, and left. It was a long way to come for such a short conversation.

Ronnie Scott then tracked down his old playing partner Victor Feldman, who was by now playing with the Woody Herman band in Lake Tahoe, Nevada. Crossing the States on buses, hanging out with Herman's sidemen, talking music again, helped him to handle suddenly finding himself in America for a reason that had ceased to make sense. Joan Crewe later had two children with Sinatra, her family from the Caledonian Road moved to New York to be near her, and when Sinatra died suddenly some years later, they helped her to look after her young family. Ronnie flew home after a brief but diverting interlude with the Herman musicians. He had to reconstruct his life – and work out where to start again musically as well.

☐ ☐ ☐

For the jazz community at large, 1955 was a year to ponder such things. News came through in March that Charlie Parker had died in New York. His last months had been a nightmare. Overweight, racked with ulcers, living on stimulants and spending whatever money he could lay his hands on on drugs and booze, he had regularly begun to foul up his gigs, even firing the entire band and walking offstage at New York's Birdland and attempting suicide by drinking iodine immediately afterwards.

Parker died in the Fifth Avenue apartment of one of the most famous of European jazz fans, the Baroness Pannonica de Koenigswarter, on 9 March at the age of thirty-four. The Baroness, a Rothschild, was immediately implicated in rumours of an affair with Parker by the down-market press; in fact she was one of the few real friends the saxophonist had, who required nothing from him. One-time sportswoman, pilot, private in the Free French Army, the Baroness had grown bored with her later years as a diplomat's wife and set up residence in Fifth Avenue's Hotel Stanhope, where she put her wealth at the service of the city's (mostly black) jazz musicians and acted for all the world like an old-style European patroness.

The graffiti artists defiantly wrote 'BIRD LIVES' on the Greenwich Village walls and subways. It was the strongest reminder of the world that Laurie Morgan had discovered in his journey of 1947, in which Bird was the Messiah, the leader to be followed to the ends of the earth if necessary. Parker's personal journey led to madness, chaos and death. His music, however, came to sound more beautiful, rounded, generous-spirited and loving every year, as the abrasiveness that seemed to be its primary feature when it first burst upon the world was gradually eroded by time. Ross Russell, in his inspired biography of Parker, quoted the words of the critic of Stockholm's *Orkester Journalen*, who perceptively remarked after the saxophonist's death: 'Together with Jackson Pollock, Dylan Thomas and James Dean, he became a symbol of protest for a whole generation. It is easy to see how these four artists shared the same rebellious mind and desperation.'

# 5

# Teenagers

'This night the switchboard lit up like a Christmas tree. Dewey would play "Blue Moon Over Kentucky", then turn it over and play "That's All Right Mama". It was just those two sides for the rest of the evening. Finally Dewey said, "Get that guy down here!"'
(Wink Martindale describing Elvis Presley air-plays by DJ Dewey Phillips in 1956 from Albert Goldman's *Elvis*, 1981)

IN THE SUMMER of 1955, Ronnie Scott decided that if the money added up, he'd form a big band. It was always a difficult temptation to resist, an opportunity in a predominantly miniaturist idiom to perform a music that packed a more substantial punch. The pitfalls were well known. Big bands were cripplingly expensive to run, logistically difficult to organise, and if personality conflicts had been troublesome with a small band they were likely to be that much worse with a big one. Yet, they still had glamour and clout. Ronnie Scott loved the power of the brass, the lissome undertow of the reeds, the explosive swing of a good big-band drummer – a task that he entrusted to the volatile but gifted Phil Seamen. Other sidemen from the old Parnell band days were drafted in: Jimmy Watson, the trumpeter who had passed the idle moments on the Tommy Trinder revue with visits to the pub between trumpet breaks, Pete King and Ken Wray from the nine-piece. It also featured a man with very different roots from the Archer Street players who made up most of Ronnie Scott's circle of musician friends.

Joe Harriott, a Jamaican altoist who had come to Britain in 1951 when he was just twenty-three years old, was already raising eyebrows as a Parkerish saxophonist; nevertheless he clearly had ideas of his own and an original way of adapting Bird's phraseology. On a good night Harriott was

62

a player of immense fire. Though he worked for a period in the rock-tinged Crombie band, where his soulful sound fitted perfectly, he had little sense of the prospects of making a niche for himself in the music business and put his spiky, unsentimental style on to the anvil of experimentation. His playing was never cool and sounded, as he often did himself, on the verge of an explosive outburst. Harriott, like many of the black Americans who were to visit Britain in the coming years, was a man who demonstrated in his life and its mixture of euphoria and reverses that the world simply looked different, and often less welcoming, if it was being viewed from behind a black face, and that was that.

The big band never gelled like the nine-piece had, from the moment of its debut performance at the Samson and Hercules Ballroom in Norwich. Harold Davison, normally a prudent man, had thought the big band a good idea even though the overheads were reflected in the doubling of the personnel, though Scott himself later said the scheme was 'one of my worst ever'. The less charitable thought that its most intense and creative activity was its poker school, famed for the unblinkingly dispassionate physiognomy of Harriott, and trumpeter Hank Shaw's touchingly prudent habit of instantly posting whatever winnings he would make to his wife.

But musically, it was living proof that an assembly of diverse talents doesn't always make a living band, and it might have been the insecurity of the outfit's musical perspective that sowed the seeds for the unrest that was frequently under its surface. Harriott was unhappy with being second alto to Dougie Robinson. Trumpeter Dave Usden and Phil Seamen even fought publicly on the bandstand in Morecambe on New Year's Eve 1955, and accompanied the ensemble's final rendition of 'Auld Lang Syne' with a rival recital of shouting, deprecations, abuse and all-round indifference to the perplexed revellers. It was not a happy ship, and the most surprising feature of its voyage was that it took so long to go down. Scott called a halt shortly after the Morecambe debacle, and went back to working with Tony Crombie. But he also put his toe in the water of promotion again, something he had not considered since the days of Club Eleven.

The dream of a club in the 52nd Street style was still strong. If it was to be done, it had to be somewhere in the West End. Soho in the early 1950s was an oasis for those who didn't, or couldn't, make sense of respectable morality, acceptable arts, conventional standards of behaviour, sex, self-indulgence and dress, mainstream religion, the right manner of speech or ethnic background. It was also an oasis for those who didn't give a damn about the law.

In the 1950s, the West End was dominated by a self-styled 'King of the

Underworld', Jack 'Spot' Comer. Jack Spot was a big, vigorous, cigar-smoking Jewish Eastender (he had fought Mosley's blackshirts in the thirties) who had owned Soho clubs that had given a good deal of work to jazz musicians. At the Modernaires in Old Compton Street, Flash Winston had a group with himself on piano, performing what Spot and the gangsters indulgently called 'yer Heebie Jeebie music'.

There was no doubt in such places about who was in charge. Spot's office telephone was actually in the music room, and a wave of his hand would be enough to freeze both musicians and dancers while he loudly carried on his business, the whole atmosphere snapping back into action as soon as he replaced the receiver – this charade would go on a dozen times a night.

Denis Rose also worked for a while in Spot's club. Rose had always been fascinated by the underworld, though his occasional unreliability was a serious risk with such employers. One night Spot told Rose: 'You'll never work in the West End again,' when the pianist and trumpeter was two hours late. The rest of the band recalled playing 'Please Don't Talk About Me When I'm Gone' at the time.

Spot eventually retired in 1956, after being cut up, literally, by the rising generation of younger operators, and bought a bowler hat and furniture business off the Gloucester Road. Though fights would occasionally happen in his clubs, and a good deal of unexplained action went on that the musicians knew better than to investigate, serious intimidation was not really Spot's way. He got results by fixing deals. He made accommodations with other gangs that the generation that followed would only deal with by violence. Soho was about to come under new management.

In Gerrard Street, in the heart of London's Chinatown, there was a shabby and dimly lit basement owned by a small-time Soho businessman by the name of Jack Fordham. During the war it had been a bottle-party club, and later a refuge for cab drivers for cards and coffee, and a 'near-beer' joint, in which male customers would be encouraged by the friendliness of attractive waitresses to spend a fortune on non-alcoholic drinks in the mistaken assumption that the waitresses might become still friendlier at the end of the night. Since such places didn't come to life until late in the evening, they were frequently hired at other times to act as occasional jazz venues. Scott and Pete King hired it once or twice in 1956 and half-heartedly considered more permanent arrangements. But 1956 was also a year for other diversions. It was the one in which the old supremacy of Archer Street was to meet its unmaker.

American rock 'n' roll first hit Britain in the middle 1950s. Bill Haley's cleaned-up version of blues-shouter Big Joe Turner's 'Shake, Rattle and Roll' had crept into *Melody Maker*'s new bestseller charts by the Christmas of 1954, the movie *Rock Around the Clock* featuring Haley and his Comets arrived in 1956 and the singer followed it up with a tour of Britain in 1957. Elvis Presley's first record, too, was a similar borrowing of the Mississippi blues singer Arthur 'Big Boy' Crudup's 'It's All Right Mama'.

For Ronnie Scott and his musical contemporaries, still assuming themselves to be the young generation but now approaching thirty, the revelation of a new audience for a new music, whose practitioners and fans were barely out of their teens (and especially a new music that seemed to be simply a louder and more amateurishly performed version of the black urban blues music that they had known for years through jazz) was a difficult thing to take seriously. But changes were coming.

*Melody Maker* had taken to printing the ten best-selling records of the week in order of popularity – the first 'charts' – so at last the criterion of success of a Tin Pan Alley song was no longer judged on the sale of sheet music, a telling indication of the extent to which the transistor radio, and record sales following airplay, had become crucial to music-business economics. The newspapers reported teenage fans rioting at showings of Haley's movie. Young Londoners like Bermondsey-raised Tommy Steele (originally Tommy Hicks) were already driving expensive sports cars and enjoying the trappings of success, and they performed for an audience that was for the first time economically attractive to the music business – an audience for the most part under sixteen.

As George Melly pointed out in his recollections of the period, the fans for a successful dance band solo singer like Dickie Valentine would have seemed young until then – maybe between eighteen and twenty-five. But this was different. A changing Britain was ensuring that the sentiment, cosy emotions, repressed sexuality and blandness that characterised the kind of pop music of the dance band era was about to receive a hammering from which it would never recover. 'Teenagers' were here.

The war had brought it about. Austerity Britain, the Britain of self-sacrifice and patient duty, was on the verge of a revolution. American investment in European reconstruction sank $12 billion into fuelling an economic boom in France, Britain and Germany. British exports skyrocketed. Meat rationing was finally abolished in 1956. A new and impatient generation needed new icons, new dreams. The children born in the height of the Blitz were born to parents who had decided that for their descendants it was all going to be different this time around. More people had more money to spend on themselves and each other; on refrigerators, cars, washing machines, televisions – and on their children.

That high-spending consumer society that the previous generation had known only from American movies and which Scott, Crombie, Dankworth and the others had seen and marvelled at in New York, had almost arrived. Commercial television had arrived too (amidst much controversy) to advertise it all.

Children had thus been given high expectations in the 1950s. George Melly, sharing the bill with Tommy Steele at a south London gig in the mid-fifties, heard those expectations cut loose after an audience mostly comprising sixteen-year-olds had listened to the opening set by the Mick Mulligan band in virtual silence. During the interval, Melly wrote in *Owning Up*: 'A low continuous hum began to rise from the auditorium. It was like a swarm of bees getting ready to swarm . . . the moment the curtain went up a high-pitched squeaking and shrieking started. I was absolutely amazed.'

Rock 'n' roll swept the nation. Not appreciating its import, Ronnie Scott and Harry Klein went to what they thought was just another recording session to be sidemen with Tommy Steele's band at the Decca Studios in West Hampstead. It was, as professional musicians went, something to be sniffed at. Nobody had prepared any arrangements, and Scott and Klein had to figure out something appropriate for themselves. Arrangements or not, Steele's records were soon dominating the charts.

But Tony Crombie was one jazz musician who had tried to get in on the act, eventually turning his touring band into a rock 'n' roll group called Tony Crombie's Rockets, and persisting with it until 1957, when it became obvious that what really made a hit rock band was a personality at the microphone who was a good ten years younger than most of the Rockets could claim to be. It didn't, however, stop them conducting themselves in the manner for which rock stars of a decade later were to become notorious. After a nationwide tour by the band, it became legendary as the outfit that no hotel would welcome twice. Crombie, a resourceful man, took to booking accommodation under implausible alibis like 'Professor Cromberg and a party of students'.

A TV show called *Six-Five Special* went out on Saturdays to cater for the new craze. Amplified music did inspire a kind of an antidote in skiffle, which was a do-it-yourself idiom based on country-and-western music and black folk art like Huddie Ledbetter's, performed on home-made instruments like washboards and basses made of broom handles and string. But for modern jazz, though, there continued to be an audience of informed enthusiasts, the days in which its practitioners could make a respectable or more than respectable living by playing a hybrid version of it somewhere between bebop and pop music had all but gone, until 'fusion' music made its appearance in the late 1960s. Pop music had simply moved on, though some jazz musicians made an attempt to cross the divide. Benny Green recalled the story of the saxophonist Wally Bishop, who in discussing his credentials to join a rock 'n' roll band was asked: 'Can you play a twelve-bar blues lying on your back?'

Bishop, a man with a liking for the occasional drink, observed: 'Yes, but who's going to pick me up again?'

Shortly after his thirtieth birthday, in February 1957, Ronnie Scott got a chance to return to the States, and an opportunity to experience the rock boom at closer range. Harold Davison was handling a tour by the Eddie Condon Sextet (a further sign of relaxation of the old union clampdown) and an exchange group was necessary to maintain the formalities. Ronnie Scott set about assembling a suitable touring group – with some trepidation, since it seemed to him that America needed a tour by British musicians playing American music like, as he put it, Damascus needed a synagogue. In the event he booked Phil Seamen, Derek Humble, Jimmy Deuchar, Victor Feldman and Lennie Bush to go with him.

The job was difficult enough anyway, but Phil Seamen made it harder. The drummer was a wonderful performer when he felt OK, but when he didn't anything could happen.

'For Christ's sake don't try to take anything over with you,' Scott warned Seamen.

'Don't worry,' Seamen assured him, as he always did.

Ronnie Scott arrived late at Southampton to board the *Queen Elizabeth*. When he got to Customs, an officer stopped him.

'You Mr Scott?' the officer enquired. 'Come this way please.' He found Phil Seamen in the company of two Customs men. 'Mr Seamen is one of your party, I understand. We have discovered narcotics in his drum kit.' Facing a tour that already seemed to be happening for no better reasons than music business politics, it was all the bandleader needed.

'Look, it's vital he comes to the States for this tour. Couldn't you nick him on the way back?' Scott pleaded with the Customs officers. They were unmoved.

Ronnie Scott rang Harold Davison and asked for Allan Ganley, a young drummer with a sensitive grasp of bop, if not of Seamen's audacious waywardness with the idiom, to be flown out to join the band for the start of the tour. Then a dock strike in New York diverted the *Queen Elizabeth* to Halifax, Nova Scotia, instead, so that the performers had to fly down to New York from there, but without their luggage. So the Englishmen simply wore as many of their clothes at once as they could manage and still stand upright. They felt they were about to become a part of the hippest musical community on earth in as unhip a condition as they could conceivably adopt.

But this was no jazz tour. The Scott band was booked into an all-black rock 'n' roll show. On the bill were Chuck Berry, Fats Domino, Laverne Baker, Bill Doggett (the jazz organist who moved successfully over to pop), a rhythm and blues package of the highest class. Six Englishmen scuttling their way through a handful of choruses of the single bebop tune that constituted their contribution before escaping gratefully offstage was a bizarre enough event in itself but the Scott band was made more uneasy by the fact that it had never performed before audiences of such a size – 20,000 or so was the average attendance.

It was on that tour that Ronnie Scott came to hear at first hand two of the saxophonists who were to become lifetime heroes. One was the thirty-three-year-old Edward 'Sonny' Stitt, a Boston-born musician of great technical command and awesome power who was coming to be regarded in the States as the true inheritor of the message of Charlie Parker. Stitt's father was a professor of music and his mother a teacher of piano and organ, in which respect the saxophonist was a striking example of the kind of sophistication increasingly common among the second wave of bebop players, bringing orthodox Western theory to bear on the harmonic labyrinths of bop. Ronnie Scott heard Stitt on a stopover in Buffalo, and when the band returned to New York to discover that Stitt was playing in a club across the river in Newark, a return visit was compulsory.

Benny Green and another London saxophonist, Jack Sharpe, were staying at the President Hotel in New York on a busman's holiday to keep the Scott band company. Scott burst into Green's room proclaiming: 'I'm going to take you to hear the greatest saxophonist in the world.' Stitt, a tall, rangy figure with a reputation for competitiveness, played stupendous music, cascades of eighth-note runs pouring from his horn. He played tenor and baritone as well as alto that night, part of his strategy to escape the 'new Bird' tag which he felt might stay on his back for life.

The other event to make a lasting impact on Ronnie Scott during that tour was hearing Stan Getz in the flesh. Getz was almost exactly the Englishman's own age, a swing-derived performer whose work was attractively inflected with bebop. Getz was a longtime admirer of Lester Young rather than Charlie Parker. He had a lighter, more delicate tone than most of the beboppers and a lyrical imagination that gave his work a fragile, porcelain-like quality rare in jazz.

The journey back to England was principally memorable as a farce. Because of the row over Seamen on the outward journey, the band had panicked and hidden its small supply of cannabis in a lavatory cistern on the *Queen Elizabeth*, none of the members having the courage after such a bad start to risk taking it off at the other end. All six musicians spent the entire trip back looking for that lost stash. They split into pairs, combed the ship, met at prearranged rendezvous to compare notes, reconsidered, started all over again. The *Queen Elizabeth* had too many decks, too many lavatories and too many cisterns for any of them ever to be sure that somebody else hadn't got there first.

When Ronnie Scott and the band returned, the seeds of an old dream were revitalised. As they had realised during the Flood Relief concert, the union ban was depriving the British public of some of the most vital and living music of the age – and a music that, by virtue of residing principally in the heads of great improvisors rather than captured in written composition, was changing all the time. Scott knew that there would be an audience for the likes of Stitt and Getz as long as they could be persuaded to come to England. And the music needed the intimate atmosphere of a club rather than a concert hall.

But local jazz wasn't doing so badly on its own. Some years previously, on a guest appearance with a local rhythm section at a south London gig, Ronnie Scott had been approached by a chubby teenager who had shyly asked him, 'Do you mind if I play?' Scott had greeted the prospect with the familiar weary resignation of star soloists out on one-night stands. But when the chubby kid played the horn it was immediately obvious he had everything – stunning dexterity of a calibre to rival the superfast American hard-boppers like Johnny Griffin, rich imagination, sensitivity to what the other players were doing, and remarkable stamina.

His name was Edward Brian 'Tubby' Hayes. In a succession of bands that Hayes was to lead in the 1950s, he proved himself to be an improvisor of a confidence and attack almost unheard of in the faintly apologetic world of British jazz. His father had been a violinist and he had himself played the instrument for some years before switching to the saxophone at the age of twelve. His entire musical background was altogether more rigorous and sophisticated than the hit-and-miss manner in which so many of the Archer Street players of the previous generation had learned, and that greater fund of knowledge had led him to want to compose and arrange as well. It was these talents that Ronnie Scott had a special admiration for, as he had for Tony Crombie and Jimmy Deuchar in the days of the nine-piece. 'Beats me how they do it,' Scott would muse. 'I can't arrange a vase of flowers.'

Ronnie Scott and Tubby Hayes seriously began to consider the prospects for forming a band. There was already a cult for the two-tenor front line since Sonny Stitt and the furiously swinging Gene Ammons had been partners in such an outfit throughout the fifties. Since Hayes also wanted an outlet for his writing, the ensemble would work with a good deal of his own material, laced with the prominent jazz tunes of the time. The name – the Jazz Couriers – closely shadowed that of one of the most popular American hard bop groups, drummer Blakey's Jazz Messengers. In addition to Hayes and Scott, and a regular pianist, Terry Shannon, it featured a variety of drummers and bassists.

And from its first performance on 7 April 1957 at Wardour Street's Flamingo Club (making its own debut as a jazz venue) the band looked a winner. It didn't get the euphoria in the music press that the nine-piece had done at the beginning of its life, because times had changed and a jazz story  ·
wasn't the big deal it used to be, but the opening show demonstrated just how formidable the combined powers of the country's two strongest tenor modernists was.

Bookings followed fast. Pete King took care of the business, taking time out to get married a month after the band was started. Ronnie Scott, though no sympathiser with the institution, was naturally present, along with other musicians and friends, and like most things, there were laughs to be got out of it. The registrar's voice bizarrely changed from perfectly regular tones to an incantatory, ecclesiastical manner when the ceremony began, as if he were doing impressions. It crippled Scott, Benny Green and the photographer Harry Morris, who snorted into their handkerchiefs throughout the event, much to bride Stella Ferguson's discomfort. In the event the newlyweds couldn't afford to buy the official prints that appeared in the music press. Instead they bought, and still proudly possess, photographs of their wedding with the word 'PROOF' stamped across them in large letters.

Plaudits began to flow the Couriers' way. Even Ronnie Scott, not given to overstatement, was convinced that the critics and the public were right when the band began winning readers' polls and press observations to the effect that here was the most assured and exciting outfit in the history of British modern jazz. Although the times had changed, there was now a large enough jazz public – notably of the better educated, more sophisticated and gently rebellious post-Beatnik citizenry much of Hayes' own age – to ensure that the band became something of a cult.

Hayes was fitfully a cause for worry because he could not control either his drinking or his habits with narcotics. But unlike the drummer Phil Seamen, who was sometimes incapable of performance, Hayes was rarely inhibited from playing at least acceptably, and often brilliantly, certainly in his early twenties. The effect of heroin use, when it finally took toll of him, was to undermine his health before his willpower, in a manner that was first crippling and then fatal. But the Tubby Hayes of the late 1950s was a man at the height of his powers.

Ronnie Scott was constantly amazed, and sometimes daunted, by Hayes. But though he felt that his partner's playing was streets ahead of his own, this diffident opinion wasn't always shared by observers who appreciated his more thoughtful, shapely and delicate style. And the younger man's drive had re-energised Scott; performing with the Couriers gave him a new lease of playing life.

The band toured the country with an American blues package at one point, under the guidance of Dougie Tobutt, a dapper, humorous road manager from Davison's office. Tobutt was another who wouldn't let the opportunity for a put-on go by. On one outing, heading for a gig in Glasgow, the band bus arrived at a transport café on the Scottish border. Tobutt hauled the vehicle up some distance from the establishment and informed his charges, many of them veterans but strangers to Britain: 'We're approaching the Scottish customs now. If you're carrying anything you shouldn't be, now's the time to lose it.' The bluesmen frantically took to clearing their luggage of drugs. Tobutt then got all the travellers to line-up outside the coach. 'I want you to hold your passports in your left hand and raise your right,' he informed them gravely. 'Now say after me, "I pledge allegiance to Her Majesty the Queen during my stay in Scotland and undertake to be of good behaviour."' Tobutt then collected the passports and took them inside the 'border post'. He hadn't cracked a face muscle throughout the exercise. It was a stunt worthy of the Sculthorpe Letter.

Bad news came through in the midst of this musical honeymoon. Jock Scott was sick. Ronnie met him in an Archer Street café and found him thinner, tired, worried. But the implications didn't sink in.

'Maybe you need a holiday,' Ronnie Scott suggested.

'Maybe I do,' Jock agreed. 'I was thinking of going to Switzerland. Would you come with me?' But there was work to be done. He said he was sorry, but he couldn't. He was to regret that decision all his life.

Not long afterwards, it emerged that what was troubling Jock wouldn't be solved by fresh air. Since the *Caronia* tour, both men had lived their own lives, never discussed intimacies, conversed more as colleagues in the same line of work. Now, there didn't seem enough time left for all the conversations that had hovered beneath the surface of their relationship. Jock became rapidly worse and his son got a call that he had been admitted to Hammersmith Hospital. He drove there one day in the summer of 1958. If Ronnie was pondering that trail from the elegant night-spots of wartime London and the heroes of his early years to an absent father's profession, and then to this unimagined moment, fate couldn't have accompanied it with more of a bitter laugh.

The gatekeeper at the hospital was the glamorous saxophone hero of Princes and the Potomac, minstrel to the wartime wealthy: Reggie Dare.

The change in Jock was hard to believe. Haggard and yellowing, he had lost a great deal of weight and his old bravura and bounce were gone. He still didn't know how bad things were, and neither did his son, but it was obvious to both that something was seriously wrong. The encounter was tense, awkward, but full of affirmations of what the future might hold. There had been so many obstacles to their getting along, which a conversation in a hospital ward couldn't blow away. There had been the episode over the *Caronia*, which Jock had always resented. There had been his son's headstrong nature, swept along by the modernist movement and by the diversions of clubland, which Jock had always felt to be distractions from the pursuit of true professionalism. He never had been able to restrain himself from lecturing his son as to how he thought a life in the music business ought to be properly conducted. Neither of them had taken much opportunity to get to know each other better during the 1950s when they were both highly regarded in the same business, were sharing the same market place of Archer Street, and could have met frequently.

After that visit, Jock saw the specialist. He had been stalled by juniors a number of times and wanted the truth.

'You can tell me,' Jock insisted.

'All right. You have cancer of the pancreas,' the consultant quietly announced.

'What are the prospects?'

'Not good, I'm afraid.'

'I don't mind what it costs,' Jock insisted to her. 'If it's a question of money.'

The doctor gently informed him that it wasn't.

He couldn't believe the news. Not many people visited while he was in hospital, apart from those musicians of his own age who had worked with him and loved him. Nissel Lakin, the drummer from the *Caronia* trip, came with parcels of sweets and cigarettes. Jock told Lakin, 'I'm fed up with this. I'm going home.' Ted Hughes, the saxophone player who took over running the band at Hatchett's Restaurant in Piccadilly in his absence, was offered the dying man's golf clubs. 'I play golf about once every fifty years,' Jock said to Hughes. 'I don't suppose I'll be needing them now.' Hughes wasn't a golfer but accepted the clubs and even became obsessed with the game. Jock Scott discharged himself from hospital and went back to his flat in Marble Arch.

One afternoon a few weeks later, at the Alexandra Park races, Ronnie Scott saw his ailing father again. Standing at the back of the grandstand, the young saxophonist suddenly glimpsed Jock through the binoculars, standing close to the railings, a shadow of himself, of the practical joker, the eternal optimist, the gambler, the balladeer, the admirer of women, of elegant music, of fancy clothes. Ronnie Scott pushed his way through the crowds in search of his father. All the walk-on players of the racing game were in his way, the small-time and the big-time, the high rollers and the amateurs, the resigned and the euphoric and the frantic losers, and when he got to the track his father was gone.

It was the last time Ronnie Scott saw him alive. The news came on 28 May that they had had to break down the door of the flat and found Jock dead, overdosed on sedatives. Ronnie tried to comfort his mother Cissie, who was deeply distressed by the news, and confided to him then that she had never stopped loving her first husband. The man who had played such a part in both their lives, but in such different and difficult ways, was no longer an encounter to be savoured through some chance meeting in Archer Street, a voice on the end of a telephone after a long silence. Jock Scott was gone. He was fifty-five.

# 6

# The Late Late Late Late Show

'They wanted to blast every highminded citizen clear out of his easy
chair with their yard-dog growls and gully-low howls.'
(Milton 'Mezz' Mezzrow, on the white high-school kids who
founded the Chicago Jazz movement)

'BLOW!' YELLED TUBBY Hayes. His partner Ronnie Scott launched a solo on
'Some of My Best Friends Are Blues', a mid-tempo twelve-bar blues that
constituted one of his rare contributions to the art of jazz composition. The
tenor was harder and more gravelly now, but zigzagging gracefully over
the chords. A packed house at London's Dominion Theatre on that night in
1958 had already warmly greeted the band's breakneck opening version of
Cole Porter's 'What Is This Thing Called Love?', even though the band they
had really paid to hear was still to come – the American Dave Brubeck
Quartet, then at the beginning of its boom years.

Hayes and Scott cut distinctly contrasting figures in the footlights.
Though both were immaculate in suits – something that the sartorially preoccupied older man had always insisted on – clothes looked as if they fitted
Scott to the last thread, while Hayes couldn't help resembling a schoolboy
who had borrowed his father's Saturday night special.

As with most British modern jazz ensembles, nobody did anything particularly demonstrative on stage. Scott would stand virtually motionless at
the microphone, the horn held slightly to one side, his eyes often closed. He
was restrained in the presentations on that night, slightly nervous but still
registering his old familiar trademark.

'Thank you very much,' he said to the audience's applause for 'Some of
My Best Friends Are Blues'. 'And now from a brand new LP which you
may have seen in the shops, entitled *Elvis Presley sings Thelonious Monk . . .*'

The headlong delivery of the Cole Porter tune had been virtually a definition of their style, preceding the melody with wild, nervy riffing like the sound of frantic footsteps on a staircase, Porter's original notes suddenly materialising as if the perpetrator had burst through a door.

Most of what the Couriers did had that crazed momentum about it, it was sealed, hermetic, impervious, music not particularly suited to the expression of human frailties of the kind that were being poignantly articulated at the time by Ronnie Scott's old playing partner, the West Indian Joe Harriott, or by the Scottish player Bobby Wellins. But it had a gleeful, bellicose appeal. On the Dominion gig, they closed an equally tumbling version of 'Guys and Dolls' with a call-and-response section that turned into a headlong unison coda, ending on a blipping high note as if someone had abruptly planted a full stop in the music. It brought the house down. The finale was a rendition of 'Cheek To Cheek' so fast that only dancing partners bound at the neck could possibly have sustained the lyric's original sentiments.

Though Brubeck himself, highly impressed with Scott and Hayes, was to say at the end of the tour 'they sound more like an American band than we do', there was an unintentional irony in his remark. Brubeck didn't really sound much like an American band at all, being preoccupied with European conservatoire music and a kind of ornate, theoretical jazz. But American modernist outfits like those of Art Blakey and Hank Mobley in reality sounded quite different to the Couriers.

The attack of the rhythm sections was the dividing line – Blakey's cymbal beat was restless and probing, the momentum sporadically lifted by huge, breaker-like rolls and admonishing tappings and clatterings. With underpinnings so strong, the soloists could afford to play less, and avoid the hysterical, fill-every-chink manner frequently adopted by their admirers abroad. Insecurities about their quality by comparison with the Americans led British bebop bands to a kind of over-compensatory pyrotechnics, like teenagers driving cars too fast to prove their mettle. The palais-band tradition was audible in the Couriers' work too, in expert but slightly fussy arrangements that sounded very close to the repertoire of a miniature dance orchestra. But the Brubeck tour of Britain was a golden opportunity for the band, and the Dominion gig – recorded for EMI as *The Jazz Couriers In Concert* – was a high spot of it.

Though the band represented as much as he'd ever wanted from playing, Ronnie Scott revealed later that year, in a passing remark during an interview, that he had not forgotten that old 52nd Street dream. He was featured in *Melody Maker* in the autumn of 1958, where he was described as 'one of the post-war angry young men of jazz'. Scott reiterated his dislike of critics, a point he made whenever he got the chance. He was asked if he wanted to be a session player and replied that nothing would please him more, except that 'the only sessions I've done recently have been rock 'n' roll, where I have to play out of tune.' But the end of the interview showed the way his mind was turning. What were his hopes for the local jazz scene? 'I'd like to see a new type of jazz club in London,' Scott replied. 'A well-appointed place which was licensed and catered for people of all ages and not merely for youngsters.'

By the summer of 1959, the steam was going out of the Jazz Couriers. Tubby Hayes had never really stopped relishing the idea of a larger band, one that could handle the growing scope of his writing and arranging.

The last date was 30 August at the City Hall in Cork. And after the demise of the Couriers, which Ronnie Scott would have continued with indefinitely if the choice had been entirely his, there seemed little enough to get excited about in the jazz world. The only versions of the music that seemed likely to attract a substantial following were the Dave Brubeck group and the Modern Jazz Quartet. They were subtle, intelligent outfits, but they didn't display that infectious creative tension audible in Stitt's band, or Miles Davis's, or the Couriers themselves on a good night. After the first tidal wave of rock 'n' roll had subsided, you could demonstrate your taste by having a recording of one of Brubeck's explorations of fancy rhythms and hybrid classicism in your collection, or the hushed, cut-glass chamber-jazz of the MJQ. They were the closest fifties jazz came to pop-chart success.

Critics were divided about them. Benny Green had by this time virtually stopped playing and was working regularly as a jazz critic for the *Observer*, a new career offered to him by that newspaper's most influential jazz fan, theatre critic Kenneth Tynan. Green was a fluent and witty writer, one of the few jazz musicians who was comfortably capable of turning the offhanded, oblique, observant and frequently macabre humour of the music business into prose. He hated the hyping of Brubeck and the MJQ and frequently laid into them in print. 'The British jazz fan is highly conscious of his own insularity,' Green began an article on Brubeck during the pianist's 1959 visit to the Royal Festival Hall. 'He yearns to be in the swim, so our promoters cater most thoughtfully for this desire by sticking topical labels on their American touring shows.' Green went on to describe Brubeck's popularity 'as one of the peculiar aberrations of current taste'.

The Modern Jazz Quartet fared little better. Green concluded resignedly that: 'For the last five years four men have sought with painful eagerness to transform the racy art of jazz into something aspiring towards cultural respectability.' That much was undeniable. The MJQ took pains to dress like a classical chamber group, and performed with a measured and meticulous deliberation, for all the improvisational gifts of its four members in other settings.

While on holiday in Majorca that year, Scott had a reminder that maybe running a club could simply be fun (which was all he'd ever really asked for) and an opportunity to make a little money, present musicians he admired, and have somewhere amenable to play. He met a drummer and club proprietor called Ramon Farran, who was the son of a Catalan bandleader and had married Robert Graves's daughter Lucia. Through Farran, Scott came to meet the writer at Canellun, the house that Graves had built in the picturesque village of Deja in 1929. The poet broke the ice by simply enquiring: 'What's the pot situation like in London now?' He turned out to be fascinated by jazz, had even acted as patron to unconventional artists like Cecil Taylor. Scott was in turn fascinated by Graves and a little discomfited by his circle too. They had all read so much, and they were so funny, but with a sense of humour impenetrably dependent on knowledge and an education Scott hadn't had the benefit of, not the wisecracking, fatalistic, self-defensive shield against fate that came from a childhood on the streets of the East End.

Graves showed Scott around his booklined study. He seemed, Scott reflected later, to have written most of them himself. 'I've tried writing,' Scott began tentatively, 'but I find it the hardest thing in the world.'

'Of course you will,' Graves replied somewhat brusquely. 'Unless you're God.'

They got on well. Scott spent a good deal of time walking and swimming with Graves. He was astonished by the old man's boundless energy, springing up the steep slope from the sea to the house like a gazelle.

By 1961 Ronnie Scott was visiting the Majorcan capital Palma regularly, often performing with Farran's Wynton Kelly-like trio at the drummer's Indigo Club, and he was to continue his visits until the early 1970s. Graves would periodically visit London, too, in the days after Ronnie Scott had become a promoter as well as a performer of jazz. 'Robert's in the club,' Scott would call through to Benny Green. 'Do you want to come down?'


The breakthrough was an accident, of course. Jack Fordham, the Soho entrepreneur, had lost interest in the Gerrard Street premises that Scott and King had occasionally used for their own jazz presentations. Fordham's principal living came from the hamburger joint – one of the first – he ran in

Berwick Street. Eventually he offered 39 Gerrard Street to Scott for a knock-down rent. It became Ronnie Scott's first club.

Pete King – who like Benny Green had by now realised that he needed to choose between a playing career and something more promising – was almost entirely involved with promotion, partly on his own account, and partly in association with Harold Davison, and worked out of his own Soho office. He caught Ronnie Scott's enthusiastic conviction that this was the moment they'd been waiting for. Then Scott went to his parents to ask for help and got a loan of £1000 from his stepfather to get the ball rolling. Sol Berger was by this time a successful partner in a textiles company, and he willingly bought a stake in his step-son's club.

Number 39 Gerrard Street had nothing but space and not very much of that. The two would-be club proprietors went to the East End in search of cheap furniture and bought a job lot of chairs which they arranged in austere lines in front of the bandstand. Pete King's father-in-law, a Manchester carpenter, came down to help build a few rudimentary tables. Then there wouldn't be room for dancing, so it was going to have to be a venue for fans who really wanted to come and listen. There was no liquor licence and the best the establishment was likely to be able to provide was tea, for years staple fuel for the Archer Street metabolism (the two men had established a lifelong 'tea bag connection' with a Chiswick wholesaler), coffee, and maybe a hamburger.

From the start, it was an unspoken agreement that the front man would be Ronnie Scott and that the club would bear his name, though King was crucial to the graft of administration even then, and would become the difference between survival and collapse in later years. King's commitment was total, and Stella was obliged by the working hours to bring up their two children almost singlehanded. But to King, Scott was the unchallenged star. Someone had to embody the club in the eyes of the jazz public. Scott was the most highly regarded modern jazz musician in Britain, apart from Tubby Hayes, and his reputation was something money couldn't buy.

The London modern jazz world of the late 1950s was a limited market and for the new contenders in it, the lie of the land was not so difficult to gauge. In Wardour Street, a stone's throw away, was the Flamingo, already in existence for two years. The old Studio 51, which opened after the Club Eleven's demise, had started life with a modern jazz policy but by 1959 was presenting revivalist and traditional music. As for the amount of music you could reasonably expect to present and still come out ahead, Saturday night audiences were good and Sundays passable, but weekdays were graveyards.

Scott and King thought the entrance prices charged by the other jazz clubs were too low ever to be able to finance really unusual acts. They never considered Americans, and anyway the embargo was still firm. They would gradually improve their modest premises so that one day it would be the kind of place where people wouldn't mind paying a little more just to be in a real club. And they would build towards making jazz a part of London life.

After scratching together the basics, they went about developing a marketing policy. What this amounted to was a weekly pooling of gags by the musicians that could be deployed as publicity in small ads in *Melody Maker*. Scott had never seen any reason why you shouldn't present any enterprise to the customers as if the whole thing were a joke, as long as you didn't treat it as one when it really counted, and that meant playing. He therefore placed an entry in the columns of *Melody Maker* of 31 October 1959 which declared the following:

### RONNIE SCOTT'S CLUB
39 Gerrard Street, W1

### OPENING TONIGHT!
Friday 7.30pm.

Tubby Hayes Quartet; the trio with
Eddie Thompson, Stan Roberts, Spike Heatley.

A young alto saxophonist, Peter King, and
an old tenor saxophonist, Ronnie Scott.

The first appearance in a jazz club since the
relief of Mafeking by Jack Parnell.

Membership 10/- until January 1961.
Admission 1/6 (to members) 2/6 (non-members)

The entry concluded boldly: 'The best jazz in the best club in town' – Ronnie Scott having learnt from the American example that you didn't lose anything by excess. If the punters didn't agree they could always vote with their feet. It was a gamble, but Ronnie Scott came from a long gamblers' line.

Scott and King had opened the proceedings with a shrewd mixture of attractions, a blend of the new and the familiar intended to cut across as many of the modern jazz persuasions as possible. Hayes was a sure-fire cert, of course, and would be appearing with the Couriers' old pianist Terry Shannon, and with Phil Seamen on drums and a brilliant new bassist, Jeff

Clyne, who had played on the streets of Edgware with Ronnie Scott's step-sister Marlene and who had revered the local heroes, the Feldman brothers, on those same streets. As for the reference to the 'young alto saxophonist Peter King', this was not a gag at his partner's expense but introducing a sensational new arrival on the scene, a thin anxious-looking nineteen-year-old from Tolworth in Surrey, who had been playing for just a little over two years and already demonstrated his intense admiration for the work of Charlie Parker – King's speed of thought and richness of resources were close to rivalling Tubby Hayes even then. The newcomer's preoccupation with Parker extended, as Benny Green observed, to his small-talk, which consisted almost entirely of analyses of the structure of various Parker solos.

In the press, Peter King was modest about his achievements. He said he was 'limited both technically and musically. But I can feel something coming.' In fact, as the more discriminating of local observers immediately realised, King was virtually there. He was already one of the few British interpreters of Parker's methods to execute the complexities of bop with an air of ease and relaxation. This was not so much discernible in the young man's demeanour onstage (his eyes would be downcast as he played, his legs splayed and knees bending with the beat like a man who had spent a long time on horseback, and he perpetually looked nervous) but in the fluency with which streams of new melody tumbled from his horn, and the momentum of his rhythmic attack.

King had never served an apprenticeship in one idiom and then switched to another. He was a modernist through and through. His very existence was a testament to the value of the players of Scott's generation having made those pilgrimages to New York and spent those long hours in Carlo Krahmer's studio listening to imported 78s. They had built a spring-board for new players that would make possible a conclusive rejection of the inferiority complex that British players had about their jazz.

The first gig also featured Eddie Thompson, a pianist whose ideas absorbed swing music, bop, the majestic 'orchestral' jazz pianists like Art Tatum and Duke Ellington and a good deal of classical music too. In featuring Thompson, the club was opening with one of the finest keyboard artists in the land.

It was an evening of magic. Scott and King had already set themselves several dates that they had eventually missed and the club wasn't really ready for business even on that memorable occasion of 30 October 1959. There were shows every night of that weekend; in the daytime frantic efforts were made to improve the place. The club was packed with musicians and friends. Ray Nance, Duke Ellington's trumpeter who was returning to the States after the band's European tour, dropped in on the Friday night to wish Scott luck. It became obvious that the all-nighters were such a magnet for after-hours players looking for somewhere to blow that the club began to charge them 2/- for the privilege, a state of affairs that caused a certain amount of hurt surprise.

Many in the business, who thought they knew only too well not only the prospects for modern jazz in London, but the temporary nature of some of Ronnie Scott's enthusiasms as well, gave the place no more than a couple of weeks. But in the event it was just what the London jazz public needed. It was informal, it didn't charge nightclub prices, the music was consistently good and it was devoted to a no-messing policy of presentation of the best practitioners of jazz in Britain. *Melody Maker* ran a spread on the club the week after it opened, with photographs of Scott, Thompson, Tubby Hayes and others. The copy declared:

In addition to presenting the top names of British modern jazz, Ronnie intends to feature promising young musicians at the club and Friday's guest stars included the new alto sensation, Peter King.

In its pre-Christmas edition, its correspondent Bob Dawbarn also commented on the new arrival as 'a highly optimistic note for British jazz. There are still too few places for the modern musician to ply his trade, but the players themselves took matters into their own hands.'

Word of mouth was the publicity machine for the most part, apart from those little ads in *Melody Maker*. Scott devoted himself to making a miniature art-form out of them in the hope that people would seek them out, promising anything he could think of. He would claim that the club would be featuring an unexpected joint appearance by Sir Thomas Beecham, Somerset Maugham and Little Richard. He would promise food untouched by human hands because the chef was a gorilla.

The place caught on. Visiting musicians from abroad, increasingly prevalent in Britain as Harold Davison and others staged more and more concerts that would tie into existing European tours, were to be seen in Ronnie Scott's, which added to the glamour of being there. There were, after all, few enough places in any town where such a rare bird as a jazz musician could truly feel at home. The drummer Shelly Manne, in London with one of Norman Granz's 'Jazz At The Philharmonic' packages, even returned to the States to open a club of his own after having spent some time absorbing the atmosphere at Gerrard Street. That the place was run by musicians was already promising to be a considerable benefit. Even though Scott and King were not in a position to pay big money, they were in the same business as the professionals they were hiring, and they were honest. Players didn't suffer the crippling paranoia, fleecing and all-round disrespect that often characterised relationships between jazz musicians and promoters.

Two problems were soon apparent. The first was that there was a law of diminishing returns about presenting British jazz players – even the very best – night after night. Scott and King soon felt the draught of this difficulty. They ran the establishment on a simple principle, based on a consultation with the rudimentary accounts at the end of each week. If there was enough in the kitty to pay the artists and the rent for another week's work, it meant the place was still open.

The second snag was the absence of a bar. Scott and King looked into the formalities and the regulations were complicated. If you were going to serve alcohol, you needed a 'wine committee'. Ronnie Scott and Pete King formed two-thirds of the wine committee and asked Benny Green to be the third, being a literary man and a correspondent for a high-class newspaper. Green duly travelled to Wembley police station to make a statement as to why Ronnie Scott's Club wanted to make a public nuisance of itself in this way.

'What is the purpose of this club?' asked the station sergeant wearily.

'It's to try to get rhythm sections to play in time,' intoned Green, straight-faced.

The sergeant dutifully took it down word for word. The club's liquor licence was also dependent on providing some form of emergency exit in the case of fire. It was rudimentary enough, and fortunately never had to be tested, being simply a metal ladder that extended upstairs into the hallway of the Jewish garment manufacturer above. Relationships with that establishment were mixed during Ronnie Scott's tenure in Gerrard Street.


Early on it became apparent that Scott and King were going to be no orthodox club-owners. Scott's guiding philosophy, as it had been back in the days of the nine-piece, continued to be that if you could get a laugh out of it, it couldn't be all bad. The word soon got around. Here was a place where all of the misfits and square pegs of a square mile of London dedicated to the entertainment of the normals by the weirdos could relax in congenial company – like writer Colin MacInnes, a deep devotee of jazz and friend of Denis Rose, like actor and playwright Harold Pinter. A man called Fred Twigg attached himself to the club, and became its odd-job man and cleaner. He took to sleeping on the premises, which worsened a chronic condition that Twigg lived with – apparitions. He often complained to the proprietors of flying creatures and gorillas that frequented the establishment at night. And in those early days, the club unexpectedly became an actors' studio as well.

Ronnie Scott had known the actress Georgia Brown from the East End, and she suggested to him that the Gerrard Street cellar would be perfect as a daytime rehearsal room for an actors' company. The company turned out to involve the likes of Maggie Smith, George Devine of the Royal Court Theatre, Michael Caine and Lindsay Anderson. (Ronnie Scott fell unrequitedly in love with an actress called Ann Lynne and visited the Royal Court night after night to watch her in performance with Albert Finney.) Scott and Benny Green found the rehearsals irresistible. They both took to standing behind the tea bar for hours, endlessly making lemon tea for the labouring thespians and eventually found their own communications with others helplessly enmeshed in fake stage-speak. 'What dost thou fancy in the 4.30?' Scott would enquire of Green.

One of the rehearsals involved George Devine donning an elaborate mask, and demanding that the actors guess the emotion expressed by his body-language only. Devine went up to the street to prepare, and promptly vanished. It transpired that the passing citizens of Soho had concluded from Devine's mask that exotic fetishistic pursuits were going on downstairs, and had mobbed him. Devine eventually tore himself away and fled unartistically down the steps. 'Fear!' promptly supplied the members of the actors' company on the appearance of the master, still sticking to instructions.

Throughout 1960, the difficulty of sustaining an audience for the local musicians continued to nag at Scott and King. The Musicians' Union ban had stopped being unconditional two years previously and international artists regularly came and went. But residencies, the maintaining of an imported star in a British venue night after night for a week, or a month, had not been considered. King, who still worked with the now highly successful impresario Harold Davison, knew that the latter would not be keen that his protégés step on his territory.

But King also knew that things could not go on as they were. He began at the British Musicians' Union, with the assistant secretary, Harry Francis, who was amenable to the idea of a new arrangement that would suit the requirements of a specialist nightclub. If the exchange of artists would be one for one, Francis was convinced that the request would go through on the British side. King turned his attention to the real nub of the problem. Since the 1930s, James C. Petrillo of the American Federation of Musicians had effectively battened down any form of trade in musical resources likely to cause loss of earnings to his own members.

Petrillo (nicknamed 'Little Caesar' because of his stocky, pugnacious, Edward G. Robinson-like demeanour) was a man with a straight-shooting style of negotiation that made him a formidable opponent. The American Federation's policy had grown out of far leaner years than the 1950s and King, as a musician himself, was generally sympathetic to the union's original position. Its inflexibility from the mid-fifties onwards was principally fuelled by the attitude of the British Musicians' Union, which was convinced that American members would receive far more attractive invitations to Britain than the other way around. King reasoned that if jazz musicians were the Cinderellas of the profession already, it was shortsighted now that times were not so hard to turn down a policy that might further the public's interest in the music generally.

Scott and King needed to pick their first guest, then worry about the bureaucracy afterwards. They chose Zoot Sims, a one-time partner of Stan Getz in the Woody Herman band and a player with much the same lyricism and raffish elegance as Getz but with a more robust and muscular delivery. Sims was popular at the Half Note Club in New York, an Italian family business by the Cantorino brothers, with a reputation similar to that of the Scott club in London for presenting good music to audiences that cared about it in an atmosphere conducive to relaxation and inventiveness. Sims accepted readily.

King then went to New York to try to sew it up. He told the music press that Tubby Hayes was taking a holiday in America at the same time, and it was only reasonable that he, as Hayes's manager, should make an attempt to arrange some work for his client. King met Sims for a beer to chew it over. They played Tubby Hayes's records to the Cantorinos, and from distrusting a project they felt they didn't really need – an English jazz soloist on a month's residency in the heart of New York's jazzland – the Italians came around to the idea, and wanted to help Zoot, an old friend. The matter went backwards and forwards inside the American Federation officials' headquarters for what to King seemed like an age. But the news finally came through that Petrillo had accepted the deal. King rang Scott in London and told him they were in business. Scott rang Harry Francis at the Musicians' Union and the swap was on. Finally they called Sims, who asked simply: 'When do I come?'

The exchange was arranged for November 1961. Ronnie Scott's Club was about to become an international jazz venue.

# 7

# California Cool, East Coast Hot

'Don't ever shrink from the belief that you have to prove yourself
every minute, because you do.'

(Sonny Rollins to Kitty Grime, Jazz at Ronnie Scott's, 1979)

ZOOT SIMS WAS a delight.

After his first show, the proprietors of London's new international jazz
club sat bemused in their locked up premises, counting the hours until they
could hear him play again. For Scott, who had probably already subcon-
sciously decided that a policy of booking practitioners on his own chosen
instrument was going to be one of the principle ways he would enjoy being
a promoter, Sims was a definition of the modern jazz musician who was
still functioning wholeheartedly and pragmatically in the world everybody
else had to live in.

He had a lot in common with Ronnie. He had been a teenage saxophone
star in a showy jazz orchestra, the Woody Herman band. He was an unpre-
tentious, unaffected, music-loving enthusiast. He knew jazz history. And
he always played the music as if he enjoyed it. Sims was the kind of player
who could have thrived in just about any sort of jazz band of the previous
forty-odd years.

Sims delivered his easy-going swing and gentle rhapsodising throughout the month of November 1961 to thrilled audiences at the club. A casual,
fresh-faced man, Sims would play without demonstrativeness, holding the
instrument still. His opening bars would establish the tune with the directness and confidence of a player completely at ease with his raw materials,
and much of his appeal was founded on the manner in which his sound
exhibited both confidence and a heady lightness, as if he were performing
a graceful juggling act in slow motion. King arranged a short tour of out-of-

town venues for Sims, and the proprietors presented him with a silver brandy flask after his last performance. Other local musicians donated such peculiarly British gifts as copies of *Goon Show* records.

Sims was also one of the first Americans to experience the off-beam goings-on that entered the folklore of the Ronnie Scott Club in its various incarnations. Somebody threw a smoke-bomb into the room on 5 November which cleared the premises, but the Californian, a man after the Eastenders' hearts, barely raised an eyebrow. Fred Twigg, the club's vision-prone cleaner, was deeply suspicious of the quiet, unassuming visitor. 'Russian spy,' he warned Scott ominously. 'He's a Russian spy.'

In an interview, the usually unforthcoming Sims declared he was delighted with playing in London, since the intimacy of a club gave him the opportunity to relax. 'It reminds me of the Half Note,' Sims said. 'The atmosphere is warm and it's an easygoing place. Musicians like it. It has the same kind of management.' Sims added that he'd like to see Ronnie Scott play in the States. 'It depends on his confidence,' the American accurately observed.

For Scott's part, he was sad to see Sims go. 'My God,' he mused. 'What an anti-climax next week's going to be.'

The Sims season proved that the problem of the European rhythm section could be resolved. This issue dominated conversations in local jazz circles. Though Ronnie Scott, Johnny Dankworth, Tubby Hayes and a handful of other performers had demonstrated some confidence in their skills as front-line performers, European rhythm sections were on the whole not popular with visiting Americans, who considered them insensitive to the essence of jazz timekeeping or incapable of relaxed swing. On top of that, the club proprietor faced the choice between accompanying musicians whose independence might upstage the honoured guest, or patsies whose very inertia would lower the drive of the proceedings to the extent that even the most sensational soloists in the business would be stretched to sound good.

The solution was Stan Tracey.

Tracey had a substantial track record by 1961. He had begun at Gerrard Street within months of the opening and was a quietly truculent figure whose playing style had allegiances to both the robust and percussive keyboard style of Thelonious Monk and the muscular lyricism of Duke Ellington. Tracey had been a teenage accordion player in the forces entertainment network ENSA, had performed in the RAF Gang Show directed by the late, great British comedian Tony Hancock. He had first come across Ronnie Scott when the saxophonist was playing a guest spot at the

Jock Scott (centre), Ronnie's alto-playing father, fronting an orchestra in his prime.

Ronnie's mother Sylvia, better known as 'Cissie'. Also in the picture, Solomon 'Sol' Berger, her second husband and the man who helped the young saxophonist through the foothills of his career.

Ronnie in his teens, with the Pennsylvania saxophone.

Ronnie considering a dance hall edict with actor and jazz fan Mario Fabrizi.

Rehearsing the nine-piece in the spring of 1953. The bandleader runs through the part, with Benny Green, Pete King and Derek Humble in hot pursuit.

The nine-piece assembling for business in Archer Street. Benny Green is holding up the band bus.

Ronnie Scott with Sonny Rollins, one of the most prolific and idiosyncratic of all jazz improvisors.
*photo: David Redfern*

Ronnie Scott on baritone with Tubby Hayes and the Couriers at the Savoy, Catford in April 1959.

Dexter Gordon's introduction to the West End on the celebrated visit to Ronnie Scott's in 1962. Gordon and Lucky Thompson were the first black Americans to play there. (Val Wilmer)

Ronnie Scott jamming with Sonny Stitt at Gerrard Street in 1964. Stitt was one of the Americans Scott remained in awe of from the first time he heard him in Newark in 1957. Gene Wright, then with Dave Brubeck, guests on bass.
*photo: Val Wilmer*

The proprietor at Frith Street, in the early days.
*photo: Val Wilmer*

The twilight world of Frith Street's 'office' – night and day, it always looked the same. The profile is unmistakeable. The opponent is the late Dizzy Gillespie.
*photo: Vil Wilmer*

Chucho Valdes and Irakere
– part of the 'Cuban
connection' that was forged
with Frith Street in 1985.
*photo: David Redfern*

Turbo-charged bebop
tenorist Johnny Griffin. He
is a regular and popular
visitor to the club.
*photo: David Redfern*

Nina Simone drew huge crowds to the club in the mid-eighties with her dramatic mixture
of jazz and soul. *photo: David Redfern*

The jazz man and the
first born – Ronnie with
Nicholas in 1965.

Rebecca, Ronnie and Mary,
Christmas 1973.

Mary with Rebecca at 3 months in Wales in 1972.

Rebecca in New York in her
teens – years when jazz
clubs were the last places
she wanted to be.

Ronnie Scott with one of
the world's best-known
jazz lovers – Rolling Stones
drummer Charlie Watts
on the opening night of
'the Birmingham branch'.
*photo: Terry Walker*

Thirty-five years and
counting. Pete King ('if we
were shrewd businessmen
we wouldn't be here') and
Ronnie Scott ('not keeping
you up, am I, sir?') in an
amiable mood not all the
punters would recognise.
*photo: David Redfern*

Paramount in Tottenham Court Road in the early 1950s, then mainly a venue for London's black male population. Tracey performed on a piano with a bass player who doubled on hi-hat (an ignominious role occasioned by the absence of a drummer) so the bassist was obliged to deliver beats one and three on the bass and two and four on the hi-hat.

When Laurie Morgan had formed a band called Elevated Music after his departure from the Club Eleven circle Tracey left the Paramount to be in it. Thereafter Tracey had played on the boats – on one occasion in 1953 on the *Caronia* with Jock Scott as his bandleader – and eventually toured the United States with the Ted Heath band. He had a punchy, muscular way of playing, possessed a receptive and forceful improvisor's intelligence and swung furiously. By the time he became involved with Ronnie Scott's Club, when many piano players of Tracey's age wanted to adopt the smooth and elegant style of Wynton Kelly or the poignant classicism of Bill Evans, Tracey was determined to tread a different path.

Zoot Sims and Tracey made an album while the saxophonist was in England, on which Ronnie Scott and the trumpeter Jimmy Deuchar also appeared. Recordings of British modernists with their American counterparts were virtually unheard of. It was also a gesture of defiance directed at the sort of jazz that might shift a lot of records. Dave Brubeck's 'Take Five', a catchy melody in one of the pianist's quirky time signatures, was in the pop hit parade that week. Bandleaders were complaining that they were having to disappoint their customers because the sheet music for Brubeck's record was so hard to get hold of.


The Gerrard Street premises began to build a reputation. It was already a strong competitor with Wardour Street's Flamingo as the leading establishment of its kind in London, and it had an atmosphere all of its own, something of that risque mystery of both the 52nd Street places and the wartime bottle-party joints, the definition of a belowstairs dive in which people who had never known what conformity meant, people who were trying to slough it off, and people who were taking a night's rest from it, would listen to a music that seemed in itself to be an antidote to much of the schmaltz that still overwhelmed Tin Pan Alley and pop music.

Down a rickety stairway into a basement, beckoned into the depths by the loudspeaker on the stairs that would relay some of the atmosphere of what was going on inside (some poorer fans would simply prop themselves up outside and listen to the stars over the sound system), getting a chance to get close to these legendary figures, even snatch a conversation with them at the bar because the place was so small they couldn't get away from you anyway.

At the beginning, in that cramped rectangle of a basement, the bandstand had been placed at the far end of the room, the coffee bar at the other. As times improved, so too did life for the long-suffering punters (even at bursting point the place wouldn't hold much more than 150, one reason for the precarious nature of its economics). A tier of seats on one long wall was built, with the bandstand facing them halfway along the other.

An evening there had an informal drama the other clubs lacked. There was the wait while players of the class of Zoot Sims or Stan Getz were ushered by Scott or King from what the club ironically termed its 'office' (a cubby-hole under the thoroughfare of Gerrard Street itself) through the parting crowd, up to the tiny stage to wait for one of Tracey's quirky, sidelong introductions before filling the room with that rich, vocal, heart-quickening sound of the saxophone.

But getting a laugh out of life wasn't always unimpeded. Reverses seemed to be coming in battalions for Ronnie Scott in the early 1960s. They had begun with the death of Jock, and followed with the death of Nana Becky in a Hendon hospice in 1960. She had lived to a great age, and had been as close to Scott as Cissie had been, for all the world was his second mother. Cissie had died unexpectedly two years later, pouring tea for the women who used to come to the Edgwarebury house to play cards with her each week. Sol had been in the back room reading, and Ronnie had been upstairs in the tiny bedroom that had been kept for him, looking just the way it always had, in anticipation of his regular visits. He remembered the doctor's words to the ambulancemen, 'I won't be needing you now,' that moment of hope that she might have recovered, then the realization of what the doctor actually meant and that Cissie was gone, and with no warning, nothing to help him prepare.

He felt that the deaths of Nana Becky and Cissie had changed him. It was as if it was impossible to be quite the same freewheeler again. It brought him to the front line in his family. When they were alive, they stood between him and age, maturity, seriousness. They were the nurturing forces of life. Now he was exposed.

39 Gerrard Street was getting on to adventurous Londoners' lists as a place to go, as was another new night-haunt close by in Greek Street. The Establishment Club was opened by two young graduates, Peter Cook and Nicholas Luard, to represent the growing fashion for satirical humour. It may have been a by-product of the expansion of higher education in the post-war years, but its target was exactly the complacent and self-congratulatory British society whose boom time had fuelled it.

The Establishment invited the savage American genius Lenny Bruce to perform on its premises. But Bruce was also drawn to Gerrard Street, about as much as the jazz club's patrons and staff were drawn to him. Lenny Bruce and Scott talked jazz, and the American gave him a pass to the Establishment to watch the act. Also on the bill were the Alberts, a British ensemble led by the performance artist Bruce Lacey who wore Edwardian suits and wire-framed glasses and performed a kind of impassive slapstick. Scott would for years dissolve at the memory of their quiz show.

Quizmaster: 'Are you ready for the sixty-four-thousand-dollar question?'

'Yes' (Bucket of whitewash on contestant's head). Pause.

Contestant (from inside bucket): 'I'm sorry, could you repeat the question?'

Kenneth Tynan had described Bruce's work as 'outspoken harangues in an idiom I can only describe as jazz-Jewish'. It might have been a phrase tailor-made for Scott and his playing companions, but they soon learned that Bruce's muse came from a darker source than theirs. Scott loved Bruce's flailing vulgarity – the comic believing then that sexual repression was at the root of many ills. It was this kind of material that got Bruce's act labelled 'sick and lavatory humour' by the then Home Secretary Henry Brooke, and a ban from future British appearances. But Bruce's real clout was as a trenchant social critic. He revealed in routines like the Madison Avenue plot to increase cigarette sales by making cancer a status symbol, an act that would sound almost like a social service today.

A succession of illustrious visitors came and went, and Stan Tracey carried on adding to his encyclopaedic knowledge – material that would shortly surface in some remarkable compositions by the pianist, including his 'Under Milk Wood' suite, which became famous not only for some memorable melodies but notably the yearning, atmospheric tenor playing of the Scots musician Bobby Wellins.

Scott and King, at that time ever-enthusiastic for ways of branching out, organised a jazz package for an all-in price of 110 guineas (covering hotel bills and club admissions in that period) for some of the London fans newly nurtured on live appearances by their heroes and heroines to catch the music on its home turf in New York. It was a once-only attempt. Scott claimed that King couldn't count in guineas. None of the partners' efforts at diversification ever came to much in those days. They lacked the will to follow it up, to make a business out of it. All either of them really wanted to do was run a jazz club.

People didn't always see eye to eye with this simple ambition. The gown-manufacturer who owned the premises upstairs was furious about noise from the basement. The offending circumstances seemed to be the rehearsals that took place in the club in the afternoons, and which brought the place some much-needed extra revenue. The argument, which passed through polite requests, irritability and finally fury, ended up in the courts. The plaintiffs eventually produced a single witness in the secretary who worked in the room above the bandstand and who insisted that she couldn't receive 'important telephone calls' because of the noise. The judge remarked to her at one point 'some people like jazz. They might consider you lucky to have it while you work, without paying for it.'

The witness insisted on two principal complaints. On the first, she said, she had discovered a group of 'buglers' downstairs, at their devilish work on the bandstand. 'I told the conductor he was too noisy but he told me he didn't want to know' – a contention that astonished the defendants, who couldn't lay hands on a bugle between them, or a conductor. On the second, the noise had similarly been so intense as to provoke a personal visit, but when she arrived in the basement, she had found it empty. The defence enquired as to where the noise could thus have been coming from, and answer came there none. Scott and Benny Green had already spent much time hovering in the upstairs passage in the presence of an official with a sound level meter while Ella Fitzgerald was using the establishment as an afternoon rehearsal room. The machine had hardly registered more than, as Green recalled, 'our own heavy breathing'.

The unreliability of the gown-manufacturer's witness in the end led to an out-of-court settlement. Scott's lawyer demanded life membership of the club in part payment. 'Whose life, yours or mine?' the proprietor asked him pointedly.

Lucky Thompson was the first black American to visit Gerrard Street. And then, in September 1962, the mighty Dexter Gordon followed. Gordon was a jazz giant in all senses. He was six foot five, with a deceptively gentle and courteous manner, and a studiously respectful demeanour with his audiences which would take the form of fastidious announcements of tunes, as if the punters were all deaf or incapable of understanding the language. '"Society Red",' Gordon would announce as his next tune, the kind of funky mid-tempo blues on which he was famous for extemporising endlessly. 'So-cie-ty Red,' he would repeat with sibilant emphasis.

Dexter Gordon and Ronnie Scott recognised that they were kindred spirits and as the run progressed they took to exchanging impromptu comedy routines during the shows. Scott would stare up at Gordon's elm-like proportions from the floor, and inform him gravely that there was no money to pay the wages. Gordon would elaborately act hurt.

He was a spectacular sight at full cry. His massive feet flapped enthusiastically as an avalanche of reverberating, boulder-like notes rolled imperiously from his horn. Sweat would form rivulets down his face, explode in cascades on the floor, close to the glowing faces of the fans. As the evening wore on, Gordon's huge collar would detach itself and fly out around his enormous neck like a sail. And at the end of the performance he would hold the tenor, which seemed hardly bigger than a toy in his hands, out toward the audience as if it were a gift or he were inviting them to share with him a tribute to the instrument.

It was the appearance of Roland Kirk in 1963 that was as big a landmark in the history of the club as that first booking of Zoot Sims had been. Kirk was the best public relations exercise any jazz club could conceivably embark on. He was a blind multi-instrumentalist from Columbus, Ohio, who had become one of the most remarkable phenomena in the music by 1963. He had been a powerful improvisor from his days in the Charles Mingus band, but had developed techniques for not only playing several reed instruments at the same time and performing simultaneous vocal and instrumental lines on the flute (that owed a little to his predecessor in the Mingus group, Yusef Lateef) but also for sustaining an improvisation over lengthy periods without interruption, by the technique known as circular breathing – breathing in through the nose and out through the mouth at the same time, a rigorous discipline for the facial muscles and lungs. The late Mal Dean, a trumpeter and a cartoonist for *Melody Maker*, even represented Kirk with an array of oxygen bottles behind him connected to his head by a tube.

Kirk also gave the club its first taste of what a new black radicalism would sound like. 'Black classical music' was what Kirk called it. Unlike many of the visitors, whose musical loquacity would be matched only by their indifference to speech, Kirk was persistently talkative as a presenter of his own repertoire, and introduced pieces with lengthy preambles peppered with anecdotes of black American history.

Kirk was only interested in producing a music that drew crowds. Many came to watch what seemed like a sophisticated freak show – since the ingenuity that went into being able to perform simultaneously a three-part harmony on a trio of saxophones would sometimes take on a sideshow bravura – but it was obvious on his debut performance at Gerrard Street that he could play a straight-ahead bebop tenor solo as seriously and inventively as anyone in the business. He proved to be that rare thing – an all-round entertainer who could play first-class jazz, and remain true to his principles. As such, he had little time for critics who dismissed him as a circus act. He even hauled one of his detractors, the critic Steve Race, on to the stand one night. Knowing that Race was a pianist of some accomplishment, Kirk insisted that they play together; it was not a dignified experience for the Englishman.

Kirk was suspicious and difficult with Scott and King at first. 'Blind and black,' King thought. 'How many times has he been ripped off?' The American wanted his money in cash at the end of each night's work on those first days, a precaution born out of bitter experience. But within days Kirk's mind was at rest. A musician-run club was a reassurance in situations such as this.

Rock players were fascinated by Kirk, who was both a passionate artist and a showman. And because the rock boom already breaking at the time was fuelled by black rhythm 'n' blues, Kirk's earthy approach and accessibility made him a draw for young white rock players, who sought out black originators for inspiration. The Beatles came to Gerrard Street to hear the great multi-instrumentalist in 1963, the year in which they had five chart hits.

Kirk was never truly a member of the avant-garde and the label only clung to him because he seemed weird and would occasionally launch into odd effects such as endlessly sustained exit notes, wild off-the-register top notes or dissonant wails with three horns played together. A number of English rock artists – including the drummer Jon Hiseman, at that time making the transition from avant-garde jazz – made a short film with Roland Kirk on that tour.

Kirk's force as a performer made him someone whose opinion you respected. On his first visit he was introduced by the locals to the playing of Tubby Hayes, a man who on the face of it was as American as you could get in his confidence and the speed and agility of his playing. 'He's very fast,' Kirk agreed. 'But the best player I've heard here is Ronnie Scott.'

# 8

# Royalty

'I love this club, it's just like home. Filthy and full of strangers. Last night vandals broke in and redecorated it.' (Scott routine)

'Certain neuroses, cultivated by a pogrom-orientated mother and a father leaning toward Utopian socialism, inevitably inclined me to a humorous point of view.'

(Cecil 'Flash' Winston's unpublished memoirs)

THE PROPRIETOR WAS urinating into the washbasin of the club's 'office' as Flash Winston came in. Winston coughed. Scott looked up in stagey alarm. 'You haven't just washed in this bowl, have you?' he greeted Winston with indignant fastidiousness.

Winston, a stocky, bird-like man, was still attempting to pursue a career as a stand up comic despite a decade of discouragement, and an attempt to improve his image with a nose job that he swore had led his mother to wail disconsolately, 'You won't be able to be buried in a Jewish cemetery.' 'That reminds me,' Winston came back without a pause, 'I said to the man in my garage, "I gotta leak in my radiator." He said, "It's your radiator, go ahead."'

Scott returned, 'You got a ready wit, Flash. But it's not quite ready yet.'

Winston saw an open goal. 'As a matter of fact, it is,' he said urgently. 'Put me on tonight, Ron. I won't let you down.'

Scott went into brief consultation with Pete King. Finally he said, 'OK. You're on in fifteen minutes.'

Scott then set about introducing Winston to the Gerrard Street audience. 'It's a great pressure, er, pleasure,' he began, 'to introduce a young man who has just finished cabaret in the north, and is now here to finish it in the south.

93

How about a nice round of applause for Flash Winston.' Following that introduction, Winston excelled himself, and even the normally unforthcoming Scott was complimentary. Winston was invited back the following night. He couldn't sleep with the excitement of the opportunity, blew the second show, and Ronnie Scott – a friend from the days when the public had never heard the names of either of them, but whose life had taken a very different path out of the East End – was forced to cancel him for a third.

But it wasn't just old loyalties that had inclined Scott to giving Winston a chance in the first place. Snap decisions made on gut feelings were his way. He and Winston had had a conversation like a musical dialogue with a fellow player, and as often as not such spontaneity led somewhere. If it didn't, what did it matter? It would be a long time before Ronnie Scott would consider that this philosophy didn't always work.

In 1963 Ronnie Scott got a new opportunity for an American trip. It involved returning to the Half Note in New York where Tubby Hayes had triumphed to make Zoot Sims' journey possible two years before. Scott went to the States with Jimmy Deuchar and saxophonist Ronnie Ross to work with a band featuring the Massachusetts pianist Roger Kellaway, who had made a reputation for himself in both modern classical music and jazz. But despite the fact that the Cantorino brothers welcomed the Englishmen and the club was comfortable and pleasant to play in, Ronnie Scott still felt like an interloper, bringing American music on to its home soil. He blotted out most memories of the trip, but the return journey etched itself permanently on his mind since his taxiing aeroplane caught fire at Idlewild Airport and the recollection of the chutes and the firemen in asbestos suits came back to him for years afterward, every time he approached the steps of an aeroplane. Deuchar and Ross found it easier to forget since they had both been drunk when the incident occurred. 'My saxophone, my saxophone,' Ross had wailed to Scott as he stumbled down the aisle to the exits. 'Fuck your saxophone,' Scott replied, pushing him out of the door.

But if that journey to the States had been memorable to Ronnie Scott principally as a reminder of the potential treachery of fate, there was also a nuance to it that would not become apparent to Scott and Pete King for another twelve months at least: 1963 was the year of the Beatles. The Liverpudlian group, itself steeped in the sort of music that had formed the repertoire of the black rock package on Scott's previous visit in 1957, was now not only an inspiration to aspiring British pop musicians – every school and youth club in the land seemed have sprouted at least one 'beat group' – but to young Americans as well. The Beatles, and the dozens of British bands that came in their wake, were soon to make such an impact in America that the quota system applying to the transatlantic exchange would shortly become irrelevant. It was perfect timing. The expansion of Ronnie Scott's Club through the 1960s would have been much harder without it.

At thirty-six Ronnie Scott was a club proprietor, but still a saxophonist first and foremost. His style was taking on a firmer, grittier edge, moving away from the delicate sound of Getz or the graceful swing of Zoot Sims. He had found two new inspirations, in Americans Sonny Rollins and Hank Mobley. The latter was a model that seemed to reveal a meeting-place between Scott's own background (palais-band work, and that peculiarly Jewish mix of romantic pragmatism that he had found a voice for by borrowing the cool elegance of Getz) and the more direct, wilful and soulful world of black American jazz.

Mobley was a Georgia-born musician three years younger than Ronnie Scott, a 'musician's musician' who had worked in Art Blakey's Jazz Messengers. He displayed an original musical intelligence, restraint and softer sound that appealed to the more introverted European sensibility, and an ability to construct his solos through highly original suspensions and manipulations of the beat. This came at a time when Sonny Rollins and John Coltrane were producing a more outwardly intimidating music by, in Rollins' case, the use of a bleak tone, oblique musical jokes, unpredictable stutterings and stumblings between loquacity and impenetrable pauses, and (in Coltrane's) a tendency toward stark and unnerving off-the-register harmonics and drenching super-development of bop harmony to generate a seamless, trance-like effect. Ronnie Scott was fascinated by both of them, but they were unswerving experimenters, and he was not. It was Mobley who seemed to retain the grace that Scott's deepest sympathies inclined to, one that seemed to retain a little of Jock's values, that 'good sound', and the 'pretty notes' he had always liked.

Ronnie Scott had become involved with a German barmaid at the club, Ilsa Fox. Ilsa was a serious jazz fan who had heard John Coltrane in concert three times before she met Ronnie Scott, and had started work at the club for a close-up view of jazz musicians she respected. Ilsa was intelligent, strong-minded, and happy to share the unpredictable timetable of a musician's life. She was dark, handsome, and exhibited some engagingly theatrical quirks, of which smoking a pipe was one. She and Ronnie found that they read the same books, Jewish humourists in particular. And toward the end of the year, Ilsa discovered that she was pregnant.

Ronnie was no nearer wanting to be a family man now than he had been in the 1950s with Joan, but Ilsa had a strong will of her own and had made up her mind. It was partly that he doubted that the life of a practising jazz musician could easily be squared with it – what had happened to Jock and Cissie was proof of it. But he was also afraid of the responsibility. Taking charge of a band was as big a step into the adult world as he wanted. He encouraged Ilsa to consider a termination, but she was delighted to be pregnant and wouldn't hear of it. The child, Nicholas, was born the following midsummer.

Once he accepted it, Ronnie Scott gave every appearance of intending to go through relatively conventional fatherhood with Ilsa. At the time he believed it, but he wasn't allowing for his familiar responses to emotional responsibility. The club seemed much more like home to him. And there, life wound on along its erratic, and frequently surreal course. Ronnie Scott and Peter King had decided the place needed a facelift. They had improved the food by the simple expedient of sending out the orders to the more competent of local restaurants, but they also wanted to smarten the place up. Preoccupation with this sort of domestic detail was a rarity for both men. But the boredom was relieved by Gypsy Larry.

During redecorations one day, a grey-haired, weather-beaten old man in a bandana entered the premises, requested a paintbrush and stayed until his death twelve years later. Gypsy Larry was unquestionably a man with a past. Some Soho regulars knew him from the early 1950s, when he was often to be seen in the company of another legendary bohemian of the area, Iron Foot Jack Neave. Jack was a man who held court to audiences of entranced children in Old Compton Street; he had white flowing hair, a black cloak and a swag bag, sold old jewellery and bric-a-brac, and the iron clamp on his right foot rang on the pavements.

Jack's varied efforts to make a mark on the world extended to founding a religion all of his own, into which it was alleged that a sizeable number of impressionable and underage girls were recruited as worshippers. He was also famous for having advertised 'The World's Most Daring Book on Sex and Marriage', forwarding a copy of the Bible to the punters on receipt of the fee. Jack eventually served twenty months in Wormwood Scrubs for running a nude show under the guise of 'The Caravan Club'. But he never lost the knack of eking a living from ingenuity and the gullibility of the public. Damon Runyon described careers like his as Doing The Best You Can.

On 6 March 1964, Stan Getz arrived. This was a major coup for Scott and King, since the virtuoso saxophonist had encountered problems over drugs with the British authorities four years previously. It was assumed that a work permit would be a tall order in the circumstances. On top of that, both men thought that Getz's fee – particularly now that he was enjoying unprecedented success in the bossa nova boom thanks to the album he had made with guitarist Charlie Byrd and singer Astrud Gilberto the previous year – would break the bank anyway. *Jazz Samba* had featured Latin-jazz classics like 'Desafinado' and 'Girl From Ipanema' – and Getz helped reveal to the world the talents of two remarkable composers, Antonio Carlos Jobim and Joao Gilberto. Getz was thus bigger than he had ever been, a stature that they were sure would be reflected in attendances at the club.

King was by now getting to know the ropes of immigration department. He began to drop some hints to people he knew about a permit for Getz, and unexpectedly secured one after some manoevring. King promptly flew to New York to see if he could set up what he figured would be the coup of the club's life so far. 'If I could fix a work permit,' King reasoned, 'would you do a month at the club at $300 a week?' Getz, accustomed to three times as much, was sure that King would never get the permission. He therefore let it ride, agreeing to come for the $300. He wasn't overjoyed to discover that the problem mysteriously melted away, though he stuck to his promise in the end.

But that was just the start of the uphill struggle to get this exquisite performer to unfurl his remarkable gifts for the benefit of a club audience in London. Everything about Getz was difficult. He had been entangled with hard drugs for years and was temperamental, unpredictable and easily riled. He took firmly against King after the episode of the original booking, and fell out with him on the first day of rehearsals with the Stan Tracey group because noisy repairs were going on in the room at the same time.

But he couldn't miss with the public, whatever the difficulties of actually getting him to stand in front of it. The club raised its admission fee to cover the season, but 'House Full' notices were displayed throughout the month. The lucky ones inside weren't disappointed. Getz was at the peak of his form. His lovely tone, his fastidious distaste at the playing of anything that orthodox musical standards would consider ugly, the tireless ease with which he would embroider and burnish the fundamentals of a song, and the gentle acknowledgements of his discreet quotation from past Lester Young triumphs like 'Lester Leaps In' and 'Dickie's Dream' all combined to make his performance a tour de force. Getz would also ensure that he chose the best songs, and some of his finest playing was to be heard on a neglected Jerome Kern tune 'Why Was I Born', held by those present to rival the version recorded by Billie Holiday in its poignancy.

For Ronnie Scott, the Getz season was a personal delight – he had been devoted to Getz's work since the American's period with the Woody Herman band in the 1940s – soured only slightly by the difficulties he and King experienced with their star guest off the bandstand. But the period also saw another woman enter Scott's life, who was to become as close to this elusive man as anyone ever had.

Early in the Getz run, a young Welsh nurse, who had come to London from a hospital in the Midlands, went to the club with a girlfriend. Mary Hulin was a jazz lover, her mother a music teacher, and she had learned the violin as a child. As a student nurse in Burton-on-Trent she had explored what there was of the local jazz scene, but she knew there were better things to be heard in the south. The presence of Getz was a magnet for her, as it was for most of those packed into the tiny basement. Both women were leaving after Getz had played, but ran into an old friend and changed their minds. A decision that made a big difference to Ronnie Scott's life.

Late in the evening Ronnie Scott spotted Mary and offered to buy her a drink. He was on form, wisecracking with that absence of his old inhibitions that would always come when he felt comfortable and was in congenial company. He could be sensitive and attentive as well, and Mary, who had no idea who he was at first, was intrigued. She was surprised by how self-effacing he was once she got behind the smooth operator of the bandstand.

The relationship bloomed. Mary had not only the willowy grace of a mannequin but was a good listener with a gentle temperament, her presence radiating relaxation and an absence of the cynicism that permeated the nightclub world. She couldn't find nursing work in London, and had a job as a waitress at a Soho restaurant. Scott said, 'If you're going to do that, why not do it here?' Mary Hulin thus entered Gerrard Street's orbit.

She was also charmed by the side of Ronnie Scott that wasn't visible on the bandstand. He was hardly domesticated, but there were aspects of his home life he cared about. When they met, he had a colony of cats in the flat. He would roll up the silver paper from the packets of Senior Service that he constantly smoked, roll them across the floor and get the cats to bring them back to him. This was a version of home life that helped Scott to relax in the face of the substantial strain that the presence of Getz was imposing on his patience, and on Pete King's.

Getz was determined to be patronising about his appearances in such a far flung outpost of the jazz world and was casual about his timekeeping. Dexter Gordon had often been late, but this was different. Getz took so long getting from the bandroom to the stand that the crowd would become distinctly restive. Stan Getz was determinedly sulking by this time and took longer and longer to make his appearances. Eventually his hosts cracked.

King had said to his partner, 'Listen, I've got to keep out of his way or I don't know what will happen.' Scott and King got into a furious row with the saxophonist, at the end of which the guest grew very distressed, cried, even apologised. The two men had come to the verge of replacing Getz with Zoot Sims.

For other musicians Getz continually made music a competition rather than a pleasure. Stan Tracey, who was really too spikey an operator to be likely to find common ground with a performer as lyrical as Getz, had serious problems with the American. Tracey, whose efforts to keep up with the demands of such a varied succession of powerful artists six nights a week, month in, month out, had turned him increasingly toward stimulants, was becoming as volatile as some of those he was there to support. When Getz publically criticised the rhythm section one night during the run, Tracey's riposte was simply to shout 'Bollocks' from the piano chair. Getz, when seriously challenged, frequently backed off.

Getz and King were left to each other for the latter part of the saxophonist's season. Scott had slipped a disc getting into his car the day after the row, was admitted to Lewisham hospital for traction. Inevitably, it entered the Ronnie Scott repertoire. 'I slipped a disc bending over backwards to please Stan Getz,' Scott said in a BBC interview.

The middle-sixties came to be viewed as a golden age for the Ronnie Scott Club musically. Following Getz into Gerrard Street in May 1964 was Sonny Stitt, the man who had made such an impression on Scott and Benny Green on the American tour seven years before. Stitt was still his old terrifying, competitive, eat-you-alive self, difficult to cope with too, but unlike Getz he would mostly get it over with onstage. Scott jammed with Stitt in Gerrard Street one night, with the Jamaican guitarist Ernest Ranglin, in the company of Brubeck-bassist Gene Wright and trumpeters Oliver Beener and Roy Burroughs from the Ray Charles band. Stitt tried to throw Scott by playing a fast blues and changing the key each chorus, but by coincidence the Londoner had been practising exactly the same device and stayed right with him.

The fans who were there that night knew that they had witnessed in action exactly the kind of musical electricity that the Kansas City clubs of the 1930s or the 52nd Street clubs of the 1940s were famous for, but this time with a twist that had a particular appeal for a London audience. Ronnie Scott's real inventiveness as an improvisor was probed and exploited by

the ferocious competitiveness of Stitt. Not a sound from the audience interrupted the music as the dogfight soared on and on. And after it, Ronnie
Scott, though he clearly felt he had experienced a distinctly unusual musical adventure, was phlegmatic in his discussion with Mary about it. He was
convinced that all jazz musicians felt like him – that they could always have
done it better.

As for Stitt, his relationship with Stan Tracey had less sublime
moments. The American even publically lectured Tracey on the stand one
night, stopping the show to grab the pianist's hands and place them where
he wanted them. Tracey restrained himself, but his seven years as the house
pianist at a time of frequent musical and racial tension in the jazz world was
often stressful and thankless. It was that kind of job.

Ronnie Scott later confessed that of all the American saxophonists capable of unnerving him musically, Stitt was the most formidable. What made
it worse was that – unlike Charlie Parker or John Coltrane – Stitt's power
didn't come from a visionary genius but from an omnipotent ability to do
what most other jazz musicians did, but far better. It meant that an ordinary
mortal could learn to play something like it, given enough practice. Ronnie
Scott knew his dedication didn't stretch that far.

On 21 June 1964 – Father's Day – Ilsa Fox gave birth to a son, Nicholas.
Ronnie Scott was, to Ilsa's surprise, fascinated. Friends said that it was
Jewish pride in the male issue. Ilsa was as positive and decisive about
motherhood as about most things in her life, 'had always wanted babies but
never wanted to be married', as she put it later. Just the same, she was
alone, living in a bedsit, and discovered within weeks of leaving hospital
that her child had a hole in the heart.

Ilsa concluded that the difference between her and Ronnie was greater
than could be explained simply by his distrust of the notion of parenthood.
However she was feeling, and whether Nicholas was happy, or sad, or sick or
well, the bond between them was something she had not been able to imagine
until it happened to her. She knew Ronnie could not feel the same. 'I don't
know how I'm going to take to a baby,' he said to Ilsa.

Ronnie Scott did, however, immediately begin to pay for the upkeep of
his unexpected family. He had been visiting Ilsa and Nicholas every day
while they were in hospital, then would visit the Willesden flat Ilsa and
Nicholas moved to almost daily. These meetings were variable. Sometimes
Ronnie would play happily with Nicholas and he and Ilsa would enjoy
each other's company as they had in the early days. Sometimes he would
be tense and preoccupied, look at his watch, prowl the room, leave early.
Ilsa suspected what the preoccupation meant. The relationship hovered

between happiness, unhappiness and farce. On one occasion, Ilsa put a sleeping pill in Ronnie Scott's tea, hoping to stall his departure and wait to discover if anyone would ring to check his whereabouts. But the drug didn't dissolve and floated to the top.

'Ilsa, are you trying to poison me?' Ronnie Scott enquired mildly.

'No, just trying to put you to sleep,' Ilsa responded, half angry, half in hysterical giggles.

In time it all came out. Ronnie Scott had begun an affair with Mary, and eventually she left the house she had been sharing in Chelsea, and they moved together into a flat at Chesham Street, Belgravia. But if they had regularised matters, Ronnie remained unpredictable: sometimes moody and withdrawn, sometimes careering off into outrageous public clowning – in restaurants, in the street, anywhere – that would reduce them both to helpless laughter.

But life did follow a pattern in that part of the day they shared through their work – the early hours. When they got home from the club, Mary would make tea, and they would sit in the two big wing chairs in the living room, and talk. They found they had a lot to share. Mary was adopted, was desperate to find her real parents, and the preoccupation struck a chord with Ronnie, recalling the tensions he felt between the fascinating, absent Jock and the staid, reliable Sol. But one night, Ronnie Scott made an observation of an entirely unexpected kind.

'Mary,' he began. 'Maybe you and I should consider not seeing each other any more.'

'Why's that?' she quietly asked him.

'Well, I don't think I'll ever be able to marry you. I just don't believe in being that tied down.'

Mary let it ride. But she felt that the conversation would surface again, sooner or later.

At the end of the year, Scott and King booked one of jazz music's best-loved artists, a man who virtually defined the image of the art in the public mind – Ben Webster. Webster was fifty-four when he came to play his first season, and had been one of the handful of jazz musicians to have helped put the tenor saxophone on the map in the 1920s. As Benny Green was later to acknowledge in the *Observer*, men like Webster and Coleman Hawkins had made it possible for players like himself and Ronnie Scott to exist at all.

Webster was by now already playing unevenly and passing into a period of his life in which he was frequently drunk onstage. When Scott and King went to collect Webster from Southampton (he refused to fly), the saxophonist was incapable of independent locomotion from the moment he left the boat and had to be shoe-horned into the back of King's mini, where he slept resolutely throughout the journey, only waking to shout 'Give 'em what they want – as long as they don't want too much!' to the mystification of his chauffeurs.

On his first appearance at the club, Webster's music was mostly as romantic, breathy and full of silky sensuality – particularly on ballads – as it had ever been. And though he was less secure on uptempo numbers by this stage of his career, and had never overly relished them, he would deliver a grainier, more laconic series of monologues, splashed over by frequent broad, palette-knife flourishes that characterised the self-confident, expansive jazz of the swing era. Midway between ballad tempo and a brisk trot, Webster would place one of his favourite tunes, Gershwin's 'Our Love Is Here To Stay', on which he would blow smoke rings of sound that both maximised the effect of his rich, shimmering tone and simultaneously highlighted the ingenuity of the composer. Roland Kirk, in the audience during Webster's season, remarked that such a sound ought to be impossible to produce on a saxophone.

The significance of having a legend like Webster on the premises was most moving of all to Scott himself. One night toward the end of Webster's visit, Mary witnessed a cameo that caught in flight what jazz meant to an old travelling poet like Webster and to her new partner. On the rickety wooden steps of the club, the massive American stood embracing the young man who had brought him to London. 'It's marvellous that I can come to a place like this in London,' Webster enthused. 'A place where I can settle down, play for a month, relax.' It was much the same insight that Zoot Sims had made. Scott said enthusiastically, 'It's great to have someone I've admired so long working here.' Mary remembered a lesson she had heard Ronnie Scott deliver to all the incoming staff of the club. 'The artists are the most important people who come here. Always treat them with the greatest of respect.'

The arrival of Theodore Walter 'Sonny' Rollins at the beginning of 1965 provided the most telling illustration of what the music of an artist entirely dedicated to the pursuit of the oblique, the subversive and the unexpected could sound like night after night in an atmosphere tailored to the avoidance of the easy option. Rollins made an impact on London musical life, in that year and again in 1966, that shook the predominantly cool and restrained demeanour of jazz style in the capital. He was in his prime then, and his musical curiosity was boundless. Such audacity and cliff-hanging inventiveness in performance forged an immediate bond with audiences. Some fans visited the club three or four times during the season to hear how Rollins would twist and tangle, bludgeon and illuminate the popular song forms that he would use as ostensibly implausible triggers for elaborate spontaneous concertos.

Rollins was thirty-four at the time of his first visit to Ronnie Scott's Club. He was a one-time alto player who had been fascinated by the riff-dominated 'jump bands' of the immediate post-war years, forerunners of rhythm 'n' blues. He concentrated on the horn playing of Coleman Hawkins to begin with, intrigued by that big, assured tone and the deliberate, measured tread of Hawkins' methods of extemporisation. A neighbourhood friend, Thelonious Monk, introduced Rollins to the playing of Charlie Parker, which he then attempted to graft on to the swing band saxophone style that gave his playing a quirkiness even at that early stage.

His individuality quickly recommended him to Miles Davis, who employed him in 1951, and six years later Rollins released a sensational improvisors' record called *Saxophone Colossus* that secured his reputation once and for all. The album was the quintessence of that development of the methods of Charlie Parker and Dizzy Gillespie that came to be known as 'hard bop'. The style was notable for a deliberate eschewing of romanticism and sentiment and a preference for rugged, vibrato-less tone, the development of themes in very long solos that would frequently run into a dozen or more choruses. It was also characterised by a perfunctory indifference to over-elaborate themes, preferring the functional and the skeletal that could be simply used as a springboard to blowing. Whitney Balliett, reviewing *Saxophone Colossus* for *The New Yorker* at the time, wrote that Rollins' solos 'often resemble endless harangues' but that the younger man's melodic imagination probably rivalled that of Charlie Parker.

At Gerrard Street Rollins got the ball rolling in a rehearsal with the Stan Tracey group that included bassist Rick Laird and drummer Ronnie Stephenson. But it was no ordinary rehearsal. Rollins began by restlessly pacing the room, bouncing booming sounds off the walls, examining the saxophone as if encountering it for the first time, adjusting the mouthpiece endlessly. Tracey and his partners waited patiently, until eventually Rollins seemed to make up his mind.

He asked for 'Prelude To A Kiss'. The saxophonist then took the tune and played it fast and furiously, slow and with passion, with impassive aggressiveness as if trying to shake out the last over-staying guest of a note cowering in the bell of the horn, with braying, spine-tingling laughter and generally performed, as he frequently did, the act of the taking the tune and shaking it so vigorously that none of its secrets and implications could possibly remain concealed. The musicians began to realise just what it was they were rehearsing. This was the rehearsal of an understanding of the American's attitude toward playing, and to absorb the spirit that under-pinned it, rather than a series of party pieces.

That this was the intention behind the American's eccentric way of introducing himself was borne out by the events of the next four weeks. Rollins never referred to 'Prelude To A Kiss' again, and the band – after, as Tracey was to describe it later, 'playing the arse out of it all afternoon' – was never asked to play it again. Rollins was a law all to himself. Dedicated to his work, and to preserving a working method that kept it fresh (immense self-discipline enabled him to overcome heroin addiction in the fifties by simply taking leave of the music business and getting labouring jobs for as long as it took him to get straight) Rollins rarely socialised with the musical community, rarely kept later nights than were obliged by the schedule and was much given to exercise, mysticism, and the sometimes off-putting pur-suit of facial isometrics. The bassist Rick Laird encountered Rollins alone in the bandroom one night, wearing a beret, gesticulating before the mirror and announcing in a Clouseauesque stage whisper, 'I am Pierre the Frenchman.'

Simply standing at a microphone with a horn was not his style for long in those days. He arrived one night at the club in a taxi, playing the tenor as he stepped out of it and down the staircase. He would frequently begin playing whilst still in the tiny office under the stairs and then emerge into the crowd with his performance already under way. He would sometimes leave the bandstand and lead the crowd, Pied Piper-like, out into Gerrard Street, with the supportive Tracey's men still furiously pumping away and just audible in the subterranean depths.

It was also Rollins' shaven-headed period, and a time of wayward experimentation with dress. Hats were a particular preoccupation – some-times the famous beret, sometimes a Stetson. He wore a mackintosh throughout one performance at Gerrard Street, and displayed an occasional fondness for more elaborate embroidery, like a row of tambourines tied to a belt around his waist.

Ronnie Scott was fascinated by Rollins and watched him night after night, as attentive as in those early days in the wartime clubs, relishing the privilege of hearing an improvisor at the peak of his inspiration. He got to know the American well during that period and also on later visits, and on their work for the soundtrack of the movie *Alfie*, which was made at Shepperton studios, and which involved Scott, Phil Seamen, Stan Tracey and trombonist Keith Christie among others.

Rollins had been invited over to write the music – the film director's son was a lifelong Rollins fan. The American was staying at the Royal Garden Hotel in Kensington and Christie and Scott began the project by visiting him there to get the lie of the land. Rollins's sense of occasion didn't let him down. The saxophone was on a sofa with a spotlight shining on it.

All three men got very stoned in the course of the discussion and eventually the two Englishmen asked to see Rollins's ideas for the score. He brought out a sheaf of manuscript paper and laid it before them. Every sheet was blank – except one. A fragment of phrasing was notated there, in a childlike hand.

'How should we treat the music?' Scott asked, puzzled by the American's apparently cavalier disregard for the responsibilities of the job.

'You should treat it lightly,' Rollins advised. In the circumstances, there didn't seem to be much choice.

In the event the *Alfie* score could only have been performed by jazz musicians. There was hardly anything to go on, which was exactly what Rollins wanted. The director would put the key scenes on the screen, tell the musicians they had sixteen seconds to fill, and leave them to it. Whether they took a long time over the job, or hurried it, Rollins' reactions would be equally unpredictable. After one long morning of preparation with an unusual degree of attention to detail, Scott took the American down to the river in his sports car for lunch. They rounded things off with a large joint. When they got back, Rollins said, 'All that stuff we did this morning, forget it.' Everybody started again.

Rollins's anarchic presence hovered over the movie to the end. At the London premiere of *Alfie*, Scott and the other musicians were present to play the music in person. They were supposed to begin the *Alfie* theme on the signal of a green light and stop on the red light that was supposed to appear a couple of minutes later, at which point the platform they were playing on would be lowered out of sight and the curtains would open. The green light came right on cue and the band eased into Rollins's playful, jaunty opening bars. The red light, however, didn't show.

They played that theme over and over, with all the variations they could think of, for more than twenty minutes while technicians sweated in the projection room to locate the hitch with the film. It was just the way the composer would have wanted it.

# 9

# Not On This Piano

'The person who sees furthest into the future is likely to be the person who sees furthest into the past.'

(Bill Evans, *Jazz and Pop*, 1965)

SONNY ROLLINS THREW everything he had into those performances in Gerrard Street – improvisation of a quality and style rarely represented on his records except possibly *Our Man in Jazz* – and he enjoyed working with Stan Tracey, applauding him in the music press with the words that brought a glow to the hearts of British jazz fans unaccustomed to American praise. 'Does anybody here know how good he really is?' Rollins enquired of Tracey's playing. Tracey was to reach late middle age, and have passed through a crisis in which he even contemplated giving up the music business, before he was accorded the status Rollins considered his due.

For Ronnie Scott's part, his relationship with Sonny Rollins always brought surprises. Some were opportunities missed, like the occasion in a New York hotel room in the small hours one morning when he turned down Rollins's out-of-the-blue telephone call asking him to come over and practise out in the country.

Rollins was a hard act for the club to follow, but the arrival of players of the highest calibre was becoming a regular delight at Gerrard Street. This in itself contained the seeds of insecurities to come. The international stars were what Scott and King had always wanted to offer to the British jazz scene, though the cost of air fares, hotels, competitive fees and incidental expenses were not going to be sustained week in and week out in an establishment that could only contain 150 people. As long as they remained in Gerrard Street, the success of Ronnie Scott's Club would continue to be a rod for the backs of its inventors.

In March 1965, the club was able to announce proudly the arrival of the first all-American *group* to play on its premises. Bill Evans was indeed something to be proud of. He was that rare breed: a jazz performer with a strongly European bias toward reflection rather than explicit emotion who could still convey all of the orthodox jazz virtues of swing, profound understanding of the blues and a strong sense of spontaneity. A bespectacled, studious-looking performer from New Jersey, Evans had learned the piano and violin as a child, and grown interested in the swing pianists at the tail-end of that music's period of mass popularity, unaware except by rumour – as most white players were – of what was really going on in the New York clubs where bebop was being forged. College and the Army further kept Evans from the new developments, but eventually the clarinettist Tony Scott brought him into the 52nd Street clubs and he was noticed by Orrin Keepnews of Riverside Records.

The pianist's growing reputation through the recordings made with Riverside led, as a select coterie of young performers of imagination and originality had found, to the Miles Davis band. (Though legendary for a substantial ego, Miles Davis didn't allow his temperament to impede his openness to the work of newcomers, a flexibility which paid off in the trumpeter's sustained ability to remain contemporary – and fashionable.) Evans stayed with Davis for only eight months and was exhausted by the experience, but the period produced one of the great jazz records – the album *Kind of Blue* – based on what were called 'modal' variations of the structure of improvisation, such that solos would be based on cycles of scales rather than on chords. It imparted to the music a mysterious, displaced and ambiguous quality more reminiscent of Indian music.

Bill Evans's ruminative piano style was perfect for it, and Davis later acknowledged that the pianist had been a considerable influence on his thinking about the new idiom. It was the perfectionist quality of Evans's approach and the subtlety of his thinking that made Scott and King realise that they would have to improve the facilities a little. The club's piano was a battered old upright that had been in use there since the establishment opened, its eccentricities by now instinctively grasped by Tracey, who knew every treacherous habit it had. But they could not expect Evans to play on it. So the two club proprietors performed the long-postponed ritual of selling the piano the weekend before Evans was due to arrive. They then set about hiring a grand piano. But what seemed like a simple enterprise requiring only solvency, or a convincing pretence of it, turned into a nightmare.

The representative of the hire company arrived at the club on the

Monday of Evans's arrival to examine the premises. When he discovered a jazz club he was appalled.

'What's the problem?' Scott and King enquired in alarm. The salesman protested that jazz pianists would have no idea of how to take care of an instrument of this class, and in any event they would never be able to get a grand piano down the steps.

'Anyway,' he complained, 'it will simply get damaged. There'll be drinks spilled all over it. Girls sitting on it . . .' His vision of what a jazz club was like was built on gangster-movie clichés. Scott and King tried offering everything they could think of, such as the value of the instrument as a deposit, money they didn't have but thought they could rustle up if the worst came to the worst. None of it made any difference. The conversation lurched on for an hour.

King eventually looked as if he'd had an idea. Conspiratorially, he beckoned the piano man close. Scott wondered if his resourceful partner had hit on the makings of a deal. There was a pause. 'FUCK OFF!' King eventually yelled in the ear of his attentive listener.

The two men began a frantic round of the central London hire companies. They struck lucky at Steinway's in the Edgware Road, which had no grands available but some beautiful uprights.

'Do you know how good this pianist is?' they pleaded with the sympathetic German manageress in despair. 'We can't ask him to play on an upright.'

'He's a jazz musician, isn't he?' the woman encouraged them. 'He vill still be able to see the rest of the boys over the top of it.'

The whole exercise was a reminder of just what a backwater jazz remained in the respectable world outside number 39 Gerrard Street, a state of affairs that in the euphoria of the previous three years of presenting fine musicians to enthusiastic audiences they had tended to forget. Eventually a friend and sympathiser with the club's objectives, the jazz pianist and composer Alan Clare, was able to arrange the loan of a grand piano for Evans's opening show. It came at the eleventh hour.

When Evans began to play, all that anguish melted away. Like Rollins, he had distinct mannerisms in performance, though where Rollins was explosive and charismatic, Evans seemed to express his apparent desire to escape more and more comprehensively into a fascinating landscape inside his own head. A thin intense-looking figure, he sat at the instrument with his head bowed over it, his nose at times virtually touching the keyboard, hands floating ethereally through a mixture of evaporating arpeggios, crisp, sinewy single-line figures that would erupt and vanish in an instant, and an ever-present rhythmic urgency that continually prodded at the otherwise speculative and other-worldly quality of his work.

Unlike many of the bebop pianists, Evans did not merely concentrate on chorus after chorus of melodic variations on the harmony – the latter usually expressed in bald, percussive chords designed to emphasise the beat – but sought to develop a solo as a complete entity with a fundamental logic and shape, his left hand developing and enriching the harmony. Like the composer Gil Evans, like Art Pepper, like Stan Getz, Bill Evans – as the New York *Village Voice* writer Gary Giddins remarked – exhibited the white jazz players' gift of 'swinging with melancholy'. Evans became another regular visitor to Ronnie Scott's Club over the years, with a variety of high-class and empathetic accompanists.

The illustrious procession wound on in and out of Gerrard Street through 1965. One of the greatest guitarists in all jazz, Wes Montgomery, followed Evans on to the premises performing with Stan Tracey, and astonished his listeners with the amiable, easy-going manner in which he spun fresh melodies from the instrument. Montgomery never read music, had taught himself to pick the strings with his thumb instead of a plectrum – because he didn't want to disturb his neighbours and because nobody had told him any different – and was, like Evans, brought to the recording studio by Orrin Keepnews of Riverside on the recommendation of Cannonball Adderley.

By the time he arrived at the club, Montgomery was already on the way towards being a big star. Not because he was a jazz player – the skills of an improvisor never led to big record sales – but because his artless way of learning the instrument had given him a rich and resonant tone unusual in a music where guitars were usually played in a spindly, single-note fashion as if they were echoing saxophone lines. He had developed a way of playing solos in octaves that was original and exciting in the context of an improvising group stretching for variation of texture, but could just as easily be adapted to the easy-listening market – which was what eventually happened to him. When the Riverside record label went under in the year before Montgomery came to London, the guitarist went to Verve Records and was encouraged by producer Creed Taylor to develop those soft, plush sounds for the commercial market and cut down on the slashing, slalom-like runs and prodigious facility for melodic improvisation that could take an audience's breath away in a club. Montgomery never lost that facility in informal surroundings, but the experience with the record business – though he went along with it, and not least for the sake of being the breadwinner for a family of six children – distressed him increasingly as the years passed.

The season at Ronnie Scott's was the old Montgomery, the cavalierly casual, effortlessly musical artist who would smile broadly at his audience throughout his set, hardly looking at the guitar, notes flying and tumbling from the speakers. Montgomery, whose early playing circumstances had obliged him to meet the demands of both a day job and performance in the evenings, was to make only one visit to Ronnie Scott's. Three years later, having barely enjoyed the fruits of the success that he had felt so confused about securing, Montgomery died of a heart attack at the age of forty-three.

The last link in the intimate circle of Ronnie Scott's family life was finally snapped in 1965. Sol Berger, Ronnie's quiet, easy-going, hardworking stepfather was found dead in bed by Rachel, his wife of less than eighteen months, and Ronnie – who had been the apple of the old man's eye almost as much as he had been of Cissie's and Nana Becky's – was immediately summoned to the house. Sol's world had been turned inside out by the events of the previous two years. Cissie's sudden death after a quarter of a century of marriage had left him lonely and confused. He had met Rachel (always nicknamed Ray), a lively divorcee in her sixties, at an engagement party in late 1962, the year of Cissie's death, and at the end of the evening intently sought her out. 'I must see you again,' the old man had insisted. 'I know we've got things in common.'

Ray, though surprised by his determination, thought him interesting and flattering, and sensed his loneliness. She needed a change in her own life, liked Sol, and knew she could feel comfortable in the quiet Edgware back street. They had married in January 1963 and Ronnie Scott had come to the party, though surprised and at first a little discomfited by the alacrity with which Sol had started afresh. But it was to be a short interlude. Thrombosis undermined Sol's health, he began walking with the aid of a stick, and he was disheartened by the discomfort after an active life. It was difficult even to fulfil his duties to the local British Legion, to which he had given a lifetime of service.

When he died, the household at Edgwarebury Gardens went into the traditional seven days of Jewish mourning. Ronnie Scott came to the house every night to take part, for which Ray was grateful, describing him to friends as 'a wonderful boy. There was nothing he wouldn't do.' But Ronnie had good cause to be grateful to Sol, who had never failed his wayward but gifted stepson when it counted, from the suits he had made for Ronnie's first band, to his investment in the first Ronnie Scott Club.

For Scott's part, he wanted to make up for missed chances, his absences during Jock's last weeks, that rare row with the mild-mannered Sol when the boy had shouted at him, 'You're not my real father anyway.' Much of what he had done with his life was eased on its way by Sol, and he knew it. Scott's gold disc, a *New Musical Express* pollwinner's trophy, remained in the front room where Cissie had died pouring the tea for her friends, until Ray's own death in the 1990s.

The club's pressing problem of insufficient space for the income it needed continued. In the summer of 1965 Scott and King found what they thought were ideal premises at 47 Frith Street, the home of the club today. But if they were getting into a different league with their public, they were also getting into a different league as businessmen. This was not the kind of establishment you could put on the road with a lick of paint and a loan of £1000 from relatives. Scott and King did the rounds in the effort to raise cash for the big leap. They even went to the Arts Council, at that time hardly involved in subsidising jazz at all.

It wasn't a fruitful meeting. The two men felt ill at ease in any event, in an unfamiliar world of modulated voices, discretion, cut-glass chandeliers, softly ticking clocks, oak tables. They were kept waiting for what seemed an age, until an earnest-looking assistant finally arrived, rubbing his hands together in what appeared to signify both bonhomie and a vigour about getting down to real business. But it wasn't real.

'Now then, about this Bonny Scott's Club. How can we help you, gentlemen?'

Scott and King looked resignedly at each other. 'Sorry, you can't help us at all,' they informed him and left the premises without so much as opening a briefcase. In the event, it was Harold Davison who came through with the means for the second incarnation to get under way.

Davison was by now involved in big-time promotion, frequently bringing the most illustrious names in jazz music to Britain for large-scale concerts and tours. His business had become part of the giant MAM agency. But if Davison was a businessman first, he was a jazz fan a very close second and he had admired Ronnie Scott since the days of the nine-piece band. He agreed to come up with £35,000 to finance the refurbishing and launch of the club in Frith Street. The transaction tied up the fortunes of Scott and King with the MAM operation, their first loss of total independence, but the money was repayable on reasonable terms and Davison remained in the background, not attempting to influence the views of the two proprietors in order to protect his investment.

Benny Golson, an eloquent and elegant improvisor on the tenor (and later a composer for Peggy Lee, Nancy Wilson and Sammy Davis Jnr) was the last American to be formally presented in the basement at 39 Gerrard Street. But though proceedings there under Ronnie Scott's name wound up on 27 November 1965, the lease still had eighteen months to run and Scott, bearing in mind the catalyst the old Club Eleven had been, intended to keep it on as a jamming centre for local players.

# 10

# Thin Air

'You sit there and you learn. You open your mind. You absorb. But you have to be quiet, you have to be still to do all of this.'
(John Coltrane to Frank Kofsky, *Black Nationalism and the Revolution in Music*, 1970)

'I have decided to break off my engagement with W. She doesn't understand my writing, and last night said that my "Critique of Metaphysical Reality" reminded her of *Airport*.'
(Woody Allen, *Without Feathers*, 1972)

THERE HAD ALWAYS been a house style at Ronnie's, even in the old days, for those who were its intimates and friends. Those who edged into the bandroom beneath the oblivious pedestrians of Gerrard Street were familiar with it: where Sonny Rollins would perform contortions with his jaws, pallid acquaintances looking like minicab drivers would sit on upturned instrument cases reading the racing pages or telling deadpan jokes, or where Pete King, arrayed expansively behind a desk like an up-and-coming boxing promoter, would greet the unwary with the most ambivalent of greetings: 'Allo boy, still creepin' about?' And there might have been Ronnie, performing his elaborate silent mime of an astronaut attempting to masturbate at zero gravity.

At Frith Street it was the same only more so, because there was more room for manoeuvre and a bigger cast. One house rule, an unspoken one, remained: neither Scott nor King could stand either their customers or their guests on the bandstand pulling rank – through money, class, bloody-mindedness, or any other reason. Jock Scott's old partners from the boats and hotel bands would continue to be welcome, get a drink on the house, sometimes a permanent loan if times were hard. Musicians who had been contemporaries of Scott and King in Archer Street but who by 1965 were finding the phone ringing less often, found that they could treat the place as home, and some got jobs there. Jeff Ellison, a drummer and long-time friend (who had been in Club Eleven on the night of the drugs raid and accidentally spared from arrest because Scott, who he was due to follow on to that exposed position on the stand, played one more number than he should) took up a regular post on the door, often a punishing job in a night-club. 'Stick with me and you'll make a fortune,' Scott had said to him. He never did, but he became Scott's regular chess-playing partner, and his quiet manner and soft smile made a change from the studied indifference of some members of what was sometimes dubbed 'the Frith Street Charm School'. An old East End principle – look after your own – always persisted at the club.

The audience changed. At Gerrard Street, the proportion of diehard modern jazz enthusiasts was massive compared to the passing trade. Going upmarket altered the percentages. It also meant that the club would have to deal with more punters who thought paying the entrance fee meant they owned the place and the musicians. People who were arrogant, aggressive or loudly drunk wouldn't get the time of day from Scott, who developed a repertoire of gags to deal with the problem ('Good evening, sir, sorry to hear you've been drinking on an empty head'), nor did he ever learn to butter up wealthy customers in the way that most West End nightclub proprietors would have considered a reflex. One night a rich hooray arrived in the foyer with two women in furs, for the latter's benefit noisily enquiring of the nearby proprietor, 'Hello, Ronnie, what have you got for us tonight?'

Scott looked down his considerable nose. 'Excuse me, do I know you?' he said in a drop-dead tone.

Professionally, Ronnie Scott's world was full of promise around this time. Life was running fast again. He was now working regularly with the all-star line-up of the multinational big band led by American veteran bebop drummer Kenny Clarke and the Belgian composer Francy Boland – and though the old nervousness still gripped him in the presence of American saxophone heroes like Johnny Griffin, the band was exciting and new, travelled widely and the diversion of its exotic gigs was comfortable enough to offset the agony of being obliged to fly to them, for which he still had to douse himself in whisky and tranquillisers. The status of the Clarke–Boland band had resulted in Scott working with musicians he had previously only admired as a spectator – like Stan Getz, for whom Boland wrote a miniature saxophone concerto on which Scott not only soloed but was congratulated for his contribution by Getz himself.

Ronnie Scott's relationship with Mary, who had moved with him to the new premises and become the club's cashier, convinced him temporarily that his self-image as a freewheeling loner maybe didn't have to follow him into middle age.

And his love of play-acting wasn't dampened by bigger responsibilities and the passage of the years. He would still lurch without warning into remarkably accurate impressions of the mannerisms of forties movie actors, even for the benefit of the younger waitresses who hadn't the least idea who the subjects were, and then when the phone rang with an enquiry from a prospective customer would charge unswervingly on in the same vein – 'Have we got a table? Certainly, sir, would you like it here, or take it away?' He would also continue to slip round the corner to the betting shop whenever a likely runner presented itself, or had a name he liked. 'I can stop a runaway horse just by putting money on it,' was one of the proprietor's favourite observations about his hobby.

The only unforgivable sin was to be boring, which meant those who couldn't think on their feet, see the funny side of fate's whims, the self-important, the priggish. Scott was free to pursue his playing career and principally treat the club as a source of personal pleasure and entertainment, because the relationship between himself and King was by now so secure that it never needed to be talked about, and the latter would take the responsibility for making sure the figures added up.

As the club's repertoire broadened out – notably to include more singers opposite pure jazz acts to sugar the pill for the new clientele – King expanded his role as the anchorman. He took charge of more of the booking. Many of the club's visitors – like Roland Kirk, Ben Webster, Zoot Sims, Sonny Rollins – had naturally become firm favourites. Scott was content to leave it with him, yet his role in the expanding club never became purely that of a figurehead. Scott had a talent for taking risks, and in the jazz club business it was a useful skill.

But out front, everything had changed. Benny Green pointed out at the time the unerring accuracy with which the musical virtues of a nightclub could be assessed just from a computation of the weekly expenses. Regular visitors to Gerrard Street could be in no doubt that many things had changed for good. On a bad night now, Scott's and King's new staff could comfortably outnumber the customers. There were waitresses, barmaids, doormen, ushers. There was comfortable furniture, soft lights. It was, at last, the place that Scott had been describing from his imagination and his memories of New York in that 1958 interview in *Melody Maker*.

London itself was different too. The bohemian Soho where artists and eccentrics of all kinds could feel they occupied a private world that ran according to their own clocks, were having trouble keeping up with the rent. Costs were rising. The pornography industry was gathering such steam as censorship was relaxed that the money it was making could outbid almost any other line of business. Scott and King were to find that out when the lease for 39 Gerrard Street came up for renewal, the rent had tripled. The days when Soho premises would stand idle while their owners scratched their heads over what use to make of them were long gone.

There was rock music. Skiffle had been big a few years before – Terry Nelhams, later to become Adam Faith, was discovered by producer Jack Good playing skiffle in the Two I's coffee bar, and Gypsy Larry had passed through a phase in which the coffee houses and modest nightclubs would give him work as a skiffle bassist – but the rhythm 'n' blues boom that was ushered in by the success of the Beatles at home and abroad had had strong roots in London clubs, notably the Flamingo, and the Marquee in Wardour Street.

The 1960s was a decade of prosperity, the mannerisms of classlessness, and a redoubled interest in the arts in the 'new meritocracy' of Labour Prime Minister Harold Wilson's Britain. Scott found his club doing tolerably well, he was hiring musicians whose work he loved, he was taking the odd glamorous session job (the Beatles 'Lady Madonna' horn part, for instance) and everything was there but the wild and raucous atmosphere of the Archer Street days. Ronnie Scott was thirty-eight when the Frith Street club opened, in a climate in which anybody who had taken a more commercial view of running a West End club could probably have cleaned up.

From the mid-1950s in the States, a change was being engineered by the descendants of Charlie Parker and the first-wave modernists. It was not wholly the inheritance as exemplified by experimenters with bop like Sonny Rollins, Charles Mingus or the composer George Russell (who announced the new campaign as the 'war on chords') who attempted to loosen the format from inside. Two men of much the same age as Rollins (Ornette Coleman and John Coltrane) and one six years younger (Albert Ayler) were about to launch an assault on the raw material of jazz that had spectacular repercussions.

There was a self-destructive formula in bop if it was played in a formulaic way. Rollins, of course, was capable of undermining the formalism in anything, but lesser players were bogged down in a game of harmonic puzzles, struggling to fire ever more crowded fusillades of semi-quavers into ever more complicated structures played at faster and faster tempos. It was as if a pinball game were being portrayed on a film played at double speed. It was hard to imagine where such an obsessive – and impassive – pursuit of technical expertise might lead, except into the kind of inertia and self-regard that would in the long run be death to any vibrancy in the music. But the public was used to it. The mixture of competitiveness and cool symbolised by late bop was popular, particularly with white audiences. It became the evidence of a certain kind of cultural arrival.

Coleman, Ayler and the prodigiously resourceful pianist Cecil Taylor were the most notable guerillas to launch an assault on these increasingly muscle-bound developments. Coltrane initially explored a ground that owed at least some inspiration to Rollins. But they all went about their work in different ways. Coleman, a Texan, had been a blues player around Fort Worth from his teens but fell out with many of the local musicians who claimed that he couldn't play in tune. He had actually reverted to some of the earliest principles in jazz – the vocalised tone, the exultant abandonment of concert pitch – and mixed them with an improvisational method that retained a close approximation to regular melody of a kind, but with random or absent harmony.

By the mid-1960s Ornette Coleman had laid most of his cards on the table. His recordings with the Atlantic label revealed his music to be as down-to-earth as a Texan barn-dance in some incarnations, and as bluesy as anything in the black tradition in others.

Albert Ayler, six years Coleman's junior, had also come up through the R&B bands, and was demonstrating by the mid-1960s that there was mileage in a return to the New Orleans tradition but with the forthright vocabulary of a new black consciousness expressed through it. Cecil Taylor was a pianist with a profound grasp of both European and black American traditions (he would insist that both had African origins) and a technique capable of impressing even classical enthusiasts who otherwise disliked his ideas. He also exhibited an all but superhuman stamina that would permit him to improvise at feverish pitch for long periods, and expressed impatience with racial oppression in his music and in his public conduct. As for John Coltrane, he was the avantist who most successfully trod a path between experiment and popularity for much of his later musical life. He influenced not simply the generation of musicians just entering the scene, but even astonished and inspired performers older than him.

Coltrane's influence widened in the sixties culture of meditation, self-examination and curiosity about Eastern philosophy and religion. But the saxophonist's journey became so single-minded in his last years that some of his former close associates could no longer play with him. It was obvious that Coltrane was prepared to make considerable sacrifices to propel his music on to the plane of sublime suspended animation that he seemed to hear in his head. When he died of liver disease in 1967, much of that work remained undone. Many musicians, black and white, took it upon themselves to carry on.

It was against this background that the developments in contemporary jazz in Britain in the 1960s had to be heard. Everywhere in the jazz-playing world, the material prospects for a life devoted to the sharp end of the music were not good, but in Britain some music of real originality had been generated at the beginning of the decade and once again the power behind it – in this case the Jamaican altoist Joe Harriott who had performed that brief and unsettled stint with the Ronnie Scott Orchestra in 1956 – had been allowed to run down.

After his stretch with the Scott orchestra, Joe Harriott's music became increasingly adventurous. Working with the bassist Coleridge Goode, a Jamaican who had come to England as an engineering student in the 1930s, he formed his own band in 1957 that included pianist Harry South and trumpeter Hank Shaw, an old associate of Ronnie Scott's from the days of the Oxford and St George's youth club.

Harriott's working life was to be dogged by illness. He spent some time in hospital at the end of the 1950s recovering from tuberculosis, but it was during that period that he began to write music and form his ideas. When he recovered, the band got a job in Frankfurt for a month, developed methods of working together that had previously never been attempted in British modern jazz, and in 1960 he recorded his first 'free form' album, ostensibly conceived without reference to anything that Ornette Coleman was doing across the Atlantic.

The band had occasionally appeared at Gerrard Street, and many of the more conventional players had little time for it. Harriott was finding the going increasingly hard temperamentally, but with the albums *Free Form* and *Abstract*, he won recognition from the source that British musicians still most valued – America. The prestigious US jazz magazine *Downbeat* gave the albums five-star ratings. It meant a great deal then. But though his original inspiration had been Parker, Harriott's music was not by any means exclusively American. Tunes like 'Calypso Sketches' were drawn from his background in the Caribbean, using local rhythms hitched to jazz.

The band could be highly inventive. Fellow West Indian Shake Keane would use a tumbler over the bell of his trumpet to give a muffled, trombone-like tone. Players would randomly begin riffing energetically behind solos and then drop out as abruptly as they arrived. Harriott would suddenly zigzag across jaunty, dancing tempos with wild, bleary howls. 'Modal' on the *Abstract* album had been entirely improvised in the studio, taken up while the band was packing away its kit and inspired simply by vibrations on a cowbell and a drinking glass. Harriott claimed his interest was to add 'colour' in jazz – loosening improvisation to paint freely in sound.

Other artists in London then wanted that freedom too. Young poets like Mike Horowitz and Pete Brown were finding collaboration with musicians an opportunity to bring poetry to audiences previously shut out by it. Poetry and jazz combined to express the resentment that many younger citizens felt at what they regarded as the cosy materialism of the British boom of the fifties. The poetry was frequently explicitly political and sexual. The music, some of it adopting the more impressionistic methods of Harriott and local performers' variations on Ornette Coleman and John Coltrane, was fragmentary, atmospheric and self-questioning. The rhythm section at Gerrard Street, often composed of Stan Tracey and bassist Jeff Clyne with a variety of drummers, would periodically be invited by Horowitz and Brown to perform words-and-music collaborations, invitations they enthusiastically accepted.

Eventually a group came out of it – the New Departures Quartet, which featured Bobby Wellins on tenor – a man who could conjure up the shrouded contours of the Scottish highlands with a saxophone style that had some distant similarities to that of Stan Getz. Wellins wrote a brooding jazz suite for the group called 'Culloden Moor', which was then developed by Stan Tracey into a larger work for a full jazz orchestra. It was this ensemble that performed 'Culloden Moor' at its only full-scale public outing at the St Pancras Town Hall in 1960.

The New Departures pioneers asked Ronnie Scott to be the MC for the night, and in a typically throwaway intro the saxophonist obliged by promptly querying Wellins's desire to commemorate such a resounding defeat for his home side.

The performance was memorable for the sheer scale of its commitment to using contemporary jazz for a truly home-grown purpose – and with considerable flexibility for improvisors within it. It was also memorable for the return of Denis Rose to the public arena for the first time in ten years. Rose repeated the habit he had been prone to even in the days of working in the gangsters' clubs. He was an hour and a half late – principally through nerves – but delivered one slightly unsteady but typically oblique trumpet solo at the close, despite the management unceremoniously dropping the curtain on to his head.

A promising and enthusiastic young jazz writer called Victor Schonfield was involved with the presentation of the New Departures concert. Schonfield was a comparative rarity in the field of jazz criticism, since his overriding interest was good improvisation, rather than a preoccupation with adversarially defending this or that genre of jazz. He was thus one of the most open-minded observers of the scene then operating, particularly since Benny Green at the *Observer* and Philip Larkin at the *Daily Telegraph* were inclined to the line that the experimental jazz of the period was destructive to the music, ignorant of its traditions, and professionally incompetent.

The German critic Joachim Berendt decided to help bring Ornette Coleman to Europe, and the saxophonist financed the rest. Coleman already knew of Schonfield as one of his most energetic supporters in Britain, and decided that the writer would be his UK promoter. Schonfield put Coleman's trio on at the Fairfield Hall in Croydon in the autumn of 1965, in a curious billing in which the other half of the show was a non-improvised performance by a classical wind quintet playing a Coleman composition. This odd state of affairs was occasioned by a union require-ment. Schonfield had brought Coleman in as a classical musician, which he thought would circumvent some paperwork and politicking. But the result was that he was then unable to present a Stan Tracey group as the support band. Schonfield therefore had to organise classical players to appear, and those that did eventually had to defy the union's discouragement to make the concerts.

Coleman then went to Europe, recording a pair of excellent live albums at the Golden Circle Club in Stockholm at the end of the year. He returned to England in 1966 to play a season at Ronnie Scott's Club and it was here, in a venue so dedicated to the orthodox virtues of jazz, that the *enfant terri-ble* really lifted the lid.

Coleman would break up the performance in completely unexpected ways. He would play a flurry of abrasive saxophone sounds, end it on a foghorn-like honk, then silence. He would edge gently back with a playful, folksy melody, drummer Charles Moffett padding softly behind him, then silence again and another flurry, or a sudden snap on Moffett's snare. He would even mischievously slip in the occasional quote from a standard, then reel mockingly away from it. Coleman's high sustained alto notes were a heartfelt cry, though oddly, considering the reaction he was getting, many of his performances at the time were actually quiet. Moffett frequently used brushes, or gentle rolls with mallets. On fast pieces Coleman would vary the dynamics – playful, squawky melodies interrupted by honks, themes that would get swing-style treatment but in a sidelong, disrupted kind of a way.

Schonfield wrote in the sleevenotes to *Ornette Coleman in Europe*: 'His lovely tone is essentially the sound of jazz, like those of Johnny Dodds, Bubber Miley, Lester Young and Charlie Parker.' The late Charles Fox, then the *New Statesman*'s correspondent, believed that the improvising he heard on the last of six visits he made to hear Coleman in that season, was the best he had ever heard anyone deliver in the flesh.

Not so Benny Green, nor particularly Ronnie Scott or Pete King. The men who had learned their craft in Archer Street circles were difficult to persuade. Their fundamental suspicion about the defenders of 'high art' and their familiarity with charlatans and con-artists of every kind made it difficult for them to hear Coleman's ideas for what they were. It was not jazz as they knew it and loved it.

Green was distinctly unforgiving of Coleman's work at Ronnie Scott's. He referred to Coleman's occasional and approximate trumpet playing as his 'Trumpet Involuntary' and concluded: 'He is not, however, without shrewdness. By mastering the useful trick of playing the entire chromatic scale at any given moment, he had absolved himself from the charge of continuously playing wrong notes. Like a stopped clock, Coleman is right at least twice a day.'

Ronnie Scott took some comfort from the opinion of Thelonious Monk, who came to the club one night during Coleman's run and publicly ridiculed the newcomer's performance. 'Why don't you get yourself a fiddle player?' Monk enquired of Coleman's efforts with the instrument. For Scott, the whole business was incomprehensible. But Coleman had unquestionably attracted attention and interest. It was a foretaste of the club proprietor's lack of the kind of energetic bigotry that actively inhibits progress. Scott disliked Coleman's music and couldn't see how it was going to take jazz anywhere. Like Green, he felt that the traditions from which jazz had emerged were being casually thrown aside. But he put it on.

It wasn't as if he hated all of the heroes of the New Thing either. Scott had profoundly admired Coltrane, despite the latter's later inclination to propel the music into ever more mystical and other-worldly territory, because Coltrane was obsessed with harmony and with trying to manipulate the saxophone into sound effects that no one had previously believed it to be capable of. Even the old-timers from the dance bands could admire him, whether they liked his music or not. It was different with Ornette. Ornette could take or leave the respect of his peers. He would go on doing what he was doing whether or not anybody listened. Ironically Thelonious Monk, Coleman's heckler at Ronnie Scott's, had gone on record earlier in his life espousing exactly the same philosophy.

The visit of Albert Ayler in 1966 made it even harder. Ayler's music seemed to the Scott club circle more unfinished and ill-conceived even than Ornette Coleman's. One night at Gerrard Street several of the musicians had attempted to make sense of an Ayler album to the extent of even trying the record player on different speeds. Many of the London players, including Scott, went to hear Ayler's concert at the London School of Economics, recorded for BBC2 (and later unforgivably wiped); it was once again indirectly the work of Joachim Berendt, who was then running the Berlin Jazz Festival and gently blackmailing mainstream impresario George Wein by threatening not to take his mainstream jazz package unless he included an avantist of Berendt's choice as well. There was no ambiguity about the blackness of Ayler's music. He did not flirt with Western techniques of construction, or seek to develop harmonic principles further as Coltrane did, or to find ways round them as Coleman did. His horn was simple, emotional, wild and loud.

Some of these attitudes were permeating through to the younger British players. In September 1966, Ronnie Scott and Pete King offered Gerrard Street to the up-and-coming local youngsters for as long as the lease was current. The impact on the British scene was as critical as the opportunity to hear American players of the calibre that Scott and King were presenting. The band of the young Plymouth art student Mike Westbrook appeared at what came to be known as the 'Old Place' on a long series of spectacular Saturday all-nighters, and with it were the new young soloists like John Surman and Mike Osborne who had absorbed the work of the American avantists like John Coltrane and Eric Dolphy. The exiled South African Chris McGregor group played there (unable to work in South Africa because it featured blacks and whites together), as did the bassist and composer Graham Collier.

Scott had originally attempted to entrust the running of the establishment to John Stevens, a young drummer and creative proselytiser for free music who had been running a gig at the Little Theatre Club in St Martin's Lane on a virtually exclusive policy of free-jazz. Stevens was unsure of the long-term prospects given the condition of the lease, and preferred to hang on to the Little Theatre which continued to be a meeting place for the most adventurous and least commercial improvisers in London for many years afterwards. The Old Place, however, became the focus of the local jazz scene. A good many of the Little Theatre's visitors – musicians and fans – drifted over to it. It became the most dynamic venue for the presentation of home-grown modern jazz talent that London had known since the days of the Club Eleven. It was a forcible reminder of how unlike New York London was (and how unlike itself in the busy clubland years of the Second World War) that the presence of two such venues in one of the world's great capital cities should seem like any kind of a luxury.

# 11

# Our Tune

'Away with all ideals. Let each individual act spontaneously from the ever incalculable prompting of the creative wellhead within him. There is no universal law.' (D. H. Lawrence)

'DO YOU KNOW this feller?'

The driver was pointing to a huge figure slumped in the back of the cab, apparently almost unconscious with drink. The figure stirred briefly to recognise Jeff Ellison, now regular doorman at Ronnie Scott's establishment. It was the sixties, so he had grown his hair long. 'Jeff, what the hell have you done to yourself?' it growled at him in anguish, before passing out. Extracting the saxophonist from the cab was like trying to get a cork out of a bottle with a toothpick. But he was eventually drawn over the threshold of the club, where his mass finally formed an immovable obstacle in the doorway through which the club's clientele, having paid for the privilege of sharing the premises with him, were obliged to gingerly step.

It was par for the course of Ben Webster's later years. Travelling always brought this behaviour out in him, as Scott and King knew from the first encounter with Webster at Southampton in the Gerrard Street days. He once had to be collected from an empty train at Victoria Station, having fallen out of the carriage and wedged himself between the vehicle and the platform, from which impasse he was eventually wheeled away on a luggage trolley. He had also been heard to enquire of two policemen who were staggering under his weight, 'Listen, this is important. What do you think of Art Tatum?'

Webster was the stuff of many after-hours tales like that. It was never much discussed that the price the saxophonist might have paid for his own affability and gentleness in the face of the society he was obliged to inhabit was chronic alcoholism.

Scott, King and the Archer Street generation didn't spend much time pondering the cultural history of someone like Webster. He was a hero, that was enough. His behaviour also had the benefit of familiarity. In a world of rock and psychedelia that seemed to them to be going off the rails musically and was too navel-contemplatingly serious into the bargain, there was always the comforting madness of Frith Street to take refuge in, and the club began to gain a reputation that almost rivalled its capacity for musical diversions. Living hard but laughing about it, being uncomplaining about reverses, taking responsibility for yourself and not making a three-act opera out of your own opinion of what was your due, this was what made sense to the pragmatic East End war-children who made up so much of its inner circle. So men like Ornette Coleman and Albert Ayler were hard to figure out personally as well as musically. They were a different kind of black musician to easygoing freewheelers like Webster, to self-contained poets like Sonny Rollins, or even to the wired-up, competitive gunslingers of the business like Lucky Thompson and Sonny Stitt.

Roland Kirk was halfway between. He had a profound awareness of the black traditions (far more so than was appreciated by some of his early critics, who seized on what was taken to be the 'gimmickry' of his street-busker image and multi-instrumentalism) but was also a consummate showman who could involve the most intractable of audiences. He came back to the club for his second visit in October 1966, by this time completely trusting Scott and King as employers. He had become a powerful draw at Frith Street, the act that even non-jazz visitors would recall long afterwards, a showman who put everything into his work. Kirk's desire to draw his audiences in had an odd twist on that second tour.

He had in his repertoire by this time a tune called 'Here Comes the Whistle Man', for which he passed tin whistles out to the crowd and invited them to blow the daylights out of the instruments at strategic points in the music. One night Kirk charged into the theme, enthusiastically blew the first choruses and gave his fans the signal at the moment the officer in charge of a police raiding party gave a similar order outside in Frith Street. As the crowd tootled gaily inside, the Metropolitan Police, sounding their own whistles – in those days whistles were regulation issue – came charging through the front door. It was a raid to enforce a technicality of the licensing laws that non-members couldn't buy a drink, something that nightclub staff tended to be relaxed about.

Kirk had no idea what was going on. Neither had the police, who eventually started pulling at the saxophonist's clothes to get him to stop. Kirk was used to over-enthusiastic fans in the front rows, and carried on regardless.

'Tell that man to stop playing,' the officer told Scott and King.

'You tell him to stop,' they replied.

An eager subordinate leapt into the breach with the words, 'I'll stop him, sir,' but experience convinced the man in charge that this was an area in which they were out of their depth.

'Let Mr King deal with it,' he conceded.

Roland Kirk was finally brought, puffing like a runaway steam engine, to a standstill. It became one of the many legendary anecdotes of the club.

1967 was a good year. Membership had gone up, and business was consistently flourishing. For Ronnie Scott's part, the improvement was sometimes a means to a not wholly musical end. He was in these years a keener gambler than usual, often out of boredom. He would spend hours in the *spieler* across the road from the club, playing cards in the company of highly unmusical gentry whose principal understanding of time was the kind that was done as a guest of Her Majesty.

Sometimes he would call Mary when the game was going against him, get her to stand at his shoulder and maybe change his luck. Like his father, who had gone racing with one of Soho's old godfathers, Albert Dimes (the man who had given Scott and King a magnum of champagne to drink when they got rich, and which lies unopened in the office to this day) Ronnie didn't dislike gangsters on sight, and in any case thought it was healthier to make friends of them rather than enemies. On occasions the place seemed so full of menacing-looking customers and their conspicuous girlfriends that more conventional visitors to the club would get up and leave in alarm.

The old gamble – how to get through the next week a little bit ahead – was still just about paying off. Increasingly ambitious projects were possible. Buddy Rich brought a big band in in the spring of that year, and established just what a powerful impact a really large outfit could have in those intimate surroundings, where the front row could shake hands with the front line. A charismatic, wisecracking, businesslike performer, Rich became, in his own way, one of the club's major draws – not so much because of the jazz content of his shows, which tended to be rehearsed to the last detail and often featured precise but unimaginative sidemen fresh out of music college, but because of the leader's own extraordinary drumming.

By the autumn of that year, it was time to make another attempt with an avantist, this time with Archie Shepp, one of the most uncompromising defenders of the 'New Thing'. Shepp was an unusual jazz musician, who had involved himself with acting, poetry and eventually academic work as well as music. He wanted his work to articulate a new black consciousness. Shepp's music in the 1960s was popular with both white intellectuals and with blacks from the ghettos, not always the case with the most unbending forms of the new free jazz.

Shepp's visit laid to rest at least one myth that tended to follow iconoclasts like him around. Waitresses at the club in those days found him to be one of the most considerate and polite of the guests. His music at the time was none the less quite the reverse. It featured two trombones in Grachan Moncur and Roswell Rudd and involved a good deal of fierce and dissonant squalling. Shepp's work expressed impatience and rebellion. Ornette Coleman's inventions, once the passage of the years defused the hysteria that had sprung from its departures from convention, came to be recognised even by the saxophonist's former detractors as being as lyrical and shaped as anything in the jazz of earlier decades.

But Shepp's most experimental phase wasn't like that. It mystified and provoked audiences and musicians alike. Jazz has had a short history. One lifetime could still span the progress from the archaic, marching-band jazz of Bunk Johnson, through 1920s classicism (formal elegance and balance as well as bluesy fire in the collaborations between Louis Armstrong and King Oliver) and then the fragmentation, sparked off by Armstrong's irrepressible individual genius into a spray of separate trajectories – swing, orchestral jazz, bebop and beyond. At 47 Frith Street, on and off the stand, the legendary figures of all those diverse persuasions would meet, play, talk it over, argue about it. Coleman Hawkins and Stan Getz were at a table one night during Shepp's season. Hawkins is rumoured to have remarked to Getz at a particularly storm-tossed moment, 'Hey, they're playing our tune.'

And it was Hawkins, sixty-three years old at the time, who followed Shepp into the club that year. He was not growing old gracefully except in his playing. For years he had ostensibly been living on a diet of Remy Martin brandy and cigarettes and was hardly known to eat. When he arrived at the club, the proprietors did their best to introduce Hawkins to food, but even a bowl of soup was mostly beyond him. Mary would try to slip an egg into the brandy, but he would, unsurprisingly, spit it out, protesting furiously. Vitamin B shots had to suffice.

Hawkins was undoubtedly past his prime, but in such a personal music as jazz, this could sometimes deepen expressiveness even when technical skills were declining. Music taken at any sort of lively tempo would unsettle him, and the effort to keep up would distract him from the flow and miraculous sense of form for which he had grown famous. His tone had become querulous, the gaps in the flow of his ideas were obvious and couldn't be explained as interpretation. Yet his old admirers were not uncharitable, particularly Benny Green in his published commentaries, who was astonished by Hawkins's courage. The old man did not let himself off lightly, even playing the slow Kurt Weill tune 'September Song' without any accompaniment that might have helped cover up his difficulties.

Ben Webster was in town at that time, and was effectively dependent on much the same lifestyle that was killing Hawkins. The younger saxophonist had by this time struck up something of a familiarity with the regulars of Ronnie Scott's Club and was frequently attended by the doorman and sometime-drummer Jeff Ellison.

In the early hours of a mornng, Webster ran out of alcohol. Ellison was at a loss as to where he could fix Webster up with a drink. The American knew that his old mentor and Svengali, Coleman Hawkins was in town, in residence at the Piccadilly Hotel. 'Bean'll have a drink,' Webster triumphantly decided. 'Let's go and see Bean.' Somehow they passed the foyer of the sleeping hotel, the bear-like figure of Webster unconcealable, not least because he would let out an ear splitting 'my man!' to anybody he could see. When they got to Hawkins's room, he was nursing his usual bottle of Remy Martin and the ice water. But he kept Webster talking, tantalised, knowing what he wanted, and never offered him the drink. Webster, for his part, was always in thrall to Hawk. It was like the imperious charisma of Sonny Stitt and Don Byas. Webster let the drink go.

Pete King had arranged for Webster to go on a short tour of Britain at the time, and the presence of Hawkins in town meant that at least one attempt to get them to play together on one of the dates was inevitable. But Hawkins' health seemed too far gone to risk it. The old man, however, wouldn't miss his chance to play with Webster. He made the gig, performed three tunes with the younger man after a shaky start, and recaptured much of his old élan even though struggling for breath before he went on stage. A local doctor concluded that Hawkins was suffering from pneumonia, a diagnosis confirmed by the club's own doctor in London. Hawkins was due to leave for Stockholm to begin a European tour, and the medical advice was he should stay right where he was. Hawkins ignored it all, checked out of his hotel and flew to Stockholm anyway. He was to die in May 1969.

Ronnie Scott and Pete King's role was changing. Neither of them had had grandiose ambitions when the club began, a little place to play in and meet like-minded people was all it was ever supposed to be. It was a line of work not generally commercial, that ran to distinctly unsocial hours, and that put immense strains on domestic life. The two men were powerfully bonded (though they would have thought it sentimental to discuss it) by both a highly traditional *esprit de corps* about professionalism and the still surviving romance of youth at large in the entertainment business. Pete King had now formed a booking agency, still using Ronnie as the front man just like the old days, called Ronnie Scott Directions, which would sometimes use artists who had visited the club for a season on packages that would tour the country. They had done this with Ben Webster and in 1967 sent out tours that featured the singers Dakota Staton and Blossom Dearie.

And if their business commitments were broadening, the club's clientele had changed just the way that Benny Green had forecast on the move to Frith Street. (Once again with Davison's help, they were able to expand the premises by buying the next-door lease as well, using its upstairs room initially for local jazz talent and then for pop and soul. The impresario Norman Granz also lent money for improvements.) The identity of the establishment had changed from a jazz club to a supper club that specialised in jazz and the old audience had to rub shoulders with the new. The dedicated followers of jazz mingled increasingly with tourists, expense account business customers, passing trade. It was the only way to make the books balance. But it was going to make Scott and King think harder about acts like Archie Shepp's in the coming years.

Sonny Rollins revisited in 1967, not with quite the same élan with which he had taken Gerrard Street by storm, and playing more frequently with Gordon Beck, an excellent British pianist who was none the less not so quirky then as Tracey and less provocative of Rollins's wayward muse. The year also saw the longest residency by a single artist in the establishment – and, unexpectedly, for a woman instrumentalist.

Elvira 'Vi' Redd, a Los Angeles saxophonist, had abandoned the temptation to consider singing the only feasible outlet in jazz for her sex; she came from a musical family with a drummer for a father and an amateur saxophonist for a mother. Redd's great-aunt, Alma Hightower, persuaded Vi Redd to play the saxophone as a child. She developed a powerful and hard-hitting alto style modelled on Charlie Parker and was soon displaying talents that should have earned her a soloist's career as prominent as Johnny Griffin's or Hank Mobley's but which, as the critic Leonard Feather had pointed out five years before, was simply invisible because she was a woman. Feather wrote that Redd was thought of 'not as an available saxophonist who plays and reads well and can hold down a chair in any man's reed section, but rather as a novelty who can't really be that good.' Redd herself remarked on the number of times that men in horn sections walked offstage as she came on. She said without rancour, 'I often tell people the fact that I'm a female is an act of God.'

She did, however, get a chance to put the record straight in her season at Frith Street, on a tour of Europe that followed a successful appearance at the Monterey Jazz Festival. She worked at the club for a ten-week stretch, and demonstrated her own brand of dismissive running commentary with awkward audiences. One night, finding herself playing to an indifferent but largely silent crowd, Vi Redd upbraided them with the words, 'I go to church on *Sundays.*' The following year she came to Europe again – this time with Count Basie. She left music in the early seventies to raise a family but returned to it in 1976.

1968. A change had come over the way the music industry bought and sold its property. As long as Ronnie Scott could remember, every square inch of the music world he knew had been mapped out by an American first. American popular culture was so dominant that players from across the Atlantic would have swamped the local music profession. Now it was all different. Or was it? British pop music appeared to have taken the world by storm, but was founded on black rhythm 'n' blues. The Rolling Stones and the Beatles never disguised their indebtedness to the very artists that Ronnie Scott, Stan Tracey and the others had nervously toured the States with back in 1957.

Rock now dominated the thought processes of record company executives, jazz did not. Yet jazz was influencing the most adventurous of the rock bands. The Grateful Dead mingled electronics, country rock and long, jazz-like instrumental jams. John Coltrane's later odysseys, mystical and semi-religious as they were, also had a strong influence on rock players – not always for the good, since musicians who weren't necessarily good improvisors in the first place were not improved by thrashing around in what they assumed to be a Coltrane-like manner. Coltrane never toyed with electric music himself, but his influence on it was heightened by the tragedy of his premature death in 1967.

Some jazz artists did attempt – for a mixture of artistic and pragmatic reasons – to absorb the more fashionable devices into their own work. Miles Davis, a dictator of musical fashions for years, was prominent in the move – persuaded both by his own long-term adventurousness and the record sales of musicians like Sly Stone and Jimi Hendrix. This new musical development appealed more to Scott and King's generation: some of it was tuneful, it was possible for good soloists to make a mark on it, and in a way it swung.

But if some jazz musicians were listening with increasing interest to the new rock, for many others it was simply the old temptation to ditch improvisation and play 'hot licks' – familiar, repeated, crowd-pleasing phrases - instead. The single-minded journeys of Coltrane, Cecil Taylor, Ornette Coleman and others were affecting another group of British jazz players. Some had turned their backs on any kind of commercial status and were exploring 'free' music with ascetic rigour, mostly in back rooms to tiny audiences – though the climate for experimental art of all kinds in the London of the late 1960s, particularly in establishments like the Arts Lab, was fairly healthy.

Ronnie Scott passed his fortieth summer in the midst of these upheavals. The music business of his youth had changed out of all recognition. The reign of Archer Street was over. Nobody congregated there in search of jobs any more. And it wouldn't be long before he could say that he had been a club proprietor for a decade.

He took to walking the streets of the city in the early hours of the morning with Mary after the club had closed. Normally he drove everywhere, but virtually gave this up. The saxophone was played less and less. He had never been able to share the confidence of his admirers about his horn playing, and would repeat to Mary over and over during those long walks, 'What am I doing with my life?' It was partly exasperation at his own contrariness. He loved music, loved those who made it, and could be an inspired exponent of it himself. But he was also a prisoner of his own sporadic lassitude, and found himself becoming prone to depressions. He believed he was being trapped by the obligations to be the club's front man. Mary heard the rhetorical questions go on and on.

'It's ridiculous,' he would say. 'What am I doing but spending my life repeating a lot of stupid jokes?'

'Why do it?' she would say.

'Because they expect it,' Ronnie would come back. 'It's what I'm supposed to do.' It was a sense of obligation as old as performance itself. The customers paid the piper, and the rent. Ronnie Scott was in the pincer of being a Jewish boy with a small-business background, devoted to a musical culture that was emotional, vibrant, anarchic, subversive, and as wide as the world. The mysterious and long-gone showbiz glamour of Jock was pitched against the counterweight of Cissie's protective love, his grandmother, Sol's textile business, the security of the little Edgware house. The same tension existed between his affection for women who were creative, witty, enterprising – music lovers, painters, designers – and that old deeprooted Jewish perception of womankind as the providers of chicken stew, cinnamon balls and clean shirts, the nurturers of homes that you would from time to time go back to.

And in Ronnie's professional life there was turmoil too. He was glad that the club existed, but the procession of legends that had entered it were a disturbance to his equilibrium as well as a delight. At least the business could provide work and a congenial environment for so many players he had admired from a distance, and he and Pete King even did what they could to help old professional friends out, whether they were playing on the premises or not. There were the calls that would come through to Ronnie Scott's Fulham flat, like the one that came from his old hero, Hank Mobley, stranded at Heathrow Airport in the early hours with just enough money to make the call.

Mobley was sick, broke, and physically worn out, and had come to London to seek help from people that he believed appreciated him and his work. Mary recalled how Ronnie had pulled his clothes over his pyjamas, driven to the airport to pick up the saxophonist, and made sure that the club took care of his accommodation and needs until he got back on his feet. Frith Street was at least an oasis in which the practitioners of a generally neglected art could find support. But as a saxophonist, Ronnie Scott was constantly plagued by doubts. He thought of trying to change his career, but did not know how to. He felt he had reached a hurdle in his own playing. It was a period of marking time, and one in which some seeds of dissatisfaction deep inside him put out shoots that were almost to drag him under later on.

□ □ □

In the late summer of 1968 Ronnie Scott, impressed with the work of some of the young players he had begun to make contact with as the Gerrard Street 'Old Place' continued to play host to local talent, decided to form a band that would marry their uninhibited ideas with his own more formal approach. He included some of the musicians of the New Wave in Britain – including John Surman, a Coltrane-influenced saxophonist from the West Country, who had made a considerable reputation for himself in the Mike Westbrook band and was noticeable especially for his unconventional decision to use the unwieldy baritone saxophone as a fleet, front-line soloing instrument in the way that Coltrane was using the tenor and soprano.

The band also included Gordon Beck on piano, Tony Oxley on drums and Kenny Wheeler on trumpet, a shy Canadian expatriate of cool musical eloquence who had worked in a succession of John Dankworth orchestras but also on the free scene too. It also included an excellent altoist, Ray Warleigh, trombonist Chris Pyne and the remarkable double-bassist Ron Mathewson. Mathewson was part of the club's house team, another musician with a prodigious capacity for alcohol whose playing seemed mysteriously unaffected by it. They were just called The Band.

Tony Oxley, who for a brief period in the new band's short life was the drummer alongside Tony Crombie, was also by now a regular accompanist for visitors at the club. He performed in an unusual manner for British players. He was not by temperament cast in a respectful mould. Nor was he of the Phil Seamen manner of relaxed, sensual swing, subtle shading and reserve about extremes that won the older man such acclaim as the English drummer who sounded 'black'. Oxley learned every trick in the book, invented several of his own, and then set about playing in such a way that nobody could be in any doubt about it, a rodeo horse of a drummer on which only the most flexible and experienced of performers could ride. Jokers would compare the standard onomatopoeia for the sound of a smooth-flowing bebop ride cymbal ('ten-to-ten ten-to-ten ten-to-ten') with Oxley's jolting tempo, and describe the latter as more like 'around-about-a-quarter-past-eleven' because he would embroider the basic time in clusters of jostling beats but still remember, in some metronomic circuit in the depths of his brain, exactly where the tempo was and come back to it at intervals with an emphatic crash that seemed to say 'told you so'.

Oxley would frequently unsettle soloists or lose them altogether. Just as Stan Tracey had been, Oxley was a house player of a completely unorthodox type who revealed that perverse, let's-see-what-happens streak in Scott. Where he could have made a point of always hiring high-class metronomes who wouldn't push the guests, he chose to make two of his

most prominent house sidemen the most intractable, challenging, unpre-
dictable and sometimes bloody-minded performers he could find. Some
visitors disliked such quirks. But some – like Johnny Griffin and the
Grammy-winning saxophonist Joe Henderson – deliberately sought out
Oxley, just as Rollins had been delighted by the opportunity to play with
Stan Tracey.

The new band didn't, couldn't, last. The personalities of the younger
players were too strong to be restrained by the kind of urbane lyricism that
Scott and Crombie liked. Scott took to calling the outfit his 'all-star aggra-
vation'. And there were soon to be other things on his mind. The expansion
of the club through the acquisition of the next-door lease was just about to
begin. Joe Henderson played the last stint in the old room before the place
was closed to knock the two downstairs rooms together to form the layout
as it is today.

The opening of the expanded club brought back conflicting memories.
Ted Heath, his old employer, the man who had helped him become a
teenage star, came to Frith Street for the opening night by Buddy Rich's
band. But Heath had had a stroke by this time and couldn't enter the
premises unaided. He was helped in by another man who had made it possible – Harold Davison – and by Tito Burns. Rich's band was forced to open
for business while some of the work was still in hand. 'First time I've ever
worked in a building site,' Rich maintained gamely from the stage.

But if Ronnie Scott's attempt to draw the new generation of players into his
own musical sphere was unlikely to succeed neither were men like Surman
and Oxley likely to see eye to eye in the long run. The new players divided
into those who derived their inspiration from jazz and those who derived it
from elsewhere. The problem of a home for young British players had
reached a crisis point. Scott and King had been forced to close the Old Place
when the lease finally ran out; they maintained they had lost over £100 a
week on keeping it open and had ended up £3,000 in debt on its account.
An effort to use the upstairs part of the new Frith Street premises hadn't
worked either. The musicians themselves had then grouped together to
form the Jazz Centre Society, an organisation dedicated to the long-term
objective of establishing a building in which jazz could be played, taught,
read about and listened to by its devoted practitioners and fans.

But there was an irony. The avant-garde players were convinced that
the music they were pursuing was of little interest to the organisers of the

Jazz Centre Society. The twist was that although the Jazz Centre's policy was almost certainly one that was more attractive to Scott and King (and which would be attempting to fulfil the role they no longer felt able to for local players) it was they who found themselves offering shelter, by donating the Frith Street premises on Sunday nights to musicians whose work at times made Shepp's performances the previous year seem like a Palm Court Orchestra.

Tony Oxley was the courier in this curious connection. Oxley was a player who could do anything that Ronnie Scott himself could require of an accompanist, so his opinion counted. If Oxley thought there was something in a music in which people scraped sheets of metal, banged gongs, performed stratospheric ear-splitting whistles way over the upper register of saxophones and listened to Stockhausen and Pierre Boulez, then there had to be something in it.

In 1970, the London Musicians' Co-operative was formed. It was the logical outcome of the parallel line of jazz that had been going on at the Little Theatre Club and elsewhere. It called its opening press conference at 47 Frith Street, and it staged Sunday night concerts there for some months. Ronnie Scott and Pete King lent their premises to the Musicians' Co-operative for nothing – members of the Co-op recalled the gesture years later. It would have been very easy for a West End club proprietor to discourage anything that might be bad for business, and on some of those Sunday nights outraged visitors were heard to leave the premises complaining that if this was the place where you could hear the best of the world's jazz then they didn't know what the world was coming to.

The club's tenth anniversary came and went, the BBC using the premises for a series of filmed concerts – including the only appearance in the club of Miles Davis, performing with an electric band. And the Kenny Clarke–Francy Boland big band, with which Scott had enjoyed a fruitful association throughout the 1960s, put in a convincing appearance.


In September 1970 Jimi Hendrix died. The most inventive and passionate electric blues guitar virtuoso of the era had been performing in Ronnie Scott's Club on the night before his death, jamming with War, singer Eric Burdon's rugged rhythm 'n' blues band. Burdon, a long-time fan and friend of the guitarist, had asked Hendrix to come to the club, and sensed from the uncertainties of their guest's performance on the first set that something was wrong. Hendrix hadn't wanted to go back on after the interval, but eventually did return and played like something close to his old self on 'Tobacco Road', demonstrating that melodic sense and the suppleness of long, B. B. King-influenced lines that lay beneath the performer of wild, squalling sound effects. 'He was a genius,' the anguished Burdon said to *Melody Maker*. 'But I knew there was something bad in his mind that night.'

Another once-only appearance by a legend was the arrival of the formidable Charles Mingus in 1971. It was a show that started out with the kind of curious overture that appealed to Scott and King. When Mingus arrived in London he found a tax demand for work he had done in Britain on the movie *All Night Long* in the mid-fifties. He strode on to the stage on his opening night roaring, 'I've just had a letter from your Queen,' and then proceeded to beat the living daylights out of the bass.

If Mingus was the repository of old values and the directness of the earliest jazz, Weather Report – the electronic band that came to London the following year – was a powerful example of the best that could emerge from the now headlong drive to fuse jazz and rock. The whole idea was paradise to the music business, which had never really had much idea what to do about jazz anyway and was forever chiding its practitioners for indifference to public opinion.

Jazz-rock. It was the perfect disguise for jazz at a time when public concentration on the idiom was wavering. All the mannerisms of pop were there – heavy backbeats, electric guitars or keyboards that sounded like guitars, dominant bass sounds. But Weather Report wasn't so easily put in its place. The band featured two excellent performers who had worked extensively with Miles Davis in pianist Joe Zawinul and saxophonist Wayne Shorter, the man who had finally replaced Coltrane in Davis's band. Weather Report's season was a milestone, but Zawinul and Shorter were fine soloists who would only later become cramped by the idiom.

And as the climate grew warmer for a certain kind of jazz playing, it grew as cold as it would ever get for some of the British scene's most creative artists. In 1972 both Joe Harriott and Phil Seamen died. Harriott had never defeated those early respiratory problems. Moreover, to be a West Indian playing adventurous jazz music in a Britain in which landlords could still demand 'no coloureds' in their advertisements would put intolerable strain on the most robust of temperaments and physiques and Harriott was not strong in either area. Seamen eventually died of his heroin habit, at forty-six, making a record (*The Phil Seamen Story*) in his last months that catalogued in music and speech his chequered history in the music business.

Tubby Hayes departed the following year, in June 1973, at the age of thirty-eight. His health had been bad for years, and his heart was not strong enough to enable him to play with his old power, but he had adopted a slower, more lyrical approach, as well as concentrating on his other love, the vibraharp – developments that gave his work a new reflectiveness that had been camouflaged by its pyrotechnics. Ronnie had visited him the night before he died, and they had talked over all the things they had in common: Tubby's father was a highly respected musician, so was Ronnie's; the parents of both men had separated when they were small children.

Ronnie Scott was forty-five. He had been with Mary for nearly eight years, and it was the most committed relationship he had been involved in since his long on-off affair with Joan Crewe. They had moved from Knightsbridge to a rambling redbrick block built around a secluded court-yard off the Fulham Road. It was easy for Ronnie Scott's old fears about domesticity to be kept under control in that partnership. Mary worked in the club and kept the same hours as him. She was popular among the musicians and was comfortable in any company. And she looked after Ronnie.

1971 had been a year that brought many changes for them both. In March, Ronnie Scott's son Nicholas had been operated on for a repair to the hole in his heart. Nicholas' will to survive astonished the doctors, but Ilsa had to cope with her son's health difficulties for many years The experience had pro-foundly disturbed the boy's father who had paced the flat all night before the operation was due, not having seriously considered, until he heard it from the doctors themselves, that Nicholas might not survive the operation.

In the Christmas of that year Ronnie Scott – who liked the opportunity to play Santa Claus even if he didn't regard himself as the world's most nat-ural father – went shopping with Ilsa to buy presents for the boy whose future they were now celebrating more gratefully than on any of his seven Christmasses past. Nicholas was recovering well and growing more robust – he was even the only boy in the ballet class of the bilingual German/ English school that Ilsa had taken him to in Petersham, one achievement that she kept from his father. Ronnie bought Nicholas a train set. Ilsa bought him a Lego kitchen and bathroom kit to put into the miniature house she had built for him at home. 'Isn't that a bit cissy for him?' Ronnie asked dubiously. 'You'll be telling me next he goes to ballet classes.' Ilsa didn't have the heart to tell him that the boy already did.

Winter 1972 brought the three-day week and nine-hour electricity cuts in Britain as labour relations plummeted. Stan Kenton's band was booked into the club during this period, and as well as being the best-balanced jazz orchestra Pete King believed he had ever heard, the booking provided one of those unintentional farces King and Scott adored. With no power, they staged Kenton's band by candlelight, and spots powered by car batteries. It was just like old times.

And at that time, too, Mary told Ronnie that she was pregnant. She had decided that she would have a baby by the time she was thirty and had already miscarried once, though all the conversations to secure Ronnie's consent to fatherhood had led nowhere – he never really visualised it as a source of more pleasure than anxiety. He tried to talk Mary out of it. Other people raised doubts too. 'Make the most of the hospital, you'll have to pay equal attention to Ronnie and the baby afterwards,' said Mary's mother Barbara, a woman with sufficient of a traditional view of men and women to doubt unfounded optimism.

Ronnie Scott had other fears about it all, those deep-rooted anxieties about accident and physical decline that represented the mirror image of his anarchic self, fears enhanced by the memory of Jock's appearance at the end, the decline of Sol, the sudden departure of his mother. He convinced himself that he was too old for fatherhood, that middle-age might have increased the risk of his child being born unhealthy. He wanted Mary to have every test she could, visited doctors with her, listened intently to advice. And when he was assured that it would be all right, he relaxed and began to look forward to it. They took Mary into hospital in the final weeks of her pregnancy assuming there was still a while to go.

Ronnie Scott went home. Mary gave birth to a daughter on the morning of 5 September 1972. The child's father – by this stage of his life having a profound loathing of life before lunchtime and not anticipating any developments yet – couldn't be contacted. Three hours after the birth, he arrived at the ward, grinning broadly. 'My God, Mary, she looks just like my grandmother,' Scott exclaimed in astonishment as he looked into the cot. So they called her Rebecca, in memory of a woman who had given the baby's father so much cause to welcome life and enjoy its opportunities. For eighteen months Rebecca shared the Fulham flat with them, and the child's perceptions of the world as a playground galvanised her father's never-distant inclinations to see it that way himself.

That summer he went motor racing for the first time in his life – an old dream since that romantic image of his ex-boss, Johnny Claes, in that big, brutal Grand Prix racer back in the 1940s – taking part in the 'celebrity races' that were run at Brands Hatch and driving in formula saloon car competitions. (He mused that in a short career at the wheel, winning two races, doing well in two others and crashing two cars he had, on percentage, come out ahead of Jackie Stewart.) Pete King and Ronnie Scott, both long-time motoring fans, made concerted efforts to rerun their adolescence in their forties.

And in 1973 the impulse took its most predictable form. Ronnie Scott began an affair with a new waitress at the club. Linda Poulton was a young aspiring singer, fascinated by the world Scott moved in. She played the guitar, enjoyed painting and sculpture, thought she might be a useful addition to the personnel of Scott's own band. Little Rebecca was not much younger than Ronnie himself had been when Cissie forced Jock to face exactly the same problem forty-three years before, and Mary was no more prepared to turn the other cheek than Cissie had been.

She knew Linda well from the club, had had many intimate conversations with her, and found out about the affair through the hints of another member of the floor staff who advised her not to go on confiding in the younger woman. Mary soon confronted the new arrival with the implications of what she and Ronnie were doing. Ronnie Scott alternated between agonising about it, considering ending it, and trying to believe that Mary's displeasure wasn't real.

Linda Poulton went to America during 1973, to begin what turned out to be an unsuccessful engagement with the Mel Lewis band. Ronnie Scott went to France to play some concerts around that time and sent a message to Mary in London saying that he had been invited to take a temporary assignment in a French big band whose tenorist was sick. Since they were going to be playing some upmarket shows, would she send a tuxedo out to him? It was all an implausible stab at an alibi. Mary sent the tuxedo, but soon learned that Ronnie had actually gone to the States in pursuit of Linda. Though she still loved him, she knew it was over. All of her friends were Ronnie's friends. Her life was in the club, where everyone knew Linda too. This couldn't be any ordinary separation. In February 1974, Mary left for New York with Rebecca.

Ronnie Scott didn't need telling that he was nothing like the phlegmatic, impervious, wise-cracking controller of his destiny that seemed to be illuminated night after night by his own spotlights. His impulsiveness surfaced in bursts, hand in hand with the romanticism that was the flipside to Jewish pragmatism, the survivor's compulsion to dream. It had shown itself in the first journey to New York in 1947, the trip for the Holy Grail. It had gripped him helplessly in the drop-everything trip to America in the mid-fifties to follow Joan Crewe and Spencer Sinatra. It betrayed him all over again by never letting on that there would be women in the world, not like Cissie and Nana Becky, who would have their own lives to live. He interpreted their pursuit of their own needs as rejection, and defended himself by becoming the child Cissie and Becky had unhesitatingly protected.

Midway through 1974, it was all going downhill fast. Mary and Rebecca were gone. Linda Poulton had come close to being a singer with the hard-swinging trio that Scott had formed with the organist Mike Carr and drummer Bobby Gien, but Mary had furiously objected. Linda left America for Australia and then New Zealand, where her parents lived.

Ronnie Scott was getting into bad shape. Finding himself plagued by anxieties about Mary and Rebecca, and unable to stop thinking about Linda either, he was becoming dependent on sleeping pills and brandy to get any sleep. He had only ever been a moderate consumer of alcohol in the past. This time, all the unanswered questions of his life rose up and nearly drowned him. He rang Linda twice, three times a week. He pleaded with her to come back.

Work went on, but only just. For the autumn of 1974, Scott's trio was booked on to a long tour of Australia and the United States with the irrepressible Parisian violinist Stephane Grappelli, who had performed at the club the previous year. The tour was to culminate in a Carnegie Hall concert in New York. Grappelli was popular everywhere he went, playing a jaunty, dancing, raffish kind of swing like an elegant conjuring act. Scott's band, built around the deep, reverberating tones of Carr's organ (Carr would add the role of the missing bassist by performing basslines on footpedals) was equally rhythmic, though the leader was by this point inclining toward adding the packed melodic constructions of early John Coltrane on top of the Hank Mobley grace.

Linda came to see him play in Sydney, and they spent a week together. The tour went on to the USA, where ABC TV recorded Scott's week of performances in Rochester, New York State, and he and Grappelli played Carnegie Hall. The concert wasn't all that it might have been. The band discovered in rehearsal that American electrical specifications fouled up the mechanism through which Carr's bass pedals achieved their proper effect. They eventually had to hire another instrument, which wasn't set up to replicate a real bass as Carr's was, with the result that the organist's dancing feet produced a distinctly ungroovy, jovially amiable sound like the clip-clop of a low-pitched xylophone.

Scott was in a bad way, barely able to get through the work, always performing with a jug of iced water on stage because the sedatives were drying his mouth. Still drinking heavily and taking anti-depressants and sleeping drugs, veering wildly between the impossible choices he had set himself, he found considerable solace in Mary's long experience of him. He and Mary even visited the children's clothing department of Macy's in New York one day to buy presents for the little girl. Confused and still badly strung out, Ronnie Scott sat on the floor, propped against a display stand, people seeming to float around him like ghosts. He fell asleep there, with Macy's customers going impassively about their business all around. Eventually the presence of the exhausted, dishevelled-looking man on the floor attracted a crowd. When he woke up, Mary was anxiously slapping his face to bring him around. She kept Rebecca and Ronnie apart throughout this tortuous period. Though she was determined that he should never lose touch with his daughter in the end, Mary knew this wasn't the time to build on the relationship. She was to spend a lot of time in the later years as Rebecca grew up trying to explain just why.

It was the fall of 1974. Ronnie Scott knew that it was time to come home.

By Christmas Pete King was seriously worried for Ronnie as a friend and as a lynchpin of the business, but was uncertain how to help. As the year came to a close, on what seemed like just another night's work, there was a sharper twist. Scott was by now barely functioning except by reflex. A drunk in the club grew argumentative, Scott tried to throw him out and frog-marched him through the aisles toward the door. The drunk turned on him and knocked the proprietor's glasses flying into the twilit room. Scott hit him in the back of the head and broke his little finger. The drunk came out of it intact, but for Scott it was clearly going to be impossible to play the saxophone until the fracture healed. Saxophone playing, the pursuit to which Scott could turn in his most extreme moods of self-disgust, was suddenly an unavailable refuge. He rang Linda Poulton in Auckland one more time. 'I feel completely useless,' Scott told her. 'I can't play. I can't do anything. Suppose I come out there for Christmas?'

In the state he was in, it was impossible for him to hear quite how the proposition sounded for a woman living with her parents on the other side of the world and trying to get on with her life. But, hesitantly, she agreed. He booked everything in a sudden explosion of energy, bought presents for Linda, went around the shops with a list of things she wanted. He arranged for Brian Theobald, an old friend of Tubby Hayes's and a one-time road manager who was currently driving a minicab, to pick him up from the Fulham flat on the morning of his flight. Seven hours before he was due to leave, Linda rang from Auckland. 'I've been thinking about this, Ronnie,' came the voice on the line. 'I don't really think it's a good idea.' In later years, Ronnie Scott would acknowledge that she was right. But not on this morning.

Ronnie Scott dissolved. He swallowed everything he could lay his hands on in the flat, left a note for Theobald outside the door telling him to forget it and that he'd be back in touch some time. Theobald arrived, rang the bell and hammered on the door but there wasn't a sound from the flat. He rang for Henry Cohen, the giant jazz fan from Dagenham who had become the

Frith Street bouncer – 'his shadow's bigger than Asia' his boss used to tell the club's audiences. When Cohen arrived, Theobald told him the score.

'I want you to take the door out,' he told Cohen.

The big man shuffled uneasily, edged toward the stairs. 'I can't do that,' he protested. 'I'll get the fuckin' sack.'

'Do it,' Theobald insisted.

They found Ronnie Scott on the floor beside the bed, the bedclothes lying on top of him. Theobald satisfied himself that Scott was alive and promptly rang Pete King, who summoned Sidney Gottlieb, an ex-East End doctor who had by now acquired a West End practice and was a long-standing friend of the club. Gottlieb would help Ronnie and Pete whenever they were in trouble. Gottlieb took charge of Scott. The doctor had concluded that whatever the musician's intentions had been before Theobald and Cohen found him, it was senseless to take chances. Scott needed round-the-clock supervision, he insisted.

Gottlieb took Scott to his Highgate home, then to a private nursing home in St John's Wood. Pete King called Mary in New York, and she came to London with Rebecca. When she arrived at Dr Gottlieb's, she spent forty-five minutes being briefed on her ex-partner's condition before she was allowed in to see him, and even then she wasn't prepared for the shock. 'He was the colour of a newspaper, had lost so much weight he looked like a little bird, propped up in that bed, and he couldn't even hold his cigarette,' Mary recalled. But he began to eat again, food that Mary cooked for him at the flat and sent over twice a day with Brian Theobald.

King wanted to do what he could to help his partner get straight, and the medical advice was that seeing Linda again would probably do Scott more good than harm. But no one really wanted to have to handle such a delicate responsibility. Eventually Mary found herself in that bizarre role, talking on the phone to Linda's parents in Auckland, begging her to make the trip, then going with Theobald to the airport to collect her when she finally agreed, helping her to deal with the traumatic encounter. For Mary's part, she found the strength to cope with it in Rebecca's face back at the apartment at night.

Ronnie Scott's stay at the home, initially under twenty-four-hour supervision, was entirely paid for by a sympathetic Spike Milligan. While he was there, Mary and Pete King set about having the Fulham flat completely refurbished. Gottlieb and other advisers had tried to talk Scott into moving house, so that he didn't have to return to the scene of so many of his nightmares. But he always refused. Making a new home out of the old one was the only possible compromise.

While he was there, Mary and Pete King set about having the Fulham flat completely refurbished. Gottlieb and other advisers had tried to talk Scott into moving house, so that he didn't have to return to the scene of so many of his nightmares. But he always refused. Making a new home out of the old one was the only possible compromise.

Scott would keep trying to practise the saxophone nevertheless, nursing home or no. The establishment was eventually forced to take his reeds away because he kept the place awake, and Theobald once found him there sitting up in bed and playing his soprano with no reed in the mouthpiece, just to keep his fingering in shape. As he got better, his attendants gained more faith in the likelihood that he wouldn't do anything dangerous to his returning health. 'I'm going to take a bath,' Scott said one night to the nurse. 'Don't worry, I'll be all right. Read your book.' The nurse agreed, settled down to read, and nodded off.

Meanwhile, in a downstairs room was one of the home's wealthiest patients, an elderly woman who refused the standard electric bell and would communicate with the staff only by shaking a handbell. Since she had never been known to take a step outside of her room in eight years' residence, it came as something of a surprise to the staff to find her charging volcanically down the corridor like an extra from the *Ride of the Valkyrie*, handbell clanging, wailing in fury. They went in to find a good deal of the plasterwork of the ceiling in her bed, and a cascade of water following it. Upstairs, the nurse still dozed outside the bathroom door. One of the home's largest members of staff took a run down the corridor at the door, and it opened unprotestingly to his charge, leaving him prostrate over the lavatory. Ronnie Scott was asleep in the bath with both taps full on. One hand absently held the shower unit above his head. They managed to placate the outraged customer downstairs. They also tried to keep their faces suitably straight when they told the story to the visiting Theobald later on.

As he improved, Scott considered psychoanalysis. He tried with Dr Gottlieb, but they weren't the right partnership. Gottlieb then recommended a Harley Street psychiatrist. The patient was uncomfortable with the whole idea, but began to tell his story, head in hands. When he looked up the eminent specialist was asleep.

'Excuse me, doctor,' he began despairingly.

'I'm so sorry,' apologised the shrink, waking up with a start. 'It's a little stuffy in here.'

Ronnie Scott perceived psychiatrists not so much as members of a healing profession but like unfortunate agents who were blighted by having a string of inept musicians on their books. 'How can you expect them to get

King's son Christopher would recall the period later, accusing his father of 'doing a Ronnie' whenever he did the same thing.

He began to mend, with the help of anti-depressants, and got back to playing again, which was an immense release. But for most of 1974 he was coupling the drugs to heavy drinking. Mary had helped him get back on his feet. She had intended visiting for three weeks and had stayed five months, feeding him and looking after him, preventing the little flat from becoming the vortex of the downward spiral it had threatened to be. But eventually she and Rebecca went back to New York. Scott was functioning again, but unsteadily.

So many of the steps he wanted to take he knew were crazy but he took them anyway. He booked himself on to a plane to the Antipodes to see Linda again, unannounced, and ended up staying with her and her parents outside Auckland, a stoned-out, drunken Jewish saxophone player nearing fifty with crazed designs on the daughter of a respectable family of Auckland Gentiles. Scott felt himself transplanted into the screenplay of Woody Allen's *Annie Hall*, having supper with Annie's Gentile parents and suddenly believing himself to have changed into a rabbi in mid-sentence.

Scott nevertheless persuaded Linda to leave Auckland with him, even to come back to London to try it again. He tried to lace the journey with the attractive proposition of what almost amounted to a round-the-world tour, returning via the States, adventures unlimited on a Diners Club card for which there was to be a fearsome financial reckoning in the months to come. She came back to Fulham and they tried to start afresh. But nothing much had really changed. The partnership lasted a few more months before Linda Poulton flew home.

Mary and Rebecca kept in touch. They would talk on the phone once a week. Mary would hear nothing against Ronnie despite the pain of those years. 'If he hurts other people he never means to, and he hurts himself just as much and maybe more,' she would say. She told him, as the darkest clouds passed and some of that old humour returned that had so charmed her in the Gerrard Street basement years ago, that they should try to put it behind them. And she never forgot all those images of how far into despair he could fall. In the worst months, Scott had sent to Mary all the photographs he had of his mother, grandmother and family. He wanted Rebecca to have something to remember him by when she grew up, to make sure that whatever happened they couldn't fall into anybody else's hands. It had been his way of saying goodbye.

# 12

# Take It From the Top

'Jazz is the expression of fleeting emotions.'
(Ronnie Scott to Kitty Grime, *Jazz at Ronnie Scott's*)

GRADUALLY, MUSIC PULLED Ronnie Scott back into the world.

He formed a quartet in the summer of 1975, following the American tour, which included the brilliant Irish guitarist Louis Stewart. It was the band he had wanted for years. Listening to the guitar always reminded him of the London of years gone by, hearing Django Rheinhart jamming until dawn with Dave Goldberg in that rabbit warren of an apartment in Charing Cross Road.

As for the club, it was not the only fish in the sea any more. The Jazz Centre Society, which had started so small, was developing a more adventurous policy of combining home-grown and imported talent than anyone had believed it could, and was attracting Arts Council funding to do it in proportions that rose healthily through the 1970s. There was also a risk that the booking policy at Frith Street, which was based on a mixture of fondness for saxophonists, the occasional presence of jazz-influenced nightclub singers to appeal to the casual and tourist audience, and great sentimental attachment to artists who were by now regular visitors, was going to be by-passed by the changing times.

Frith Street was Ronnie Scott's beat. He had no social sphere outside it, didn't need one. Mary wouldn't stay with him now, he knew that, though he believed that she still loved him. And he increasingly took to visiting the establishment's downstairs bar, a tiny room in the basement where the musicians would relax between sets. The barmaid there was French, another jazz fan and sometime painter called Francoise Venet. Francoise brought her own jazz records to work and played them over the downstairs sound system. Ronnie Scott began to confide in Francoise, tell her what he had been through, try to explain why it had shocked him so much. He distrusted analysis, thought that it might simply become a way of life, like it was for the people you laughed at in Woody Allen movies, but musicianspeak had no vocabulary for coping with what he was feeling.

The company of jazz musicians was a Catch 22. It was funny, colourful, intuitive and diverting but it was a predominantly male world and the inhabitants of it tended to be uncomprehending of mental difficulties, if not actually unsympathetic. Francoise became the understanding figure Ronnie Scott needed, and they were attracted to each other. Francoise was the daughter of a cartoonist, and took to drawing and painting the performers who were coming through the premises. She was also a skilful photographer. Francoise was soon to move into the Fulham flat.

She found that her new partner's sense of humour – a self-defence which had never left him even at the worst times – was shared by the professionals whose company he loved. And excellent artists were continuing to come and go in the club through the latter part of the 1970s – like Dexter Gordon, Sarah Vaughan, Dizzy Gillespie, Stan Getz and Art Blakey.

Scott particularly admired Gillespie, one of the pioneers of the music that had taken him over when he was hardly out of his teens. To have visited the 52nd Street clubs when Gillespie's playing, and his mannerisms, and his jokes were the talk of the London jazz circles and to find him there, answering an invitation in the reverse direction thirty years later, was sheer fascination. Gillespie, for all his clowning and bonhomie on stage, was pungently realistic about the jazz business. One night in the back room where they talked and played chess, Scott began talking with the trumpeter about the magic of jazz, the pull that kept musicians in thrall to it.

'It happens so seldom,' Scott said to Gillespie. 'Ninety-nine per cent of the time you play within boundaries. Then sometimes something happens and you break through it for a night, or an hour, or eight bars.'

'That's what the incentive is,' Gillespie agreed.

'How often do you think it's happened to you?' the Englishman enquired.

'About once every two years,' Gillespie unhesitatingly returned. The answer was an unsentimental reflection of the merciless demands of combining a sophisticated improvised music with the necessity to tour continually to make a decent living.

The club had become an institution. The comedian and writer Spike Milligan regularly visited, a jazz fan who became an invaluable friend. Princess Margaret visited the club, once occasioning what was regarded as a highly risque gag about her friendship with the comic actor Peter Sellers that Milligan persuaded Scott to read out to the audience. The papers next day were indignant. When the Princess arrived on the premises, doorman Jeff Ellison thought for a moment that at last the club might acquire a status that the music it presented had deserved for so long.

'We're fashionable now,' he said to Scott. 'With visitors like her, it'll make all the difference.'

'Who needs fashionable?' Scott enquired phlegmatically of Ellison. 'It means you're in for five minutes and then people forget all about you. We go on the way we always have done.'

In 1978 Mary sent young Rebecca over for a holiday. The little girl was by now a self-possessed, independent and funny six-year-old, full of mannerisms that reminded her mother of Ronnie – the same jokes, the same hilarious impressions, though Becky's memories of Ronnie were not much more defined than Ronnie's had been of Jock, and she was later to recall the eeriness of addressing a stranger at the end of a telephone as 'Daddy'. But the trip, intended as a two-week holiday, was to become a problem for all of them, Rebecca in particular.

Ronnie Scott was working in the club, keeping the same old hours and, though he was intrigued by the daughter he hardly knew, had no idea how to handle the relationship. Much of the responsibility for looking after Rebecca consequently fell on Francoise. And this responsibility was soon extended because immigration difficulties prevented the child from being returned to the States when the two weeks were up. Francoise stopped work to look after her but resented the responsibility. She found a school for her – which Rebecca was indignant to find herself despatched to – when the visit ran on into months, and eventually life at the flat became so tense that she finished her stay at the house of old friends Harry and Harriett South. Pete King bought Rebecca two colossal dolls as big as herself that Christmas. After frantic weeks of enquiries, Mary was finally able to bring the girl back through Canada. She had to leave the dolls behind.

Ronnie Scott and Francoise then took a step that the saxophonist's friends would hitherto have considered unthinkable. He had already put down firmer roots than ever before by buying the Fulham flat, a cheap deal for a long-time tenant. Now his relationship with Francoise seemed secure enough to risk finding out what 'settling down' actually meant. After all, Pete King and his family seemed to have an agreeable existence in the suburbs. Maybe in those years of rejecting all that, he had just been punishing himself.

Ronnie and Francoise bought a big semi-detached house in West

Hampstead. Ronnie could practise the saxophone without bothering any-body, they could keep a dog and a cat, put an end to living in a shoebox. But for Ronnie Scott there was something comforting and womb-like about a little flat in a beehive like the apartment in Fulham. The open spaces of comfortable, middle-class territory like Hampstead seemed to shout at him. The couple stayed at the house through 1979, and set about building a life in it. There was to be a music room for Ronnie, the first he had ever had. There was to be a painting room for Francoise. They made plans, chose a decor, hired builders.

But there were too many decisions to make on things that Ronnie Scott had never taken the remotest interest in before, and had too little experi-ence of how much time and energy they could take up. Builders filled the house, with noise, dirt and themselves, and Ronnie and Francoise found it increasingly trying. Francoise was unsure why he had changed and put it down to such a disruption of his former habits of life.

He kept up an old hobby – betting. He would still gamble ferociously when the impulse took him – though he always insisted that he wasn't an addict of the horses as Uncle Mark had been, or as Jock had been, that there were limits to how far he would go or how much he would lose. But he ran the risks that made it exciting. On a tour of Wales with the quintet he formed in the late seventies, Ronnie Scott even lost the wages for the outfit in a Bangor betting shop, bored whilst the others were spending the after-noon talking guitars in a local music store owned by an enthusiast. By the last race he had £40 left out of over £700. He took a flyer on a combination forecast with the last of the money, and though the odds were stacked mas-sively against him the bet came up. He won back the £700 and came out £300 ahead. He would still wistfully say that he wished he had back the money he had lost, willingly swapped for his winnings over the years. But it was too much of a diverting recreation to leave alone. Francoise would watch him glued to the television sports on Saturday afternoons, one hand on the telephone.

Great music continued sporadically to be heard in that smoky, and increas-ingly seedy, low-ceilinged room (when the original decorations faded, nei-ther Scott nor King were the types to notice the difference) but the proprietors had to face the fact that they were in business and businesses all around the country were ruefully reflecting that they had known better days. The recession was biting and the weakness of the pound against the dollar meant that American artists demanded higher fees just to keep up. Promotion had never been more crucial to the survival of the establishment. Scott would use a gag in his routines in later years that ran: 'We'd like you to eat, drink and enjoy yourselves. Pretend you're on the *Titanic*.' In 1980, that was more or less the situation they were in.

In the course of trying to sharpen up the club's image Pete King and Brian Theobald (the man who had broken into Scott's flat in that oblivion of 1974 and who was now running the club's touring arrangements) were having to cope with the mixture of shyness, laziness, diffidence and single-mindedness about simply playing jazz that characterised their front man. It had already become obvious that Scott would hardly ever record, even when the prospects were lucrative, insisting that he hated hearing himself on disc, that he found the studio inhibiting and even disliked live performance when he knew the tapes were running.

He was a good salesman for the club when actually working on the premises, and that mixture of mischievousness and unwillingness to be obseqious that had been his trademark throughout the club's life enhanced if anything the effect. He had done a legendary double-take on the soul superstar Isaac Hayes one night, who had arrived in the foyer wearing a massive fur hat. Scott didn't recognise him, looked at the hat and remarked, 'When that has puppies, can I have one?' Hayes wasn't amused, and promptly left.

Scott's unwillingness to go out of his way to sell himself or the club extended to the Michael Parkinson television chat show, which King and Theobald saw as one of the only peak-viewing showcases for jazz. Parkinson loved the music, and usually included jazz acts for the musical interlude. After some wheedling, they managed to persuade Parkinson to include Ronnie as a guest, during a week in which the Woody Herman orchestra was in the club and not doing good business. But when the contract came through for the show, Ronnie Scott didn't want to do it. King rarely tried to talk his partner out of decisions, but sensed that a good performance on *Parkinson* might save Herman's season.

They eventually persuaded Scott. He found himself appearing as a guest with songwriter Arthur Schwarz and the actor Robert Powell, and didn't push himself with them, exhibiting his usual reserve in unfamiliar company. After a while he actually appeared to be asleep, legs crossed, his trousers ridden up above his socks, head lolling back. Parkinson turned the conversation to ambiguous song titles. Powell and Schwarz were stuck. The host sprang it on Scott, convinced he wasn't even listening. The saxophonist barely opened his eyes, and without shifting the loafing pose muttered, 'The Party's Over

– it's all over my friend.' It wasn't so much the gag as the delivery. Parkinson and his guests cracked up, so did many of the studio staff. Woody Herman's band played a spot on the show, and the club was packed for the rest of his run.

The club's economics had always been such that a short down period would cancel out the virtues of months of good business. In 1980 there was a new and more pressing problem. Value Added Tax had forced King, grumbling furiously, to become a reluctant bookkeeper for the government when it replaced Purchase Tax in the early seventies. King found that though he ought to be saving some of the operation's proceeds for the bill that would one day come, the demands of the artists were more pressing, and easier to sympathise with.

King received an enquiry from a VAT officer to make an inspection of the club's books. He duly set up an appointment for the inspector, then got another call not long afterward, ostensibly on the same business.

'I thought we'd just made an appointment,' King said, mystified.

'Well, who are you expecting to see?' asked the government man. King told him. There was a short silence. 'Ah. That's not us, that's a long way up the hierarchy.' It was an ominous signal.

When the Customs and Excise arrived, they threw the club into crisis. After a long investigation, they left Scott and King with a bill for £40,000, backdated to when VAT began.

It was a potentially fatal blow. The two men could lay hands on £20,000, and undertook to pay the rest in instalments. But business wasn't good enough to keep up with the payments.

'If you'd been shrewd businessmen you'd have seen this coming,' somebody said to King.

'If we were shrewd businessmen we wouldn't be here at all,' King replied.

The club's accountants could see no other route but receivership. However, if the receiver was open enough to permit the two men to try to buy back their premises once the tangle had been sorted out, it might be possible to stay in the jazz business. The receivers were Martin Spencer and John Pappy, at the time trying to pull the Chelsea Football Club out of its difficulties. Spencer took on the job on 16 July 1980, looked at every detail of the club's operations, suggested ways of cutting costs and stayed with the operation for a year. At the end of that time things hadn't got much better. 'Look, you're losing this. You'll have to sell,' Spencer eventually informed Scott and King.

The premises went on to the market in the following year. The estate agent's brochure claimed that the club ought to have annual profits of £100,000. Initially Scott and King were surprised by the number of people they had previously regarded as supporters who tried to take advantage of their difficulties and buy the lease themselves once they knew of the situation. But there was an unexpected saving grace. Charles Forte, the original landlord of the premises, had included in the first lease a clause to the effect that it could not be reassigned. Scott and King had to be the owners. They also had somehow to raise the money to cover the obligation or go bust. They were looking for £110,000. It might as well have been a million.

Maybe as a reaction to life not seeming fair any more, or his gathering discontent with Hampstead home-owning, or his progress into his fifties, Ronnie Scott's gremlins came back. His fits of depression grew harder to cope with, until Francoise finally left to return to France in 1981.

Another younger woman entered his life, a student who had visited the club with an older sister, who was renting a room in the flat of Joe Green, an old associate of Scott and King. She played the clarinet and wanted saxophone lessons. That the whole scenario already smacked of a French farce was perfectly obvious to Scott, who this time knew what he wanted to do was crazy and proceeded to dive resolutely in. To begin with, the newcomer was intrigued by the idea of a relationship with the middle-aged owner of a world-renowned nightclub who was also a famous saxophone player. But Scott soon descended into the depths he thought he had left behind, and as he did his new partner thought twice about what she was getting into.

The close proximity of comedy and tragedy in what followed was of the kind that Scott's own sense of humour was founded on, but it would take time before he was to be able to turn it to account. The student lived in Brighton and shared a house with college friends. Scott took to visiting there without invitation, often getting drunk in the bar on the train. Sometimes he would find himself in desultory conversation with her house-mates who, he began to realise, were treating him with a kind of bewildered sympathy, as if he were suffering from a peculiarly ignominious form of dementia. 'Relationships end, you know,' Ronnie Scott heard an eighteen-year-old boy declaring earnestly to him over the teacups. Another suggested that he ring the Samaritans.

She loved piano music, particularly Chopin, but couldn't afford an instrument of her own. Ronnie Scott bought her a piano in Brighton on the proceeds of a bet, tried to have it delivered without telling her. The boy who ran the household came out of his room as the delivery men were struggling up the stairs. He immediately looked shocked.

'Oh, I don't think so,' he muttered anxiously. 'I don't know if she wants it in her room. I don't know if she wants it at all.'

'All right, if she doesn't want it I'll take it away again. I just want to surprise her, that's all . . .'

It was no good. The routine was worthy of Laurel and Hardy. They took it all down again, then brought it back when its intended recipient returned and enthusiastically welcomed it. But the gift didn't save the relationship. She was tired of it, Ronnie Scott wasn't. Soon after she finished her course, he lost touch with her.

He called Francoise, asked her what she thought about him selling the Hampstead house and moving back to Fulham. 'It's not up to me, it's up to you,' Francoise said. 'Do what you feel happiest with.'

But Ronnie Scott was hurled back into the dark by the experience. This time it was Ilsa who was on hand to take the mother's role, coming to the flat to cook for him. Once again he had seriously lost weight. Ilsa was surprised to find that hardly anybody seemed to visit, except Spike Milligan, whose relationship with Ronnie deepened at that time. Familiar with mental pain himself, the comedian would send cabs to Fulham, ferry Ronnie to his Barnet home to talk, drink, listen to music.

He tried to stay on the road just the same, but he was increasingly cancelling gigs, and was a hard partner to travel with. John Critchenson, his piano player from 1979 (and gradually to become a close friend), recalled long hours on motorways spent in total silence broken only by the band-leader's occasional weary ejaculations of 'Oh shit' and 'Aaah fuck'. Critchenson would sometimes wait for elaborations that rarely came. Often he would say, 'Listen, I'm going to turn the radio on, your scintillating conversation's sending me to sleep.' Scott didn't resent these rejoinders, and the close proximity month in month out bonded a relationship with Critchenson that the piano player was later to describe as almost brotherly.

But it had its volatile moments then. Sick or healthy, loyalty to a band was one of the few things Ronnie Scott could be stung to rage about. When Critchenson began to divide his time between the Scott band and saxophonist Dick Morrissey's funk outfit with guitarist Jim Mullen, Scott initially confronted the pianist with the observation that it was them or him. But the bandleader relented, saw the relationship with Critchenson as something worth saving, musically and personally. He rang through one night to say: 'You're the pianist I want to work with. I'm going into hospital now, but when I come out I'll be better, and I want you there then.' He made no other stipulations.

Once again, Ronnie Scott was caught by surprise by emotions he had never come to terms with. Francoise knew, as Mary had known, that he was mortified by the havoc he caused, and that his regrets were not a self-indulgence. She missed him as much as he found he was missing her. Eventually she would come back to England, and back to him, though they wouldn't live together again.

All these diversions had made things harder for Pete King, on whose shoulders the strain of the club's financial crisis had fallen. He would ruefully shake his head at his partner's preoccupations. 'Every time he gets into something nice, he goes and fucks it up,' he would complain to Stella.

She agreed. 'But he stays friends with them, in the end,' Stella pointed out.

It was all true. The calls from Mary and from Joan Crewe in America would keep on coming. He and Francoise became very close. But it was hard for Ronnie Scott to concentrate on the crisis in the club. Often he would cast a look of entreaty at King and ask: 'What shall we do?' When accountants told them to quit, it was King (partly motivated, he later said, by a desperation about what else he might do with his life) who flatly refused to, and Scott who would almost humbly confirm: 'Pete says we go on.'

One night in the autumn of 1981, when the remarkable teenage gypsy guitarist Bireli Lagrene was in residence, Pete King was attending to the club's sound system when a stranger came over to him and said, 'Hi Pete, how are you?' King couldn't place him but knew he was from the record business. The visitor began to ask about the fortunes of the club, said he'd heard that things were bad. King was impatient and preoccupied at first, but he could see that the other man was genuinely interested and didn't simply seem like someone gloating or anxious to step into their shoes.

'So you want to pay off the debt and carry on?' the man asked.

King nodded.

'Are you going to be running it yourself?'

'Yes.'

'Just the same way you always have?'

'We don't know any other way,' King replied.

'If you're going to be running it, then put me down for £25,000.' The speaker was Chris Blackwell, boss of Island Records, who had built his business out of West Indian music and who had been known to Ronnie Scott and Pete King since the Gerrard Street days. King swears he cried as Blackwell walked away.

They tried other avenues too. The Greater London Council under Labour leader Ken Livingstone had a reputation for interest in the progressive arts, particularly where ethnic minorities were concerned, but after several preparatory conversations about it and a meeting with the council's supremo, Lord Birkett, nothing was followed up. They went to the Arts Council too, for only the second time in nearly two decades, but once again got nowhere. Despite the nature of the music they presented, Ronnie Scott's Club was still perceived in establishment cultural circles as part of Tin Pan Alley, not the elevated arts. Its proprietors were middle-aged Eastenders with no comprehension of the language of arts lobbying, the convolutions of committee politics, the limitless patience and detailed reading of minutes and technicalities. They were worlds apart.

Eventually it was the old stagers who came through. The Musicians' Union, partly through the good offices of jazz fans Brian Blain and Johnny Patrick, and with the support of the general secretary John Morton, agreed to lend Scott and King £30,000. With Blackwell's contribution they were halfway there. Then they went to Charrington's, the brewery that had held the club franchise. At first, the firm believed it might be throwing good money after bad, but eventually agreed to help, though adding to the obligations the repayment of the outstanding debt. With a final contribution from the Performing Rights Society, the lease was secured. It was a remarkable testament to the affection and respect in which Ronnie Scott and Pete King's long contribution to the British music scene was regarded, in some quarters at least.

Slowly, they and fate pulled the club round.

The proprietors' part in it was principally down to Pete King. King had always privately conceded that when it looked as if there was no hope, his motivation to forge on was both love of his work and terror about his job prospects. As a long-retired saxophone player who had then spent the prime of his life running a jazz club, he was beginning to see himself in these troubled times as an expert in an unsustainable line of work.

Necessity and a profound affection for jazz, its practitioners, and the club's crucial place in the jazz firmament made King throw himself wholeheartedly into a rescue. As in the early days of Ronnie Scott's surreal *Melody Maker* ads, the club needed to go out to the public more and, in particular, dispel the widespread belief that 'Ronnie's' cost an arm and a leg to spend an evening in. King developed a shrewd membership scheme whereby for a small annual sum members were offered very cheap admission on weekdays. It brought in a new and younger public, one that could help to guarantee a longer term future.

Yet it had to remain a jazz club. If there was no alternative but to turn the establishment over to cabaret or pop music to keep it afloat, Scott and King would reluctantly but finally have concluded it was time to throw in the towel. But they didn't need to. After a decade in which jazz was marginalised as a minority interest, popular taste was swinging back.

Ronnie Scott and Pete King didn't know it yet, but a sea-change was happening in other London clubs. Not well-equipped, big-time, high-profile establishments like theirs, but one-night-a-week clubs in modest rooms used for other purposes the rest of the time, with audiences mostly under twenty years old, dancing to the selections of an increasingly eclectic and creative group of disc jockeys who had grown tired of the regimentation, predictability and anonymity of the seventies disco. In the States, breakdancing and hip-hop developed alongside more participatory, assertive pursuits like rapping (spontaneous, highly rhythmic street-life poetry) and graffiti art. Dancing styles became freer, as a tightening recession and growing youth unemployment in the West intensified urges toward self-expression and the search for alternative notions of self-respect. The upshot was, you could dance to anything – and improvisation was gaining respect as an approach to art and life.

Some of the new British DJs, like the young jazz fan Paul Murphy, rediscovered the jazz classics, combed the racks in the specialist shops for old Blue Note discs, encouraged the audiences to develop dances to tracks Art Blakey and other hard bop stars had laid down twenty years previously. The exoticism of Soho clubland was promoted again, with the filming of Soho chronicler Colin MacInnes's book *Absolute Beginners* in London, featuring a jazzy score arranged by veteran compositional genius and long-time Miles Davis partner Gil Evans.

Gradually, these changes began to filter through to the box office at Ronnie Scott's Club. Takings went up. Jazz began to acquire a cachet it hadn't had since the fifties, as a badge of sophisticated taste and discrimination. Regular favourites of Scott's and King's, like the irrepressible veteran drummer Art Blakey, found an enthusiastic new audience in Britain for fundamental values of hard-swinging jazz.

Blakey came to Ronnie Scott's as regularly as the seasons. Approaching seventy now, but still playing like a typhoon, he had seen his kind of jazz go in and out of style over the decades but never wavered from a barging, jubilant, gospel and blues-drenched version of bebop that had also furnished a demanding apprenticeship to some of the best improvisors in the business. And Blakey's most celebrated apprentice of the 1980s was undoubtedly Wynton Marsalis.

Marsalis was the New Orleans-born trumpet virtuoso (son of pianist and teacher Ellis Marsalis and one of several gifted jazz-playing siblings) who joined Blakey when he was barely eighteen, left the Frith Street audiences gasping at his precocity at the beginning of the decade and who was touring as a bandleader two years later. In 1982 Marsalis brought a group of his own for a once-only visit to Ronnie Scott's Club as leader.

From the promoters' points of view, it wasn't a success. Marsalis disliked the place, took issue with some of the European dates Pete King's associate Brian Theobald had booked for him, and left London before his full run of engagements at Frith Street were complete. But the appearances he did make, even if his heart wasn't in it, were enough to confirm the single-mindedness of his approach, and his superlative technique and mature grasp of the subtle beauties of the music. Marsalis was the diametric opposite of the jazz radicals of the 1960s, unconvinced that the search for a contemporary music necessitated dramatic departures from the past.

Yet his reinterpretations of the methods of Miles Davis's groups of the early sixties – Marsalis's principal preoccupation at this time – came uncannily close to capturing the spirit of one of the greatest bands in all jazz. His trumpet solos exhibited a poise and far-sightedness rare in an improvisational art, sweeping over the harmonic architecture they were based on, oscillating between long, serpentine melodic figures and periodic percussive accents to sketch out the beat, resolutions in unexpected places, juggling of perfectly shaped notes and occasional muttering off-pitch ones for contrast. Marsalis echoed and developed Miles Davis's scalding collaborations with his percussionist Tony Williams in the unpredictable accelerations and decelerations of the time delivered by a remarkable and original drummer, Jeff 'Tain' Watts.

Though Marsalis's unwillingness to play out his season on the 1982 trip left a bruise on Scott and King that time wasn't to heal, his brief visit was an indelible memory to those who were present and his musical authority, expertise and obvious love of jazz and devotion to its history perfectly equipped him to be the role model for young musicians he was to become as the decade unfurled. He was eventually such a walking definition of the revival of interest in jazz that he adorned the cover of *Time* magazine under the headline 'The New Jazz Age'.

Marsalis did return to Ronnie Scott's Club the next year, though not as a performer. He arrived at the door with a group of friends and fellow musicians, intending to hear a show by his old employer, Art Blakey. The door staff, knowing of the previous year's tensions called for the proprietor. 'Sorry, you're not welcome here,' Scott said, when he realised who the visitor was. Marsalis looked aggrieved, but didn't make a fight of it.

'Why didn't you let him in, man, he's a musician like us,' Art Blakey asked later on.

'I don't give a fuck if he's Jesus Christ,' Scott replied without ceremony. A man with a notoriously bad memory, Scott always remembered what he perceived as disloyalty. But the club didn't go short of superstars.

Nina Simone was a legendary performer on a wave of renewed popularity, and a series of visits in the early eighties brought packed houses. A dramatic and sometimes spine-chilling exponent of both gospel and soul and the European legacy of Weill and Piaf too, Simone was proof that purist notions of what jazz was or wasn't had truly lost their currency, since no two of her performances were exactly the same, her piano playing was wilful and quirky, and her blending of many of the world's musical persuasions had long prefigured the eclecticism of the 1980s. However balefully quiet Nina Simone's performances could be at times, they always veiled the ever-present threat of that whiplash timbre when she turned the intensity up, and the way she could establish an atmosphere of dangerous intimacy with an audience gave a fierce resonance to every word she uttered.

Simone was also exactly the kind of unpredictable and volatile individual that Scott and King rather liked as proprietors, because it appealed to their downbeat sense of theatre. They always accepted an artist's eccentricities without complaint as long as they felt the performer had earned the right to be ungovernable, and would actually show up and play with reasonable consistency. For Nina Simone's part, though her mannerisms often seemed to threaten an imminent eruption, liked the club and its audiences, and regularly turned up, though she would often arrive on the bandstand straight from a cab, wearing a fur coat and white trainers and carrying a Tesco shopping bag. She also insisted on being provided with a chicken kiev and a bottle of champagne on the house. The club's driver Joe Green would run her back to the Grosvenor House hotel in the small hours after the show, and one night he discovered the fridge in her suite was bulging with chicken kievs. As in many areas in her life, Nina Simone had just wanted to make a point.

Another unpredictable favourite of the early eighties at the club was the trumpeter and singer Chet Baker. Baker had been a star of the West Coast 'cool school' jazz movement of the 1950s, as much for his soft, romantic singing and James Dean physical charisma as for his obliquely inventive trumpet playing, but narcotics addiction had knocked gaping holes in what should have been a continuously fruitful career, and by the time he was appearing at Ronnie Scott's Club he was fragile, prematurely aged, and musically inconsistent. But audiences hung on the sublime moments that glittered among the ashes of his talent. On a tune like 'Love For Sale' Baker's trumpet sound would border on evaporation, his wraith-like breath hardly seeming to disturb the harmonics of the instrument on its way through the metalwork. On vocals, his pitching was often awry, but his rhythmic sense and swing unerring, and the result on a handful of bars was frequently more expressive than a concert-worth of music by more polished but lightweight artists.

When he wasn't playing, Baker would usually be curled up in the cramped 'office' at the back of the stage, among the drumkits and sound equipment, huddled as if trying to make himself vanish, occasionally talking in his slow, semi-absent manner, sometimes terrified to face his audience, sometimes playing – as Ronnie Scott later put it – 'like an angel' at just the times when he appeared least capable of standing, let alone making inspired music. Baker's distress, like that of many artists, became a predictable, if regrettable element in his audience appeal. The jutting cheekbones, the fathomless lines in a sunken face, the crumpled seated posture with the trumpet pointing toward the floor, they all became the Baker people expected to see. Yet he could achieve an almost unbearable poignancy on themes like his favourite 'Almost Blue' and 'My Funny Valentine', shift pace from plush mid-register phrases to sudden flares, as if a shaft of sunlight were suddenly entering a shadowy room. It was the kind of spontaneous and personal music, made without regard for marketing niches, or column inches, or leisure-industry fashions, that Ronnie Scott's Club existed to nurture.

Off the bandstand, Ronnie Scott's relationship with his daughter Rebecca, now ten, was settling into something that almost resembled a pattern. He would visit New York twice a year at least, and when he did he would take Rebecca out for walks in Greenwich Village, a locality where the vivid streetlife, recalling the cosmopolitan optimism of the East End, took him back to his own childhood. One night in 1983 they pursued the same expedition, winding up in a Chinese restaurant where Mary was waiting for them, then went to check out the jazz at the Village Gate. As the night wore on, it was as if the years of pain and doubt had fallen away from Scott. He ran through his repertoire of rubber-face caricatures, and the ten-year-old stayed with him for every move, until the club's audience came close to finding the unadvertised show almost as diverting as the one on the stage, Mary was so captivated she asked a photographer to capture the moment on camera

By 1984, with the threat of closure a fading memory, it began to look as if celebrations for the coming twenty-fifth anniversary might herald the beginning of a new era rather than simply an expression of astonished relief at having come as far as this at all.

# 13

# Old Times

'Jazz allows you to sound fifty when you are fifty. When you are nineteen you should sound nineteen. Jazz allows you to tell the truth.'
Max Roach to Kitty Grime, *Jazz Voices*)

IN NOVEMBER 1984, a month after the twenty-fifth anniversary celebrations,
Denis Rose died.

His departure was a shock, even for those old hipsters, the ageing delin-
quents who had, as the beat jargon went, 'lived for kicks' in the war years
and the 1950s, who had tried to express – as Charlie Parker had instinctively done – an impassivity to everything but playing. Rose was so much a
part of that world, so languidly and expertly a professional at the art of survival in the big city, and so generous and obsessive a teacher of the music
he loved, that his loss seemed to cruelly resolve that episode that had begun
in the shattered London of 1942 and which had seemed like an everlasting
*now*. He had been forgotten by everyone but musicians, but accepted his
obscurity, playing piano in Denman Street pubs, teaching occasionally in a
room full of music and copies of the *Racing Chronicle*. 'I'm free,' he would
say. 'I can play what I like. I don't need to shave, and I don't need to be on
the spot all the time like Ronnie.'

The funeral was on a bleak November day in New Southgate, north
London, the old stamping ground of Rose and Laurie Morgan. Ronnie Scott
was particularly distressed by the death of Rose, a man whom he felt had
set him on the right path when he might never have understood the
mechanics of the music sufficiently to discover it alone. Ronnie Scott and
Laurie Morgan were there as the rain slanted over the gravestones. So was
Tony Crombie, Lennie Bush, Jeff Ellison, Pete King, and many others.
Rose's family put a toy piano on the earth where the musician was buried.

It was not a celebration of Rose's immense virtues, and it was not a wake. It was a dour, grey occasion, and one to prompt some personal reflections. Laurie Morgan, staying in the Midlands with the retired alto saxophonist from Club Eleven days, Johnny Rogers, had remarked before Rose's death that it was a pity that so many of the pioneers had gone their separate ways. 'We'll have to be careful that we don't just meet at funerals,' Morgan had said.

In early 1985, Pete King and his wife Stella took their first holiday for years, and in the process forged another link in the chain that hauled Ronnie Scott's Club back to the shore. It wasn't the holiday King might have planned, it started inauspiciously with lost luggage and interminable diversions, and it resulted in the least likely of bedfellows becoming passionate partners, but it changed the character of the musical calendar at Ronnie Scott's more than any other single event in the rocky years after receivership.

Pete and Stella King were invited to Cuba.

Ronnie Scott had previously visited the country as a performer, participating in the spectacular annual music festival. He told his partner that the cultural agencies of the tiny, beleagured island were anxious to treat Pete as an honoured guest, with the aim of promoting trade. 'For Christ's sake, go,' Ronnie told Pete King. 'The musical quality out there is incredible.'

This was a fact that the capitalist world had woken up to already. Irakere, one of the leading Cuban bands, and with two sensational soloists in trumpeter Arturo Sandoval and altoist Paquito D'Rivera in its ranks, had recorded for CBS in 1978 – becoming the first Cuban ensemble in two decades to work for a US label. The next year the American company and the Cuban government started co-promoting high-profile local events, and the world began to notice what a wealth of talent the island had been harbouring.

This was the climate in which Pete King, as the business half of one of the most famous jazz clubs in the world, was invited to Havana. But it was a trip in the best traditions of the club's disputes with fate. On a freezing February day the plane from London was iced up and missed the connection in Madrid. The recommended detour involved flying to Montreal and then down to Mexico City, and by the time Pete and Stella arrived there in the middle of the night, dressed in tracksuits and carrying a single overnight bag, their luggage was long gone in another direction. The two Londoners didn't make a happy couple on the plane from Mexico City to Havana, and their complaints were overheard by a man in an adjoining seat.

'If I can be of any help, Mr King, please let me know. By the way, how's Ronnie?'

It was the regional representative for the ICI corporation, a long-time fan of the club, who had recently seen an American broadcast of the British TV coverage of the twenty-fifth anniversary. He took charge of weary travellers, gave them a lift to the British Embassy in Havana, helped them sort out the tangled logistics. And the tribulations of the journey were forgotten as soon as the Londoners witnessed the Havana Jazz Festival. King was astonished by the playing standard. Though he had witnessed the exuberant and vivacious appeal of the country's music at first hand in the club, through the regular visits of American-based Cuban bands like Mongo Santamaria's and Machito's, the younger generation of Cuban performers (frequently highly trained in classical music as well as steeped in the American jazz traditions absorbed in the pre-revolutionary period) delivered a completely fresh and distinctive mixture of African music, jazz, salsa, soul and European classical ideas. Though Irakere, one of the foremost Havana bands, was now without its most spectacular soloists (Paquito D'Rivera and Arturo Sandoval had by this time both left) it was still a thrilling and theatrical ensemble in live performance, and pianist Gonzalo Rubalcaba and fusion bands such as Afro-Cuba were not far behind.

King immediately struck a deal with the Cuban cultural agencies to stage a long festival of the country's music at the club the following summer. He knew the Cuban musicians' expertise and freshness would be a hit with the London audiences. The new bands also sidestepped a growing problem in making attractive bookings at the club. Many high-profile international jazz performers were becoming increasingly expensive to hire, and several of the most prominent younger ones were coming to dislike the atmosphere of nightclubs, preferring to tour concert halls. The Cubans, keen to build bridges with Europe, were relatively inexpensive. They were also new faces, and Ronnie Scott's Club perpetually faced the marketing problem of repackaging familiar acts.

Not long after King's return to London, Zoot Sims died of cancer on 23 March 1985, in New York, at the age of fifty-nine. For both King and Ronnie Scott it was a loss that hurt more than most, and their attachment to the easy-going tenorist who had been the first American to perform as a guest in that shabby basement in Gerrard Street twenty-four years before ran deep. Sims died on a Saturday and Scott, for whom the American saxo-phonist held a special place as a player, a friend, and a milestone in his own life, immediately decided to fly to the States.

The banks were shut, but Scott and King managed to scrape together the money for the fare between them. When Ronnie Scott reached New York he called Mary's number. Rebecca came on the line.

'Where's your mummy?' Ronnie asked her.

'She's gone to Zoot's memorial service,' Rebecca replied.

'Well, that's where I'm going too,' Ronnie said. 'If she calls you, don't tell her I'm here.'

Sims's memorial service was at St Peter's Lutheran Church in Manhattan, and the attendance was massive. Benny Goodman, Annie Ross and Sims's old employer Woody Herman were there, and a procession of other jazz artists included in a gathering that probably numbered eight hundred. Mary was waiting inside, trying to find Annie Ross, whom she had agreed to meet. Dan Morgenstern, the jazz writer, came over and remarked, 'There's an obituary for Zoot in the *New York Times* and Ronnie's mentioned several times in it.'

In that instant, she saw him arrive at the church out of the corner of her eye. Though the occasion was sad, Ronnie had exhibited an old relish for a surprise. But when he and Mary sat together in the church and the pastor in turn surprised him by inviting him to come to the lectern to remember Zoot in his own way, Ronnie Scott was frozen to the pew.

'Mary,' he hissed to her in anguish. 'I can't go up there. What am I going to say?'

'Just improvise,' Mary told him. 'You'll find the words.' She reminded him of what it would mean to Louise, Zoot's widow.

In the event, he found a way through it. But he couldn't help insisting that he wasn't really the one they should be asking. He didn't know if words existed to account for the gratitude, love and admiration he felt for Sims, as a player and as a man. Scott and Sims between them had seen the music world change out of all recognition – and the wider world still more so. The Englishman recalled sitting in the bandroom with Sims when the American astronauts first landed on the moon. Sims remarked: 'Jesus! They're walking on the moon and I'm still playing "Indiana".'

With the Cuban music festival set up for a six-week summer run, audiences also witnessed unmistakeable evidence that the revival of fortunes and inspiration on the British jazz scene was no mirage. That young players now found it natural to consider a life devoted to jazz, that enthusiasm for it no longer made them oddities or outsiders, was symbolised by the arrival of Loose Tubes, a big cooperatively run orchestra that had formed the previous year from the nucleus of a student band run by composer/teacher Graham Collier.

Loose Tubes didn't have a leader, but its unofficial presiding young genius was a pianist by the name of Django Bates, an urchin-like figure who would frequently appear on stage wearing frock-coats and outlandish hats and who quickly demonstrated himself to be a keyboard soloist to rival anyone on the instrument in the length and breadth of the land.

Loose Tubes was different from all the famous big bands – Woody Herman's, Buddy Rich's, Thad Jones and Mel Lewis's, the Kenny Clarke-Francy Boland band – that had appeared in Ronnie Scott's Club before. Except in one respect – it retained all the wide-screen, visceral excitement of a traditional jazz orchestra's roaring brass effects and big, slamming, percussive impact. But it didn't follow the regimented course of repeated 'riff' patterns behind soloists, it didn't use orthodox big band materials (the pieces were usually generated by the band members themselves, and from a much wider variety of sources than the jazz heritage alone) and it was prepared to take chances at every opportunity.

The material would draw on African hi-life, bop, soca, funk, rock 'n' roll, Latin dance sounds, and free-jazz. Sometimes it sounded like fairground roundabout music, sometimes like English traditional folk-music being played by John Coltrane's Ascension band. The Quebec-born trombonist and occasional MC, Ashley Slater, once announced in a TV interview that he had been attracted to the playing of Django Bates because he was one of the few young jazz pianists he'd come across who 'didn't sound as if he was trying to clone off Chick Corea'. They all intensely disliked what they characterised as the Radio Two notion of how big bands should sound, and sensed there was a growing audience for a new concept in big-band jazz.

Enterprisingly, the British Musicians' Union extended its old creative relationship with Ronnie Scott's Club by fronting some money for a short season devoted to young British players, which included Loose Tubes' confident and impressive week.

Three generations of British jazz players, including others from the bloom of its youth, were also showcased on the jazz media event of 1985, when the Rolling Stones' drummer Charlie Watts, a longtime jazz fan, put together his own big band for a season at the club, drawing on the best

British musicians from several schools of jazz. Watts's criterion for selection was simply the players he liked.

This gargantuan orchestral project cost Charlie Watts, who had been a swing band fan since childhood, £30,000 to stage, and caused him to quip, 'I had to buy the club to put this on.' An illustrious line-up included Stan Tracey and Bobby Wellins, and the tenorist Danny Moss – looking for all the world like the middle-aged proprietor of a country pub – and Alan Skidmore and Don Weller from the Old Place generation, contemporaries of John Surman and Tony Oxley. And there was Courtney Pine on tenor too, a young black Londoner who loved Coltrane and also loved the incentive of trying to surprise a group of calculatingly casual jazzers some of whom obviously thought they'd heard it all before.

Pine was the most conspicuous figure in the renaissance of vitality in British jazz. The country's West Indian community had been influential in local jazz for years, its traditional musical materials of calypso and then reggae music from the Caribbean merging with blues, soul and funk influences from the States. But apart from a few remarkable Caribbean jazz players (Joe Harriott, Shake Keane, Harry Beckett, Harold McNair) and some South African expatriates, the community of British jazz players was mostly white from the 1950s to the 1970s, and so was the audience.

Pine's generation of young black Londoners were already becoming aware of a movement in their midst that was turning into a fast-flowing current. On the Guildhall School of Music's jazz course, an open and enterprising project that enlisted students by raw talent rather than paper qualifications, there were reed players Philip Bent, Jeff Gordon and Steve Williamson, and vocalist Cleveland Watkiss, among many others. Saxophonist Gail Thompson and trombonist/arranger Fayyaz Virji were formally trained in the enlightened music department of a high-flying south London comprehensive school, Kingsdale in Dulwich. Such a range of opportunities didn't exist for would-be jazz musicians even a decade before. It boded well for the growth and maturity of the British jazz scene, and for Ronnie Scott's Club as one of its focal points.

Lack of role models and the economics of working-class West Indian life in Britain had mostly kept blacks from the jazz world from the fifties to the eighties. Then a growing number of refugees from pop and funk bands began looking for bigger challenges, and soon there were enough to form an all-black orchestra, the Jazz Warriors. The seeds of the Warriors were sown in the saxophone section of the Charlie Watts band in that Ronnie Scott's season, as Pine and baritone saxophonist Gail Thompson discussed a thrilling dream in the off-stage hours. For the new generation of black players, influences were as likely to include the soul sounds of Al Green, Marvin Gaye, and James Brown as John Coltrane or Charlie Parker. Courtney Pine, whose opinion counted for a great deal in this movement's early days, was also reluctant to use the orthodox jazz venues – including Ronnie's – as outlets for the new players and their music. There was a belief that the new audience was going to come from venues like Brixton's Fridge and Astoria, rather than from upmarket West End nightclubs. Many of these young players, however, were regular visitors to Ronnie Scott's Club as a location for rewarding research. Scott's own band, at this point featuring drummer Martin Drew, pianist John Critchenson, trumpeter Dick Pearce and bassist Ron Mathewson, was often on superb form at this time, intelligently exploring precisely the territory between hard bop, Latin jazz and the relaxed, deliberate ensemble house style of Blue Note records in the sixties that the newcomers regarded as the sounds of a golden age.

And though the choice of music was much more of an apparent anachronism on the Charlie Watts season – a kind of private party in which a rich enthusiast hired his favourite players to perform an old-fashioned repertoire that wouldn't have been out of place in the Savoy Ballroom – it had considerable charm and certainly wasn't played the way the swing heroes of the thirties would have done it. It was also a showcase for an extraordinary diversity of British improvisors, of all persuasions and all ages. Saxophonist Evan Parker, for instance, had never passed through the bebop apprenticeship many of the older players in the orchestra had, and had started from a basis in the ideas of Coltrane and the sixties free-players. His solos treated chord structures only as guidelines rather than as harmonic prescriptions, and he often hurtled off into distant galaxies of raw, multiphonic atonalism that bore little direct relationship to the legacy of Ben Webster, Lester Young or any of the other swing-orchestra legends Charlie Watts loved. Reflecting on his devotion to jazz, Watts later declared to Q magazine: 'I love people who can improvise, same as I love painters and sculptors. They seem like amazing things to do with your life.'

Charlie Watts wanted to use his prestige and his considerable resources to show the world what the widest possible span of British jazz music now sounded like. And for Ronnie Scott and Pete King, the Watts Orchestra's players represented what British jazz had been able to become since the days of their own apprenticeship, when local jazz confidence was low and everything seemed better done by Americans.

It was, however, not to be an occasion for unseemly displays of emotion. Pete King propped up the bar as the band got underway, talking to The then*Times* critic Richard Williams. Watts, whose grasp of jazz drumming was enthusiastic but technically adequate rather than catalytic, had hired two excellent percussionists to flank him – the avantist John Stevens, and the Jazz Couriers' old drummer Bill Eyden.

'What do you think of it?' Williams asked King as the ferocious gal-lumphing and hammering got into its stride.

King gave it weighty consideration, puffing out his considerable chest. 'Needs another couple of drummers,' he finally returned.


In the autumn of 1985, some of the old habitues of Club Eleven decided to stage a reunion gig in its memory. Nearly all of its heroes were still alive – save for Denis Rose, to whom the show would be dedicated, and pianist Tommy Pollard, who had died years before. Ronnie Scott himself wasn't keen at the outset. He thought, as he put it, that nostalgia wasn't what it used to be. He disliked going back on his past, an activity that seemed to imply the sentimentality that he and his colleagues had always gone out of their way to ridicule, and which reminded him that he was nearing sixty, a prospect he didn't especially relish.

Jim Godbolt, the ex-promoter, jazz historian and editor of the club's house magazine, was the instigator. He managed to persuade the BBC to include a film of the performance in the schedule for a week of jazz pro-grammes in December 1985. And so on Sunday, 1 September, they got together to play it – two bands with Dankworth and Scott as the leaders, just the way it used to be. Crombie, the languid, free-swinging drummer behind Scott's ensemble, Laurie Morgan with his busier and more idiosyn-cratic style behind Dankworth's.

It wasn't just a sentimental occasion, for which allowances would have to be made. Some of the players who had not stayed in the music business were a little rusty, but their own surprise at how much fun it was shone through the music. John Dankworth, sometimes a cloistered-sounding soloist, played magnificently on a swooping, passionate version of 'Lover Man'.

Scott, notably on the classics of the bop repertoire, was as loose and flow-ing with ideas as at any time in his life, as inventive as on some of those out-of-town gigs with his quintet where he often played with less inhibitions than in 'the office'. And he sounded like a performer at ease with his materials. Not simply with bop, because he didn't play the music according to the style of one of the old heroes like Dexter Gordon or Sonny Stitt, but with much of the music that had come after it and which, in his own way, he had absorbed into a way of improvising that was truly his. And at the end of his solos, looking

166

relaxed and comfortable, he smiled with pleasure at his companions. It was a rare public softening of his usual studied indifference. He referred to the missing members, Rose and Pollard, in the announcements between tunes, paying a tribute to the contribution of Pollard ('who we regret is no longer with us – in fact he's no longer with anybody') and his mentor Rose, without whom the cause they were all celebrating might never have existed.

The club's finances were now beginning to straighten out. Box office takings were improving, and the programming was starting to hit a balance between a jazz enthusiast's ideal and a commercially rational policy. The jazz content always remained at the top of the list. There continued to be the annual visits of Art Blakey, and his delicate former pianist Cedar Walton began regularly to appear too, often with Billy Higgins, one of the most subtle drummers in jazz. There was even Anita O'Day, who had left such an indelible image on older jazz audiences with her appearance in the 1958 cult movie *Jazz On A Summer's Day*, wearing a hat with the wingspan of a bald eagle and singing 'Tea For Two'. Ms O'Day, who appeared during 1986, was a touching example of the way in which the club's booking policy respected creative musicians with a profound understanding of the nature of their art. In a repertoire that took in favourites like 'My Funny Valentine', 'Green Dolphin Street', Antonio Jobim's 'Wave', and 'S'Wonderful', the spirited sixty-seven-year-old singer was sometimes unsteady in pitch and insecure in her communication with her musicians, but those old skills that had mesmerised the Newport Festival audience so long ago – light, darting scatting and audacious dragging and speeding of the beat – were still in tune, and reminded anybody who needed reminding that jazz is a music that lets you be the person you are, or the person you've become, passing years and all.

Ronnie Scott's Club also lost contact with another great vocalist during this year, when it parted company with Nina Simone. Ms Simone's visits always packed the house to bursting, and for a performer with a reputation for single-mindedness and short temper, she had none the less given audiences who loved her a hundred per cent of her glowering energy and soulful power. It was too good to last. On the 1986 booking her timekeeping was slipping, until one night she didn't appear at all. Pete King was frantic, began ringing everyone he could think of who might have a clue as to the singer's whereabouts. A call then came through to him from a restaurant in the Fulham Road.

'Isn't Nina Simone working for you this week?' enquired a voice at the end of the line.

'She's supposed to be,' said the unhappy King. 'She hasn't shown up.'

'I know,' said the voice. 'She's at the next table.'

She had her reasons. But normal relations were hard to patch up.

In January 1987 Ronnie Scott celebrated his sixtieth birthday by not celebrating it, as usual. But he and King did make a concession to age they almost certainly wouldn't have considered in earlier years. A salesman from the private health insurance group BUPA visited the club, offering a special deal for those working in the theatrical and entertainment business. Neither man felt that the company's services were imminently necessary – King, for all his workaholicism and late hours, went road-training four times a week and pumped iron at Gold's Gym in the West End every day – but they joined anyway.

And as Ronnie Scott passed sixty, BBC Television broadcast its 'Jazz Week', a virtually unprecedented event for national TV, running nightly programmes that took in the work of the increasingly eclectic and inventive Loose Tubes at the Bath Festival (a predominantly classical music event, and therefore an indication both of the Tubes' rising status, and the growing acceptability of jazz in the wider world) and rising saxophone stars Andy Sheppard and Itchy Fingers. The BBC inadvertently took the gloss off the decision by deciding to axe one of its longest-running slots dedicated to new jazz music in the same year, when it took off the prestigious Radio Three *Jazz Today* show and its dedicated and erudite presenter Charles Fox, but generally the current seemed to be running the right way for a change.

In February 1988, Al Cohn, the jaunty and tuneful Brooklyn-born tenor saxophonist who shared his long-time partner Zoot Sims's ability to make tenor saxophone solos sound as natural and easy as whistling in the street, died in a Pennsylvania hospital at sixty-two. With his departure, another popular regular visitor to the club (Cohn had been less dependent on the jazz life than some, working on theme music for American TV and arranging for Broadway musicals, but a Frith Street booking could usually tempt him back) and one of Ronnie Scott's favourite players, had now joined the growing list of the permanently unavailable. Of the best Lester Young-influenced white saxophonists who had devoted their lives to the celebration of grace, gliding lyricism and good humour in their music, only Stan Getz, the most graceful and romantic of all of them, was left.

The expatriate British bass virtuoso Dave Holland appeared at Ronnie Scott's Club in the same month, and his band once again astonished audiences with its blend of spontaneity and discipline. The most significant night in Holland's professional life had occurred on the same premises one summer night in 1968, when he was twenty-two years old, not long out of the Guildhall College and playing bass in the house band behind singer Elaine Delmar. Miles Davis had been in the audience, heard Holland's work and invited him to join his band in New York on the strength of it. Holland, who could make the upright bass sound as springy and effervescent as an acoustic guitar, never looked back from that point. Nor did he relax from investigating the cutting-edge of jazz in partnership with performers younger than him, and by the mid-eighties he was working with New Yorkers on the borderline of jazz, hip hop and soul.

In the same month came the remarkable sixty-year-old Chicagoan saxophonist Earl Lavon 'Von' Freeman, formerly partner to such creative artists as Sun Ra, Andrew Hill and Dexter Gordon, and a man who would almost certainly have acquired a reputation for originality nearly as enduring as theirs had he chosen not to restrict his playing opportunities almost entirely to his home town. Freeman came to London to appear with his much better-known son Chico, in a polished and powerful band that also featured Kirk Lightsey on piano, Lonnie Plexico on bass and the Art Ensemble's Don Moye on drums.

Freeman's was the kind of performance that stuck in the mind long after others had evaporated, not simply because it revealed the older man to be – like Miles Davis, singer Betty Carter and composer Gil Evans – the kind of senior player who thrives on younger partners, but also because the event spurred the younger Freeman into a freewheeling exuberance quite unlike his frequently rather sober and calculating performances. Von Freeman was like a performing encyclopaedia of the saxophone sounds that had drifted out into the smoky twilight intimacy of Ronnie Scott's Club over nearly thirty years. He was old enough to remember Earl Hines, Fats Waller and Louis Armstrong coming by his parents' house for a social visit, and his unique style took in Lester Young, Coleman Hawkins, Ornette Coleman and John Coltrane – three decades of saxophone development.

Pete King was gaining the confidence to branch out with the booking policy, now that a jazz audience seemed to be developing that would visit the club in the expectation of hearing interesting music, without necessarily minding whether they'd heard of the main attraction before or not. In early April 1988 came Billy Bang, the forty-year-old violinist from Mobile, Alabama, one of the few violin players to have developed a technique appropriate to the vocabulary of the post-1960s jazz avant garde. Bang's methods owed little to the mellifluous swing of Stephane Grappelli, more to the ferocious loquacity of a Coltraneish saxophonist. But he drew consistently on the blues, and he swung hard. Bang began his show with the words: 'This is the music that's played in my neighbourhood. I'm glad to see my neighbourhood is growing.' It was a pertinent observation about a changing musical climate.

Nor did Bang pull his punches just because he was in front of a mainstream nightclub audience rather than a dedicated handful of devoted buffs. His band played long, wriggling, improvisations on very few tunes, but touched base with gospel and blues materials often enough for the listeners to remain gripped and intrigued. Drummer Dennis Charles's solos, which seemed to proceed with a kind of half-speed deliberation, highlighted the leader's declamatory eloquence all the more.

Following Bang, and also from the sixties free-scene, was Farrell 'Pharoah' Sanders, the hoarse-toned, impressionistic tenor saxophonist who was one of John Coltrane's final partners in the controversial band of the mid-1960s. Neither Bang nor Sanders had the kind of antecedents to make them obvious candidates for either Ronnie Scott's, or any other non-specialist nightclub, but the healing passage of time had enabled both men to be perceived in middle age as pioneers on their instruments whose innovations not only made perfect sense but could even be danced or sung to. In the dance-jazz clubs springing up around the country in the late eighties, Pharoah Sanders's once-fearsome sound was regularly to be heard on rediscovered anthems like 'You've Got To Have Freedom'.

In late April 1988 Art Blakey came back. Now sixty-eight years old and losing his hearing, Blakey was still supplying a steaming rhythmic undertow to his bands largely by feel and vibrations, leaving the organisation to a succession of musical directors. This time it was a pared-down band (trumpet, trombone, and a single saxophone), but still delivering the same old irresistably raunchy blues, revamped standards and virtuoso features for the sidemen, on this occasion including the brilliant young pianist Benny Green, whose party-piece medley touched on such early jazz keyboard stars as Art Tatum and Teddy Wilson more often than it referred to contemporary piano gurus like Keith Jarrett.

It was the epitome of business as usual. Pete King, though he was fifty-nine years old, bearing much of the responsibility for the club's survival, and driving back to his Barnet home in the small hours of the morning six nights a week, felt in good shape and optimistic about the future.

Until one day in late April when he noticed chest pains while mowing his lawn. After a cup of tea and a rest they went away. Four days later, lying in bed at 8.30 in the morning, they came back and he lost the feeling in his arms. Stella King rang the club's doctor Sidney Gottlieb, held out the phone while King described his symptoms. Gottlieb summoned an ambulance at once, but road blockages on the M1 interminably held it up. Stella struggled to move her husband into the car instead, and drove him by the back routes to Gottlieb's house. The doctor immediately confirmed a major heart attack, and the health insurance policy came through long before King had anticipated cashing it in, when he was taken to intensive care at the Wellington Hospital in St John's Wood.

The hard years of the early eighties seemed to have left their mark after all.

# 14

# Outro

'Sometimes I know that I should never have been a musician. But – occasionally – it's as if somebody else has taken over and everything seems to work. That's when I feel I'm doing what I was meant to do.'
(Ronnie Scott, 1986)

THE TWO MEN in suits sitting in the sunny room overlooking Lord's cricket ground didn't look like cricket fans. They gripped bunches of flowers in restless hands. They were representatives of what might loosely be described as the Soho cash economy – local villains, in other words. They were waiting for signs of life from Pete King. Like a scene from *Goodfellas*, two serious-looking representatives of the fringe businesses so traditionally fundamental to Soho life were sitting waiting for a colleague from the same patch to confirm that he was planning to stay in business.

'What are you two bastards doing here?' King, drifting in and out of consciousness, had realised he had guests.

'We've been waiting an hour for you to wake up,' they informed him. 'We came to wish you a speedy recovery.'

King was only disappointed that the hospital staff didn't seem to share the Frith Street penchant for grim comedy. When the doctors were urgently examining him on his arrival at the Wellington, King had recollected that the London marathon was scheduled for the following Sunday and that he had planned to participate. 'Does this mean I can't run?' the deadpan King had asked the physicians, and they didn't think it was funny.

But in every other respect he was inclined to think, if this is a heart attack, maybe it isn't so bad. His room was like a grandstand seat at Lord's, and was swamped with flowers, calls from all over the world, visitors trying to charm, cajole, bribe and intimidate their way on to the premises to shake his hand, try to top the graveyard gag delivered by the last visitor.

Art Blakey, Scott and King's guest at Frith Street at the time, was one. Dizzy Gillespie was in town, charmed his way inside and put in an appearance. Ronnie Scott was there every day. King always asked for news of the club, about how Jimmy and Bonnie and Dorothy and Monty, the club's regular staff, were coping in his absence, about how life could go on without him. Eventually the hospital put an exclusion order on everybody but Stella, Ronnie Scott and Pete's children Christopher and Sharon.

Out of the hospital, Ronnie Scott was confronting the possibility that his closest friend and his indispensable associate might not be able to go on. He also knew for certain that it was a role he wouldn't be able to shoulder himself. 'I knew I couldn't do it,' he reflected later, and with his customary candour. 'I knew I couldn't be bothered to do it, either.'

For his part, King was to look back on the period and observe: 'Working with Ronnie, you feel you're with someone who's mainly interested in playing the saxophone. That's OK, he's the star because of the way he plays, and the person he is. I never thought for a minute that I was going to croak it, but if I had, or if I couldn't have gone on, then other people would have had to run the business side.

'What was interesting about this was finding out they were there all the time. If you're a workaholic like me, you never think that anybody else can do it like you, until you have to face it. Then you find out they can't do it like you, but that's because they do it their own way, a way you'd never have thought of.'

So the club, in its spontaneous, downbeat-optimistic, jazzlike way, ran on. Ronnie Scott kept doing the jokes, introducing the bands, blowing the horn, just as he'd always done. That was enough. Everybody else lent a hand to service a machine that, in its Heath Robinsonian way, had become strangely efficient.

The summer's bookings were in hand anyway, and King, from his hospital bed and then from the end of a telephone in his Hertfordshire home, was never out of touch. He also heard a few weeks later that Chet Baker, that ghostly presence whose physical being seemed at times to be evaporating into the air leaving nothing but his shy, haunting music, had died in strange circumstances in Amsterdam, falling from a hotel window.

The summer's bookings, as they had consistently been for three years, were substantially occupied by Latin-American bands. If Zoot Sims, Dexter Gordon, Sonny Rollins, Hank Mobley and the other saxophone giants had been performing musical chairs at Ronnie Scott's Club in the 1960s, Latin-jazz dance bands seemed to be covering a substantial part of the role in the 1980s, and into the nineties.

Prominent among the early visitors under that banner were Afro Cuba, an ebullient contemporary ensemble that showed that the new generation of erudite and skilful Cuban players lived in a much bigger world than their forbears, bringing the strands of African, American and Latin ideas back together in fresh ways.

So did a spectacular Brazilian band led by percussionist Airto Moreira and singer Flora Purim, usually assisted by the powerful tenorist Gary Meek, one of Ronnie Scott's favourite players. Purim's delicate, feathery Latin scat (close to the sound of flute or a soprano sax) on material from Milton Nascimento and Chick Corea, and the sound of Moreira's fizzing cymbals, ending in the celebrated *tour de force* of his famous unaccompanied tambourine-and-whistle solo, became almost as reliable an annual draw as the vaudevillian blues singer George Melly's 'Christmas pantomime'.

The dignitaries of this movement were Irakere, the majestic Cuban ensemble which had visited Frith Street in the honeymoon of the Havana Connection in 1985 and by the late eighties was mingling its thrilling Latin dance repertoire with such things as dramatic programmatic tributes to Duke Ellington. The latter was the work of pianist/leader Chucho Valdes, whose homage was a distinctly personal and active one, moving subtly from Dukish stride to abstractions that almost suggested avantists like Cecil Taylor or Don Pullen, then back to Art Tatum. Valdes had become Irakere's undisputed pole star after the departure of its firecracker trumpet virtuoso Arturo Sandoval for a solo career.

Sandoval wasn't to everybody's taste musically, but nobody could dispute that he was a sensation in some arena of jazz/latin/music/theatre that he seemed to have gleefully invented for himself. He came to Frith Street in August 1988, proved himself to be a showman to his toecaps, astonishing audiences with displays of whistling, accurately pitched high notes, charging runs, suddenly hushed muted figures, machine-gun bebop and tongue-in-cheek showband finales. His material covered Cuban music, Miles Davis jazz-funk, tributes to Clifford Brown and Dizzy Gillespie (a father-figure to him, as to many young trumpeters) and constant confirmations that no tempo, however frantic, could seem to throw his composure.

The club continued to head into a favourable wind, despite Pete King's setback. King would never have dreamed of blaming anyone but himself for taking the survival of the club so exclusively and personally, but he came to believe that the stresses and fears of the early eighties, facing bankruptcy and – maybe worse – the prospect of a life without the jazz world and its unique diversions, had done the damage. He accepted that others could do the work he had done, cut his hours down, and balanced his life between the enduring securities of his home and family, his passion for cars and motor racing, and the club.

The continuing upturn in the general fortunes of jazz certainly helped, though briefly it seemed to be benefiting other recently-arrived jazz entrepreneurs more than Scott and King. Running a jazz club had seemed a virtually certifiable activity at the time when the seeds of King's illness might have been sown. But by 1988 it had become almost obligatory for anyone fronting anything from a wine bar to a disco to claim some allegiance with jazz.

Though no street in the UK – or anywhere else – ever looked likely to resemble the teeming 52nd Street portrayed in jazz fan Clint Eastwood's cult movie *Bird!* – Charlie Parker's loosely, though imaginatively reworked life story – in 1988 running a jazz club almost seemed like the kind of proposition you could go to the bank manager with, and many did.

A new jazz magazine, augustly titled after an old Thelonious Monk tune, *Straight No Chaser*, thought it worth making a clubland guide into a regular feature in every issue. A slightly older jazz and new music magazine *The Wire* refined tasteful minimalist graphics, and made an ability to appreciate the music seem like a badge of sophisticated good taste and intellectual independence. *The Wire* began art-directing its cover photography to make it resemble a fashion magazine far more than a music enthusiast's, and with headlines like 'The New Men' for up-and-coming young local musicians, it began to give little known jazz players a cachet far more glamorous and mysterious than their former identity as icons of a bizarre minority taste.

Jazz DJs became as influential as musicians. Young men like Paul Murphy and Gilles Peterson and a young black DJ-cum-promoter operating as Baz Fe Jazz emerged as a new breed of jazz messengers, turning classic old bebop albums into refuges from uninspired chart material for young clubbing audiences, who spontaneously evolved new dance steps to match. Saxophone teachers started reporting unprompted references to old swing stars like Johnny Hodges, let alone John Coltrane, being made to them by pupils barely into their teens.

Jazz club rivals began to surface. In north London's Stoke Newington, a tiny bar offering a mixture of much artier decor (contemporary jazz paintings and photography, designer grey-and-pink colour scheme instead of tobacco-stained browns and dusty lampshades, arcane continental alcohol and good vegetarian food) quickly made ground as The Jazz Café.

Its owner Jon Dabner, an energetic ex-schoolteacher, was reported as saying: 'In the first few weeks it was packed with loud yuppies who didn't care much about the music, the people who spend all their time sniffing their wine corks. But soon people started coming regularly just for the music.' Down the road at the Vortex, an art gallery and artists' suppliers that turned its café into a jazz club, there seemed to be more than enough business to go round too. The same thing started happening all over London.

At Ronnie Scott's Club they were suspicious, partly out of bitter experience, partly reflexive bloody-mindedness. After all, if Courtney Pine sold 75,000 copies of his first album *Journey To The Urge Within* and saxophones had begun to replace guitars as photographers' props, casually slung over the shoulders of cool young men in ads for cutting-edge designer suits, it still made very little difference to fellow musicians of Ronnie Scott and Pete King's generation, or the talented one that had followed them, for that matter.

There were no associate professorships, artist-in-residences or celebrity tours as the kind of rewards for seniority familiar from the dinner-jacket arts – not that the Frith Street circle would have cared if there were. More to the point, there wasn't much of a change in the weather for fine players like Alan Skidmore or Don Weller, musicians who would be pleased with a year that netted them the national average wage.

Ronnie Scott didn't believe the 'jazz revival' was built to last. The word 'jazz' was now being used to market all manner of products, from motor cars to perfumes, but it had as peripheral a relevance to the real nature of the music as it had in 'the Jazz Age' of the 1920s. Ronnie Scott was moved to remark that as far as television went, 'You could hear more jazz on the commercials than you could on the programmes.' He did like, however, the music on Eastwood's *Bird!*, the most successful movie representation of the mysteries of jazz playing, apart from his all-time favourite, old hero Georgie Auld's work behind Robert DeNiro on *New York New York*.

The club had always been a place where musicians swapped ideas, paid homage to contemporaries and elders and generally stirred the jazz melting pot. But as the old one-way traffic of Britain's relationship with American jazz changed, the homages turned increasingly to dialogues. Steve Williamson, Courtney Pine's young contemporary, met the American alto virtuoso Steve Coleman there, during Coleman's appearances with Dave Holland's band, and the two men exchanged reflections on ways forward to the extent that Coleman became producer of Williamson's debut disc.

Following the early success of Loose Tubes, British musicians were able to prove they had a sizeable following that would accompany them to Frith

Street – so much so that the club was able to showcase local players with growing frequency. In April 1989, there was the twenty-one-year-old Scots saxophonist Tommy Smith, with a substantial career already behind him, opposite the powerful blues singer Irene Reid.

A series of fine young British singers appeared on the premises. Claire Martin was an intelligent mainstream singer, with a flexible technique and a telling shrewdness in her choice of materials. Ian Shaw exhibited the same confidence and brains, with an added spicing of theatricality and humour and he could comfortably handle both torchy soul singing and ballads, liable to move from Motown songs to 'Danny Boy' in the space of one set. Sue Shattock was less secure in her materials, but added to the fast Latin scat of Tania Maria a wistfulness on ballads and a thin-ice journey between confident assertiveness and mild panic that made her a promisingly unusual prospect.

As 1989 dawned, the year of the club's thirtieth birthday, it was easier to see the wood for the trees in the wider jazz world, to distinguish the work that would count from the 'designer jazz' Ronnie Scott was so impatient with. 'We've come out of the other side of the jazz revival,' *Wire* editor Richard Cook told *The Guardian*. 'The media have all done their jazz think piece now, and their jazz fashion spread. Courtney Pine's been on *Juke Box Jury* and all that. The hype's fading and now it's down to whether the music itself stands up.'

Music that stood up at Ronnie Scott's in the thirtieth birthday year included expatriate South African trumpeter Hugh Masekela's half American, half African ensemble, with its direct, conversational music, embracing songs of resignation, jubilation or defiance. It captivated audiences, particularly when Masekela broadened the references with his slow, evocative rendering of Bob Marley's 'No Woman No Cry'.

But so did bop, Scott and King's first love. There was George Coleman, one of the fastest bop players in the world, a classic itinerant sax star in the Sonny Stitt mould, specialising in fast blues coloured with double-time runs, piercing whistles, R&B sax honks. There was Charlie Parker's forties frontline partner, trumpeter Red Rodney, by 1989 an amiable, square-set and energetic sixty-two-year-old, recovered from the narcotics tribulations of the 1950s. Rodney played beautifully, opposite the new British teenage prodigy Nigel Hitchcock, justifiably hailed in many quarters as the new Tubby Hayes.

In August came the spectacular George Russell Living Time Orchestra. Four nights of music made the excellent *The London Concert* record with young Britons like Andy Sheppard, Steve Lodder and Ashley Slater in the line-up. Russell had been a pioneer as far back as the mid-forties, when he had written a hit for the Dizzy Gillespie band ('Cubana-Be, Cubana-Bop'), and then developed sophisticated new theories to change the methodology of jazz improvisation, based on cycles of scales ('modes') rather than chords. Russell's band would fan fifteenth-century madrigals into rhythmic infernos of free-jazz and rock, or unleash an irresistably swinging mid-tempo orchestration of the entire Miles Davis trumpet solo on 'So What' from the classic *Kind of Blue* album. It wasn't the kind of music nightclub punters could carry on a private conversation to, nor did it obey conventional notions of tonality or resolution, but it was thrilling music and its energy swept the audience into its lap.

If Ronnie Scott's was trying to advertise just what was unique about it in the run-up to its thirtieth birthday it couldn't have picked a better follow-up to George Russell's tumultuous visit than to bring the great tenor saxophonist Joe Henderson. This was the beginning of a rise to dominance of the saxophone world for Henderson, one of Ronnie Scott's all-time favourite saxophonists, that culminated in him winning a Grammy award, and performing on President Bill Clinton's inauguration ceremony.

This time Henderson came, as he had so many times before, as a 'single', joining Ronnie Scott's own regular partners, including the pianist John Critchenson. Henderson was always refreshing as much for the ways in which he didn't resemble currently marketable saxophone playing as for the way he did – avoiding prolonged high volume and high pitch as signs of increased intensity proceeding in a lugubrious, sometimes all but dolorous tone, but generating astonishing new melody with every chorus, as if such fertlity were effortless.

In October 1989 came the thirtieth anniversary. Neither Scott nor King were renowned for getting misty-eyed about dates in a calendar, but since this particular milestone was occurring at a time of what looked like relative prosperity, it meant a lot. If Scott was touched, he wasn't letting on, however. 'Like a prison sentence' became his favourite observation about the proceedings. 'Thirty years in a jazz club.' He would sometimes vary this with: 'Thirty years? It seems like yesterday. And you know what a lousy day yesterday was.'

Even by the standards of some of the quirky professional partnerships of Soho nightlife, Scott's and King's was remarkable for its drop-dead fortitude – a quality that had kept the ship afloat when nothing seemed capable of saving it. The BBC sent in a documentary team from its *Omnibus* arts programme to share in the fun, and the result was an ironic, touching and revealing sixty-minute tribute to the club and its founders. Dizzy Gillespie, Sonny Rollins, John Dankworth and Georgie Fame appeared to tip their hats to the lugubrious pioneers. English musicians of Ronnie's generation (Stan Tracey and Kathy Stobart) and of the young 'jazz renaissance' (Ashley Slater and Django Bates from Loose Tubes, Phil Bent from the Jazz Warriors) reminisced and improvised in words and music.

Two regular attenders at the club – prominent politician Kenneth Clarke for the Tories and John Prescott for Labour – overcame their differences to recall the establishment's central place in their shared enthusiasm for jazz, and in accepting Clarke's lift back to the House of Commons after the interviews, Prescott was heard to mutter in mock alarm, 'I could get deselected for this.' The writer, comic, film-maker and human incendiary device Mel Brooks also held forth expansively on one of his favourite places on earth.

The film brought to the general public, perhaps for the first time, some insight into the peculiar chemistry of the fuel that had kept Ronnie Scott's Club running. It revealed that by a mixture of offhand obsessiveness, optimism, indifference to business advice and unshakeable faith in their own intuitions, the proprietors had started and sustained the ideal place in which to listen to this mercurial and elusive music, and into the bargain run the kind of establishment in which the musicians themselves could feel relaxed, understood and welcomed in.

At the end of the show, Scott and King's back view, facing that tiny stage, accompanied a typically economical conversation about what it all meant. They often finished each other's sentences ('like an 'old married couple' as Ronnie Scott later wryly observed), and King's statement of his own feelings, like blood squeezed from stone, exhibited a reluctant eloquence that touched hearts even among viewers who'd never been near the place. 'It's now become of world repute,' King said slowly, as if anticipating objections. 'And I guess in a way . . .' (interminable pause) '. . . we're . . . very proud of it.'

During the celebrations that October, Scott – in an interview with this writer in *The Guardian* – described the changes that had swept over jazz in Britain over the thirty years the club had been at work. He anticipated objections that more orthodox employers of artists and entertainers might have had to the condition some of his idols performed in by recalling the hypnotic influence of America on Britain when the enterprise was young.

'These people were idols for us,' Scott observed. 'It was hard for us to believe we were actually talking to them, let alone hearing them play. Our generation was like that, and it's different now, people aren't overawed by America, but to us it was the place where this music was born. When those guys came here it was a chance to see they were human, that they're wonderful, and that they fuck up like everybody else.'

Pete King also pointed out that trying to tell a hero like Ben Webster to shape up was almost inconceivable to them – 'He was a great jazz musician, decades older than us, and we respected him.'

Ronnie Scott recalled, 'I wrote a letter to a customer who complained that Ben had talked more than he played one night, saying I'd rather hear Ben talk than ninety per cent of tenor players play.' It wasn't just a flip put-down, but an honest reflection on the gravitas of a player of Webster's experience, and the wealth of experience of music-making that inhabited his every pore. 'If we've helped raise the standard of jazz played here,' Scott said, 'I think it's because people have been able to understand the approach of some of these great players to their music – you can get the content off records, but not the approach. It never stops being an education to me.'


Pete King was by now back on his feet. He was leaner, fitter, worked shorter hours and looked after himself. He was also encouraged to discover that an ancient truth of the club's existence – that British bands couldn't top the bill and draw big crowds – continued to diminish in significance. Loose Tubes, for instance, had gone on building its audience there to the extent that it was as reliable a draw as many more celebrated Frith Street imports. But it played its swan-song at the establishment in September 1990, much to the distress of a sizeable following.

The Tubes did leave Ronnie Scott's with something to remember. Having developed a reputation for performance in such unlikely locations as hotel elevators, the escalators of department stores, and on the street, the band wound up one finale at the club by marching out still playing, doing an erratic circuit of Old Compton Street and Dean Street (emptying restaurants of baffled customers on the way) and returning for the last chorus. On one such perambulation, manager Colin Lazzarini even tried to persuade the band to march to 10 Downing Street in the small hours to serenade Margaret Thatcher, but a stop for breakfast en route took the momentum out of it. Trombonist Ashley Slater declared from the stand: 'For those of you who think Loose Tubes is the most fantastic thing in the world, well, you're going to have a very empty rest of your life.'

Symptomatic of an apparently warmer climate for jazz in Britain was the fact that in 1990 Jazz FM, the country's first all-jazz radio station, arrived. It took more of a substantial slice of blues, funk and vocals to get it noticed and the interviewers sometimes sounded bemused and got their facts wrong (mercilessly pointed out by sharp-eared observers from the Frith Street Charm School in the club's typically acerbic house magazine *Jazz At Ronnie Scott's*, or *JARS*) but its existence seemed at first to confirm that jazz had finally emerged blinking into the daylight. Whether this was a good thing for it or not was yet to be established. In the event, some bad decisions and early-days profligacy almost capsized the station when it was hardly under way, its original enthusiast founders were replaced by hard-nosed radio professionals, and new programming policies reduced the jazz and improvisational content more and more. Like the Jazz Café, which moved from its modest premises in Stoke Newington to much bigger and more expensive ones in Camden Town at much the same time, Jazz FM was carried away by the modishness of jazz in the media and spent money that couldn't be recouped once the fashion palled.

Ronnie Scott and Pete King knew all about financial instability, but they had never made this mistake. They were convinced that if the artists were right, and the place had the kind of history and atmosphere that couldn't be injected overnight by architects and interior designers, the public would come. The dust on the lampshades and the gaffer tape binding up splits in the upholstery remained. Eminent lighting designers repeatedly offered their expertise to Scott and King and were turned down. Marketing wisdom suggested that the club could be capitalising much more extensively on its reputation than it did, and that the audience gathering or departing in the foyer could be hit much harder by spin-off Ronnie Scott's merchandise than it was. But Ronnie Scott, for all his indifference to most aspects of club administration, wasn't having any of it. 'It's a jazz club, not a shop,' was his opinion, and nobody was much inclined to try to shift him from it.

In October and November 1990, Ronnie Scott took a rare step. He recorded an album with the quintet, his first session as a leader since 1977. As one of the leading saxophone improvisors in Britain for almost a half-century, he had nevertheless recorded very rarely, continuing to feel inhibited by the process, and disliking hearing his work played back to him. But this was live, in the club, for the establishment's own label Jazz House, and caught over a prolonged period, so Ronnie Scott was almost able to forget the tapes were on.

At sixty-three, he sounded as if he was on a playing roll, and it was one that has continued to the present time. It was as if all the voices of the horn players he had ever admired had percolated through his contradictory spirit and settled to a sound that was more truly his than ever, one that revealed dimensions of his life he usually concealed, but also celebrated the remarkable saxophone history of the century's African-American music as well. Typically, since it was clearly a serious work that encapsulated almost everything he cared about in playing jazz, he gave it a throwaway title. The disc went out under the name of *Never Pat A Burning Dog*. There's no tune of that title on the session, naturally.

The repertoire was in the mould the quintet had adopted from the early 1980s – soulful mid-tempo pieces suggestive of McCoy Tyner and John Coltrane's earlier collaborations, gentle Latin swing, torchy ballads played softly and obliquely. On McCoy Tyner's 'Contemplation', with its insistent but dreamy swing, and following Dick Pearce's economical, Miles Davis-like trumpet solo, enters Ronnie Scott. His treatment was a model of lyrical construction, not too fast, texturally varied, revealing early Coltrane and the delicate deliberation of Scott's old hero Hank Mobley in glimpses, the high notes hoarse but delicately controlled. John Critchenson demonstrated why Scott came to believe their playing relationship was so special, keeping Tyner's solemn, bell-like chordal sound in the background, but shadowing his boss's ability to give every chorus of a solo a shape and character of its own.

Ronnie Scott always liked the breezy relaxation of Latin jazz, with its light, dancing feel, and its invitations to soloists to pace their variations at odds to the underlying pulse. The band makes a delicate account of Jimmy Dorsey's 'I'm Glad There is You', Scott paying his dues to the man he believed said almost everything worth saying about tenor-playing in this idiom – Stan Getz. Ronnie Scott arrives to coast bouyantly on the beat, sometimes gracefully fanning the notes, sometimes crackling through them in double-time, as if he were alternately displaying and shuffling a deck of cards. His control of timbre, letting the sound of a single note change colour as it glows and fades, went back long before Stan Getz, to all those last dances at the palais, the nights on the boats, to Jack Lewis's lessons, to Jock's love of the 'pretty notes', and to Ronnie Scott's own romantic nature. He always played ballads with an almost painfully poignant, violin-like grace, and the sound of it could conjure up the image of the player onstage, eyes closed, smoke curling up from the cigarette perched behind the levers of the horn.

During the period of the recording, trumpeter Dick Pearce had a bad motorbike accident, which made it impossible for him to finish the project. Mornington Lockett, a powerful, bluesy, rhythmically compelling tenor saxophonist of the kind that Ronnie Scott always admired, came in to cover on Freddie Hubbard's classic 'Little Sunflower' and stayed with the band to augment it when Pearce was back on his feet. He gave the band a clamorous urgency that recalled the old gunslinging two-tenor lineups of the past, not least Scott's great Jazz Couriers partnership with Tubby Hayes. Lockett's blustery drive contrasted well with Ronnie Scott's more ambiguous manner, as Hayes' had done all those years before. And Scott's experience now broadened his playing immensely, controlling dynamics as if his sound were floating in and out of range of the listener, slyly quoting from other tunes.

But if Getz, that troubled and troubling genius who had caused Scott and King such a mixture of pain and pleasure over the years, still had a hold over Ronnie Scott, it ceased to be an affection he could gratify by first-hand contact in 1991. Getz had come back from major surgery and played again with much of his old magic before this date, but this time there was no reprieve. Ronnie Scott had had a bad feeling about his old hero and called his number one night. A voice on the line from the States said, 'He's not well. His sickness is back.' Within hours Mary, who was friendly with the Getz family in New York, called Ronnie Scott to pass on the news that Getz's daughter had told her the great saxophonist was dead.

Though Ronnie Scott had always believed that grading musicians was futile, and knew there were many players he had admired and even envied over the years who were largely unknown to the general public, Getz always occupied a special niche for him, and the thought that it would be impossible to hear that tremulous sound in a live performance ever again was deeply saddening to him. He wrote to Getz's daughter Beverley to express his condolences, and he told Mary that he would love to have something of the artist's to remember him by, perhaps an old mouthpiece. Scott eventually heard back that Getz's belongings were tied up with the lawyers, but in the end his son sent over a mouthpiece which he hoped would fit the bill. As soon as he saw it, Ronnie Scott – who knew the rubber Otto Link mouthpieces Getz used only too well – knew it was one that Getz would never have played in a million years. He returned it, and had to be content with memories of a jazz genius that spanned forty-five years of his life.

The recession was beginning to bite the recently expanded jazz business and some of the recently founded clubs were already feeling the squeeze. Promoters started to notice it first when the audiences would just about pay to get through the doors but then spend nothing when they were inside. And for places running on tight margins, often with high start-up costs, these were serious developments. Jazz FM, the London radio station, was already running into trouble, not generating enough advertising revenue, and having overspent on the decor and technology of its central London studio in its first year. The Stoke Newington Jazz Café, having moved to much more expensive premises in Camden Town, had hit cash-flow diffi- culties that looked terminal.

But, with typical Frith Street perversity, Ronnie Scott's Club expanded.

During the thirtieth birthday celebrations in 1989, Ronnie Scott had been featured in a Sunday newspaper profile, and in the same issue there was an in-depth study of the regeneration of the country's second city, Birmingham. Pete King had never much liked the place, but Ronnie Scott read the article and was impressed by the city council's initiatives in rebuilding the central area and putting the arts at the top of the agenda in it. Conductor Simon Rattle's high profile there with the City Symphony Orchestra completed the picture. Scott and King judged the name 'Ronnie Scott's Club' to have such a widespread currency over thirty years that maybe the growing prosperity of the London establishment could energise a regional outpost.

King knew a club-owner in Birmingham, a man he had gone motor- racing with, who knew the scene and started preparatory investigations. News came back that the council would be delighted for a club bearing the Ronnie Scott logo to be part of the Convention Centre complex. Scott and King then met Alan Sartori and Barry Sherwin, two Birmingham business- men who ran the Rep Café Bar, part of the new Rep Theatre.

Sartori and Sherwin came south to meet the two Londoners, and the four men got on well. A deal was struck for Sartori and Sherwin to be the franchise holders of a second Ronnie Scott's. The two local men would carry the financial responsibility, run the premises and own the lease. Scott would lend his name to the club, appear there when he could, and the London organisation would send its bookings on to the Midlands where schedules permitted.

Ronnie Scott took an interest in the project that surprised King, accus- tomed as he was to his partner's usual indifference to the business side of club life. Scott felt it conveyed some of the excitement of the early days of planning the Gerrard Street club, and imagined it as Frith Street translated. But it wasn't as easy as that. Sartori and Sherwin sent their designer to London to look at the Frith Street club, but the version that was built in Birmingham was such a free variation on the theme that Ronnie Scott didn't recognise it as a relation. He hated eighties and nineties interior design with its hard surfaces, ice-cream parlour lighting and wine-bar look.

He went to Birmingham when the project was nearing completion in the summer of 1991, and forcibly informed Sartori and Sherwin that he couldn't stand it.

'This is nothing to do with me,' Scott fumed. 'Take my name off the door. I don't want to have anything to do with it.'

Scott's ideas about what a jazz club should look like were formed on 52nd Street in the 1940s. If times had changed, that was fine but he didn't feel he needed to endorse something he disliked by hanging his name in a flourescent light outside it. He didn't like the bar, which looked to him as if it had been designed for a disco, he thought the wrought-iron furniture was ugly, and he couldn't imagine how it could ever feel like home to him, as the London premises did. But Sartori and Sherwin listened. They were anxious not to alienate the man whose endorsement was crucial to the project, and they accommodated as many of Ronnie Scott's objections as they could.

Ronnie Scott's, Birmingham, opened in the autumn of 1991. Rolling Stones drummer Charlie Watts had by this time invested in another of his lifelong jazz dreams, a small band with strings accompaniment that sounded like the classical/jazz crossover music that Charlie Parker had briefly recorded for Verve in the early fifties. Watts's Charlie Parker was, almost inevitably, the other Peter King, playing on the opening night of a Ronnie Scott Club for the second time in his life, and the trumpeter was young Gerard Presencer, a stunning bebop virtuoso hardly out of his teens – just as King had been when he astonished the Gerrard Street audiences that October night back in 1959. Ronnie Scott himself, by this time reasonably content with his second establishment, played opposite Watts with his own group.

The Birmingham club didn't altogether go the way Scott and King had envisaged over its first year. Local audiences were different. Drawn from a smaller population, and with less of an itinerant character, the hard core of jazz fans was not high enough to sustain the kind of specialist policy that could just about work in London – so there had to be a higher proportion of soul, R&B and pop-oriented jazz music to make the figures add up. But it worked. The idea even spawned its own offspring, and by 1994 negotiations were underway to start a similar scheme in Sheffield. Ronnie Scott's Club was becoming a national institution.

Exactly the kind of specialised programme that was a doubtful starter in Birmingham was the season by the great American saxophonist Phil Woods in London in July 1992. Woods was by this time sixty-one, a saxophonist who had spent all his life devoted to the work of Charlie Parker with an intelligence and perception rare even among the legions of talented musicians who had followed the same path. Woods's special request was that his band should play without amplification. Pete King drew a sharp breath at this. Though audience sizes had risen, the notion of remaining in respectful concert-hall silence was fading, to the extent that Scott had taken to installing curtly admonishing notices on every table more or less telling the occupants to listen to the artists or go home.

But, as had so often happened before, real commitment and invention in a jazz performer acted as its own crowd-control device. Woods's astonishing chorister's purity in the alto saxophone's high register, swooping all the way down via trembly mid-range sounds to a deep and romantic vibrato created a hush in the busy club that would have made a dropping pin sound like a broken window.

Although one of the best-loved and most infectiously entertaining of the strictly jazz-angled regulars had ceased to illuminate the premises when Art Blakey died in 1990, there were plenty of others who preserved and extended the beauties of this lissome, ambiguous music. The multi-instrumentalist and one-time Dizzy Gillespie sideman James Moody kept coming back, playing with irrepressible gusto and the same engaging surrealism that made his announcements as engaging as his playing. His work was repeatedly packed with wriggly runs, slurs, exclamatory clucks, tone changes and wide intervals, and his showpiece wacky song 'Benny's From Heaven' (an alibi for an illegitimate infant) which is delivered as a mixture of mumbling barbershop declamations and yodels, worked every time. But in the audacity with which he skidded around the harmonic implications of the chords, in his slurry tone and abrupt, challenging hoots, Moody repeatedly showed himself to be an object lesson in original horn technique.

And even when the recession started to bite – about a year, Pete King reckoned, after it hit everybody else, and an indication that for a while at least, sufferers tried to cheer themselves up by going out on the town – they would always queue up for the unique singer Betty Carter, who got better and better as she got older, shying away from some notes as if they were hot, taking constant chances, delaying resolutions with all but unbearable capriciousness and into the bargain bringing a constantly freshened supply of new young sidemen with her who, as she put it, she could teach the standards without them knowing 'how it goes'.

By 1992 the press was starting to go back on all the jazz revival stories, which didn't surprise Scott and King who'd seen it all before. The Jazz Café went bankrupt and was sold to club-owners Subterrania, Jazz FM was in crisis, and some of the eighties new faces (Andy Sheppard, for one) were having trouble with contract renewals. But there was a silver lining. Blue Note eventually signed Stan Tracey (the most creative elder statesman of British jazz) and Andy Sheppard too, GRP took young inventors Phil Bent and Tony Remy, and M-Base virtuoso Greg Osby came to Britain specifically to work with East End hip-hop band Quite Sane. The old rules had changed.

1993 began badly for Ronnie Scott with another unscheduled departure, the death of a hero and friend, trumpeter Dizzy Gillespie. But memories of Gillespie's immense *joie de vivre* and love of music were so strong that the upshot of thinking about him so vividly seemed as positive as everything he had achieved in his long and inspired life. Ronnie Scott flew to New York to be present at Gillespie's funeral, which was like a state occasion.

The New York trip was a difficult journey for other reasons too. Ronnie Scott's daughter Rebecca was now a strong-minded and independent twenty-one year old who had formed impressions of the distant relationship with her father that were different from the ones Mary had sought to engender. But she was coming around to music, which she had avoided for most of her teens. Though she had shown musical promise as an eight-year-old, when she choeographed her father's own soprano saxophone account of 'Send In The Clowns' for a school dance project, and made rapid strides at the piano (the great pianist John Hicks had been an occasional teacher), Rebecca had avoided music since, and hated jazz clubs and jazz music, the smoke and the audiences. They represented a life she didn't feel was hers.

Rebecca had instead found her own enthusiasms through a passion for horseriding as a teenager. She grew devoted to a spirited, intransigent horse they called Shenanigans. Ronnie Scott rode the horse at its Brooklyn stables in 1985, and then went with Mary and Rebecca to Kaplan's Restaurant in Manhattan to discuss the possibility of buying it. Mary was adamant she could handle the cost, but secured Ronnie Scott's help with the upkeep. Rebecca became a talented gymkhana rider on Shenanigans, and the horse went with her both to the New York Military Academy, where she graduated as a stable sergeant, and to Johnson and Wales University in Rhode Island. But as she passed twenty, and entered a business course in Providence, she came back to piano playing, and also took up the drums. This was a long throw-back. As a five-year-old Rebecca had been tantalised by the sound of the great percussionist Max Roach in a New York club, and tried to imitate the drum patterns on his kit after the show. Roach had been charmed, and presented her with his sticks. At twenty-one, this long-buried ember was rekindled.

'Ronnie has always been there for us,' Mary later said. 'Through all the trials and tribulations, we have managed to keep a caring relationship. I will always cherish our friendship.'

Though Ronnie Scott continued to be doubtful about some of the new-comers to jazz, and believed that their technical prowess often ran way ahead of their creativity, he had his personal preferences. He loved the ecstatic mix of Errol Garner-like stomping stride piano, dashing blues, Latin vivacity and Bill Evans-like rumination of the French pianist Michel Petrucianni, who memorably performed at the club. Barely the height of a toddler, working with special raised piano pedals to negotiate the obstacles caused by the bone-wasting disease he had lived with since early child-hood, Petrucianni was the living embodiment of the life-enhancing opti-mism and energy of jazz.

So in his way, was a much older pianist, Horace Silver. If Art Blakey had finally hung up his sticks, his first partner from the original Jazz Messengers in the mid-fifties, was still rattling out an attractive version of that indefati-gable gospelly bop, showing how strikingly he could make a little go a long way with rimshot-like repeated notes, interminably protracted one-chord riffs suddenly erupting into scuttling runs, and a roster of original composi-tions that will go on being played as long as jazz exists.

The Cuban connection loosened a little, but a strong flavour of Latin American music continued to permeate the menu. One of the most aston-ishing of Latin bands to play at Frith Street was the one led by Hermeto Pascoal, the legendary fifty-eight-year-old multi-instrumentalist and com-poser from Lagoa da Canoa, Brazil, whose early works impressed and influenced Miles Davis and Gil Evans and who did much to launch the careers of such Latin jazz stars as Airto Moreira, Flora Purim, Milton Nascimento, Dom Um Romao.

Pascoal's waist-length white pony-tail and Robinson Crusoe beard, as well as his tendency to perform bop solos on such instruments as tea-kettles, and the boiling energy and enthusiasm with which he approached every set was a surefire hit with the Frith Street audiences, and exhibited an engaging anarchism rarely to be found in a music world increasingly businesslike. The band was packed with percussionists, and the exchange between drummers Marcio Bahia's and percussionist Pernambuco's even threatened Airto Moreira's celebrated percussion finale for intrigue.

And some British musicians continued to pull crowds. Though Loose Tubes had broken up, performers like the West Country saxophonist Andy

Sheppard clearly had skill, originality, and a perception of late twentieth-century music quite different from anything Scott and King could have imagined in their own youth. Sheppard signed with the prestigious American-owned label Blue Note, and his bands mingled free improvisation, Latin and African music, and the methods of Carla Bley, George Russell and the late Gil Evans. Sheppard's bigger groups bristled with fine players, and also brought their own fan-club of visitors who wouldn't necessarily come to Frith Street otherwise – but the spectacular American trombonist Gary Valente staggered the club's audiences with a virtual jazz-trombone history lesson, beginning with a hoarse, repeated single-note shout, then a bleary, swooping, muted passage that could have fitted into Ellington's Cotton Club band, before easing the group into a bluesy dirge that triumphantly mingled New Orleans polyphony with more contemporary references. At the other end of the dynamic range British guitarist Martin Taylor, playing unaccompanied as the departed Joe Pass had often done before in the club, even triumphed on one night over a table-full of necking, shouting hoorays stacking up empties by the crateload, to play a set of remarkable unity of melody, rhythm and bass-line playing to the point where it no longer resembled a novelty-act of extraordinary technique but became a delicately integrated music.

Scott and King were shocked by two tragic 1994 losses even closer to home than Blakey, Getz and Gillespie. One was the quiet Scotsman Jimmy Deuchar, whose swing, melodic shape, and a rounded, mid-register sound that suggested the solos of such graceful American trumpet stars as Fats Navarro and Clifford Brown. They recalled how the shy Scotsman had always made his choices on musical grounds, even rejecting an offer from the highly successful Ted Heath Orchestra when Ronnie Scott formed his more adventurous and bop-oriented nine-piece in the mid-fifties. 'He had a wonderful ear, natural swing, and nothing fazed him as a player,' Ronnie Scott said at the time. The other was Jeff Ellison, the mild, sympathetic and funny ex-drummer who had become, as King described it 'part of the furniture' at Ronnie Scott's. Scott himself regarded his regular chess partner Ellison, with whom he shared a birthday, as a friend and a confidante, and deeply regretted his loss. But, as in all things, there was a laugh to be got out of it if you looked hard enough. Fellow drummer Laurie Morgan made a speech about Ellison to the mourners at Golders Green Crematorium. He recalled how Ellison had been booked to do a New Year's Eve party gig with a pianist who never showed up. The drummer agreed to carry on by himself.

'Can you play "Dancing In The Dark"?' the party-goers asked him.

'Can you play "Auld Lang Syne"?'
'Sure.'
Smack-thump-bang-bang-click-bang-tap-tap.
'They even asked him back for next New Year's Eve,' concluded Morgan, to hysterical giggles.


Now a rich and varied, art-form, jazz has been through a variety of incarnations in the latter half of the twentieth century. Though an Afro-American phenomenon at heart, its many voices have inspired imitation, and eventually creation, all over the world. Much of this has naturally been due to the highly effective exporting of American culture since the Second World War. But much of it has also been due to the remarkable adaptability of jazz. It came into being as the expression of the resignation and hope of slaves who had discovered the hard way what their emancipation actually amounted to. It readily lent itself – not so much as an articulation of oppression but often as an emblem of it – to the underground cultures of alienated people everywhere. Jazz was prominent in the soundtrack to teenage movements like the styliagi in Russia, the zazou movement in France, the beatniks in Britain. The peculiar voicings of the vocabulary and harmonies of jazz became a secret code – not so much for those who went in for organised resistance, but for those whose backgrounds led them naturally toward contracting out.

There was often a strange disparity between the followers of the cult and its heroes in the 1950s. The former might have been the sons and daughters of bankers, doctors, the prosperous and the powerful. The latter were for the most part the sharp working-class youth, the backers of horses, frequenters of low life, familiars of the underworld. So it was with so many of the founders of British modern jazz musicians – like Tony Crombie, Laurie Morgan, Denis Rose, and Ronnie Scott.


Ronnie Scott, though he understands the origins of the music he loves as well as anyone, has always loved it best as an expression of individuality. He has rarely believed it was within his gift to conceive of a radical new direction for the music, to invent a concept that would reshape the way musicians work together, even to be a composer. It has been for him, a facet of an already highly expressive personality the one most readily performed before an audience that doesn't necessarily include his closest friends. And it contains within it that ease with vernacular intonation in music that is drawn from blues, from the black American tradition and from Yiddisher wedding-and-barmitzvah culture; the seduction of a kind of professional respectability in the business engendered also by his Jewish background and by the distant, ambiguous identity of Jock; and a pull in the other direction toward nihilism from such an early and influential membership of that coterie of young rebels in the early 1950s.

Asked if he's considering renovating his current battered tenor, Ronnie Scott will say, 'I've thought about making it nice and shiny, but I thought it might make me look old.' At sixty-eight, still in good health and in his prime as a player, with the clubs that now bear his name currently reflecting the revival of popular interest in orthodox jazz and of many new variations on it too, he can take stock of a life in which he has gained respect inside and outside 'the business', and created with Pete King (a wit and a jazz lover whose inclinations are sometimes camouflaged by his leathery mannerisms) an environment in London in which musicians can play at their best and at the same time given jazz an appropriate home. Some complain that Scott and King are musical conservatives, but Ornette Coleman, Archie Shepp and Cecil Taylor have all played in the club. Many more will testify that those who are serious about music feel that their work is valued by the proprietors, even if the overheads of a West End nightclub have pushed their policies toward a middle road. When Robert Wyatt, the ex-Soft Machine drummer, paralysed his lower limbs for keeps in an accident in the early seventies, he had only ever played in the club a handful of times, and Ronnie Scott had once or twice jammed with his band. Almost the first piece of correspondence Wyatt received after his accident was a cheque from Scott and King. There are many examples of the same generosity.

Ronnie's son Nicholas has gone into the entertainment business too, as a clown and children's entertainer and a member of Equity. Rebecca is increasingly enthusiastic about the drums, and on a 1994 trip to London with her mother spent more time with Ronnie Scott than she had in years, talking into the night with him, beginning to find the common ground that had eluded them both for so long. Ronnie has recovered much of his old relaxation, and has thought a good deal about the turmoil of the past decade. He won an OBE for his services to jazz a few years ago, and would have dearly loved his mother and grandmother to have been at the investiture, even though for his own part he inclines to the view of his friends that OBE simply stands for 'Other Bastards' Efforts' .

□ □ □

191

Though jazz is a small world, it has its giant figures – Louis Armstrong, Charlie Parker, Miles Davis, the list of front runners would take up at least two hands, and that of the powerful subsidiary influences far more. And then there are the disciples, the men and women who take more personal visions of what they have learned out into the world, into all the backwaters and tributaries, the welcoming and the hostile climates that jazz has penetrated in this century. In his various roles Ronnie Scott has performed the unique and precious role of bringing confidence, example and firsthand contact with visionaries to the British jazz scene, for so long such a beleaguered outpost.

If you ask him about his career, he will usually try to deflect you, tell you that, 'It's made a happy man very old.' Probe a little deeper and you find that though the club and its guests have been mostly important to him, it's the saxophone that is his first love, just as it was when Sol and Cissie bought him the Pennsylvania when the bombs still rained on London.

Ronnie Scott's Club remains a nightclub with a difference. There is still little or no obseqious attention of the sort you might get in an upmarket restaurant (some people claim it borders on rudeness), but the upside of it is that you are largely left alone to enjoy the music by staff not constantly rooting for business, and the character of the place as an establishment primarily devoted to celebrating jazz is maintained. Scott himself, though his stand-up comedy routines deliberately pay little regard to post-seventies racial and sexual politics, is none the less popular with his staff, has hired countless musicians of immense ethnic variety over the years, and is regarded by many of the world's finest jazz musicians as a personal friend and a playing equal. Above all, the virtues of a jazz club being run by one-time or still practising jazz musicians rather than entrepreneurs continue to be immense. Guests are more relaxed working there, the management understands the way they think, Scott's announcements methodically namecheck every member of a band.

Scott and King have performed an inestimable service for music in this country. They have resisted the overwhelming cultural pressure in Britain maintaining that jazz is neither serious like straight music or fun like pop, and proved over and over again on their own stage that it's both. They have, as John Dankworth said on the 1989 Omnibus film, shown that a Soho night spot can also be a 'recital hall, a concert hall, a place of learning'. They have helped make the British more aware of one of the great musical forms of the century, given British musicians the opportunity to work closely with visitors from other countries and helped pave the way for the new interest in jazz music. Another thirty-five years may well be beyond even the legendary ruggedness of the two founders (though it would be unwise to put money on it), but the name of Ronnie Scott's Club is indelibly inscribed on the history of jazz, and jazz-consciousness, in Britain.

As the update of this book is completed, in summer 1994, Renault are advertising a car called the 'Be-Bop' and Yves St Laurent promotes a 'jazz collection' of perfumeries, but for Ronnie Scott these things are transitory changes of fashion that mean little to the way the music is played, talked about, adored by its admirers. As for his own playing, which is his first love, he has grown phlegmatic with the years. Though he will still be a fan, still sit at the side of his own stage in admiration of a performer he respects, he no longer feels the compulsion to try to take the style of a hero apart and absorb it himself. When he played at Frith Street in October 1994 on a night when his daughter Rebecca was on the premises, he rose on occasions above even his own exacting standards, swept through the material as if discovering its pleasures for the first time. Mary congratulated him on it when he came offstage. 'Good, was it?' he enquired with his customary economy, peering at her over his glasses. But when he plays well he knows it, and he grows more comfortable with the gifts he uniquely possesses.

'The feel becomes more important, the truth of it,' Ronnie Scott says now. 'You accept yourself for what you are. If it's not Stan Getz, or Mike Brecker or John Coltrane, at least it's you. For better or worse.'

# Index